Roy Newquist

Showcase

By the same author:
COUNTERPOINT

SHOWCASE

ROY NEWQUIST

INTRODUCTION BY *Brooks Atkinson*

ILLUSTRATIONS BY *Irma Selz*

William Morrow & Co., Inc.   *New York, 1966*

To Ruth—whose patience matches my wondering and wandering.

CONTENTS

Foreword   9

Introduction by Brooks Atkinson   11

Edward Albee   17
Julie Andrews   31
Ann Corio   45
Hume Cronyn   59
Sammy Davis, Jr.   81
Agnes de Mille   91
Dame Edith Evans   107
Janet Gaynor   123
Sir John Gielgud   135
George Grizzard   163
Julie Harris   181
Helen Hayes   195
Calvin Jackson   211
Danny Kaye   225
Ernest Lehman   239
Jack Lemmon   257
Tanya Moiseiwitsch   277
Gerry Mulligan   289
Phyllis Newman   303

CONTENTS

Mike Nichols   *317*
Peter O'Toole   *331*
Robert Preston   *349*
Harold S. Prince   *371*
Rosalind Russell   *387*
Jessica Tandy   *403*

FOREWORD

I would not be offended if any critic called this book an exercise in self-indulgence, because that is precisely what it is. I am a book reviewer and a writer. I am not, nor have I wanted to be, actor, singer, dancer, or entertainer of any type. But I have a passion for being entertained, and a passionate admiration for those people whose bits of magic entertain me most. And like a star-struck kid I've wanted to meet, in the flesh, those people who have given so much to me.

I admit that there is a naïveté in my approach. I hope—and assume—this is overcome by the perception, wit and depth of each very lively artist at hand.

I admit, too, that most of the interviews are roughly governed by a pattern—autobiography first, attitudes next, etc. This was essential, however, to establish the person upon his or her basis of authority before striking out toward universals.

You will also find that four of the personalities included in *Showcase*—Hume Cronyn, George Grizzard, Tanya Moiseiwitsch and Jessica Tandy—have a great deal to say about their association with the Tyrone Guthrie Theatre in Minneapolis. I am pleased that at least a rough profile of the Guthrie, its operative methods and its success, is thus drawn, for I believe it is the most important theatrical development in the United States in decades.

So here, then, are about half of my favorite people in the entertainment world. A year or so from now *Showcase II* will present the other half. It will be a further exercise in self-indulgence.

For one of the continuing glories of our world is the presence of those artists who become, for 90 minutes of film or 150 minutes onstage, more important than ourselves. We owe them two things: the joy of respite, and (perhaps more important) the opportunity to nudge a crack in the plaster horizon that is all too prevailingly our ceiling of life.

Watching or hearing something good is like being in love. Watching or hearing something great is like making love. And we can't knock either the emotion or the act.

Greater exhilaration we'll never know.

R.N.

INTRODUCTION

As an interviewer Roy Newquist must be doing something right. By some sort of personal alchemy he has cozened theatre people into giving good accounts of themselves in this book. Dispensing with gossip and publicity angles he has set them to talking about their profession, which is the subject that becomes them most. Like professionals in any field they are obsessed with a passion for perfection, and they are willing to do the hard work that passion entails. What they say in the following pages about their early experiences and about their colleagues and their audiences is engrossing and illuminating and is likely to arouse your respect for their profession. For theatre people are very serious about the theatre, and Mr. Newquist has managed to set them to talking seriously.

The public (some actors refer to the public as "private persons") is inclined to dismiss theatre people as triflers and egotists who live in a fantasy world. There is a lot of cant in that point of view. In the first place, everyone lives in a fantasy world. Social life is a fantasy; so is business life. When the stock market collapses the thousands of investors emerge rather painfully from what turns out to have been a costly fantasy world. The worlds of salesmanship, industry and politics are no realer than the stage.

In the second place, I doubt that captains of industry are more

brilliant or as brilliant or know as much about life as Dame
Edith Evans, Sir John Gielgud, Agnes de Mille and Hume
Cronyn, all of whom are alert and articulate and have some wise
observations to make in this book. Nor are theatre people egotists
by profession. In the following unstudied self-portraits they
emerge as modest. Janet Gaynor recalls of her Hollywood experience: "There was very little temperament. We were professional people, you know." No one in any profession could be
more candid, modest and sensible than Ann Corio. There is no
ego in Jessica Tandy. She says: "It's only the work that is ultimately fascinating"; the money, the glamor and the notoriety
she regards as ephemeral. Although acting is a highly personal
art, Julie Harris is selfless. She is not interested in exploiting her
personality: she is solely interested in depicting the character
she is playing.

Edward Albee remarks that the theatre is a cruel and vicious
place. It would be difficult to challenge that harsh statement, for
failure is the theatre's commonest experience. After several
weeks of hard nervous and physical work by professionals in all
the departments of the theatre, most plays fail and some of them
fail with wounding rapidity. Because of the nature of theatre
the failure seems to be a blunt rejection of the personalities of
the people involved.

But theatre people manage to absorb failure with something
approaching equanimity. Note on the following pages a devotion to the theatre and a gaiety about it that keep the theatre exciting as an institution, no matter the state it may be in at any
particular period. Theatre people are alive only when they are
working in the theatre. Looking back on some strenuous years
when she worked around the clock, Tanya Moisevitsch remarks:
"I loved every minute of it." This delicate and intangible collaboration among many people to stage a play lights a fire that
is sacred to each one of them. Although the fire ignites them it
never burns them, and I think Mr. Newquist's interviews illus-
trate that point.

To a professional critic it is entertaining to observe the degree
to which most of these people fear, hate or loathe critics. Dame
Edith Evans, who is obsequiously admired by critics on both

sides of the Atlantic, refuses to meet critics. When Mrs. St. John Ervine invited her to lunch, Miss Evans refused until she was assured that Mr. Ervine, a critic, would not be present. (I had the pleasure of meeting Miss Evans socially a year or two ago. It seemed to me that she sustained the blow as resiliently as Millamant.) Hal Prince, one of Broadway's *jeunesse dorée*, has a phobia about critics. Although he doubts that they have the power usually ascribed to them, he says they killed *Poor Bitos* in two weeks by the dullness of their praise. Mr. Prince would prefer bright reviews that sell tickets to his productions.

No one likes criticism, including Presidents of the United States and even drama critics. Sir John Gielgud says that he never likes what critics say and doubts that any actor does: "If the critics are unkind you think they are malicious, and if they are kind you think they haven't noticed the things you did really well." But looking back over his career he adds: "I don't think I find that they've often been unfair to the plays I have appeared in."

To the people in this book who have a neurosis about critics I should like to offer some creative counsel: Never object to criticism unless it's true. True criticism is devastating. It is and should be written sparingly.

Brooks Atkinson

Showcase

"*Writing for me is something of an act of discovery—of discovering what I'm thinking about.*"

EDWARD ALBEE

Without the alternately fiery and brooding talents of Edward Albee contemporary theater would be poor, indeed. His special genius, first apparent in *The Zoo Story*, has grown into mighty and challenging plays that have offered, season after season, the most notable and noble challenges to the prevailing light laughter of lighter comedy and the diversion of the forgettable musical. It is still too early to judge the life and influence of plays like *Who's Afraid of Virginia Woolf?* and *Tiny Alice*. But it is not too early to acclaim the intensely gifted Mr. Albee for proving that theater without innovation, without progress, without courage, is not really theater at all.

ALBEE: I don't know where I was born. I spent a few days just after that event in Washington, D.C., and then came to New York.

I've been in and around New York City ever since.

Education consisted of attending a number of private schools. I was thrown out of Lawrenceville, went to Valley Forge Military Academy which I tried to wreck, so I got out of that, and went to a prep school from which I was graduated. I attended Trinity College in Hartford for a year and one-half. I didn't really want to go to college, so that period completed my formal education.

I started going to the theater when I was about six. Other kids would go to Saturday movies but my family sent me to see plays and musicals. I suppose that's where my interest in the theater was born. We've taken care of twenty-one years very nicely, and I can quickly dismiss another period because from the age of twenty-one until I was twenty-nine and a half I wrote bad poetry and worse prose. Not until I was twenty-nine and a half did I hit upon the idea of writing plays, and that brings us to the only important years.

My first play was *The Zoo Story*. After that, in rather rapid sequence, came *The Death of Bessie Smith*, *The American Dream*, *The Sandbox*, *Who's Afraid of Virginia Woolf?*, *The Ballad of the Sad Cafe* and *Tiny Alice*.

And now we're in the present tense.

N.   This is a rough question to phrase, but is there any way you can state your objectives—in terms of what you want to write and what you wish to bring to an audience—as a playwright?

❧   ALBEE: It's a rough question only because the answer is impossible. I don't really know what my objectives are beyond the desire to write plays as well as I possibly can. I've settled upon the idea of playwrighting as—if not a lifetime occupation—as my occupation for the next ten to fifteen years. It seems to be something I do with a reasonable degree of success (perhaps more artistic than commercial success), but more importantly it's something I enjoy doing very much.

When you ask a writer what his objectives are he's got to do that tricky business of going after-the-fact and talking about the effect that his work has had upon the audience more than his intention in working. After all, what is the creation of a work of art? Whether it's a good or a bad work it's a matter of getting out of his system something which is lodged there. The creative process is terribly difficult to examine, and perhaps bad for a writer to talk about, because it leads to self-consciousness. What the objectives of a writer are beyond being as good a writer as possible I cannot say. I know that the work I do is *said* to have a number of objectives—to shake complacency, for example, and lead to an examination of our mores. This probably is part of the intention, but when I'm writing a play I'm concerned only with the reality of the situation in the play and the validity of the characters and in making the stuff that's in my head as real as possible.

I'm not a didactic writer. I don't start with thesis, and then create characters, and then create a situation to illuminate the predicament. I don't work that way. Writing, for me, is something of an act of discovery, of discovering what I'm thinking about.

N.   You mentioned shaking complacency—

❧   ALBEE : It would seem that this is what I'm accused of doing. It's a nice accusation—I don't mind it at all. But I'm basically concerned, as I said, with finding out what it is that I am thinking about, and what the play is all about that I feel I have to write. It's an act of discovery for me. You see, I'm interested in *seeing* the play.

N.   Is it possible for you to pin down the origins of your plays?

❧   ALBEE : I really don't know the origins. They're difficult to trace. With the exception of *The Death of Bessie Smith*—which I wrote for specific reasons after reading, on the back of a record album, how Bessie Smith died—I can never remember the specific origin of the plays I write. When I discover that I am thinking about a play I've already gotten the idea for a play. As for the exact moment it came to me—it's awfully hard to answer. Again, of course, one can do it after-the-fact, when you find out what other people think the play is about. Their suppositions sometime bear resemblance to what one assumes one's intentions must have been.

I'm not trying to come on as primitive or naïve, here, but it's dangerous for a writer (or at least for me as a writer) to start with a thesis, and it's probably damaging for future work to try to relate the implications of what one had done in the past to something one is trying. The spontaneity goes out the window.

N.   What has your reaction been to critics who either haven't understood or resented your plays?

✿   ALBEE: That rather depends upon the critic's motive, of course. One can shrug off critics who don't understand because they're obviously people who are incapable of understanding. The ones who pretend they don't understand because they disapprove are criminals of a sort. The ones who condemn because they disapprove are, I think, misusing their function as critics.

Now, this might sound as though I think I should get only favorable notices from the press: I don't suggest this at all. But it does seem to me that any work of art must be approached from two levels. First, from the point of view of how well the person who perpetrated the work of art accomplished his intention, and second, from a relation of that intention to the entire historical continuum of the theater. Unless the critics do both of these things they are failing in their task.

As it is we have some very good critics and some terrible ones. Some responsible ones and some very irresponsible ones.

N.   How do you feel about the level of criticism in New York? And about the power the critics are assumed to have?

✿   ALBEE: Critics have an enormous amount of power —primarily, I suspect, because the audiences let the critics speak for them. The average audience will assume that what a critic says about a play reflects its tastes—which it does not necessarily do. Critics consider themselves (primarily) as reporters who report on an event that occurred on the night of its literal opening. It seems to me that there's something of a lack of double responsibility—a lack of responsibility on the part of the audience. Let me put it this way: if the audience would stop accepting the critic as the man who reflects his taste, and thought a bit more on its own, the audience would see better plays. And if the critics would stop thinking of themselves as instruments that reflect the taste of the audience, the critical standards would rise.

N.   To turn to the theater in more or less general terms —what do you think of the state of American theater at present?

ॐ   ALBEE: Everyone says that American theater is getting worse and worse and the stage unhealthier and unhealthier. Well, I've been going to the theater since I was six (though I suppose that only in the past fifteen years have I gone with a practiced eye) and frankly, I find today's theater far more exciting than it ever was in my earlier years.

The whole postwar movement of avant garde theater in Europe has rejuvenated our theater enormously. Fighting this is the apparent growing apathy of the audience, the desire for much more escapist entertainment rather then engagement entertainment, and the prevalence of all the dreadful things we know about the commercial theater—the pressures of commerce, the money made by the hit and lost by the flop.

But perhaps the thing that makes theater interesting and exciting to work in is the war to be fought against apathy.

N.   I'd like to turn to *Tiny Alice*. In a recent interview with Sir John Gielgud he remarked (and I'll paraphrase) that the difference between the modern play and an established old one—one by Shakespeare, for example—is that the "line" of the modern play isn't solid and apparent, that the actor is harder put to make his own links. Are you aware, as a writer, of this distinction between the "old" play and *Tiny Alice?*

ॐ   ALBEE: Yes. There are worlds of difference between Shakespeare and *Tiny Alice*. However, I don't know whether or not plays have gotten any more difficult for actors to perform. I've always felt that Shakespeare was one of the trickiest playwrights, offered the greatest challenges—the fact that only three or four actors in the world can perform Shakespeare accurately suggests that. Perhaps the unconscious has been moved into a bit more by modern playwrights, and things are done more by suggestion and inference rather than by direct

statement. (After all, playwrights can't go on repeating for-
mulas that have been accepted and acceptable in the past.)

I don't know whether the theater has really grown more
complex. One of the problems in any avant garde play (I don't
like that term very much, but one has to keep using it because
it's a term everybody understands or pretends to understand) is
that the same subjects are approached from a different point of
view. It is this area of unfamiliarity in the point of approach,
this actual point of departure, that confuses so many people.

The statements that are made in plays—in Shakespeare's
time and in ours—are primarily the same. There aren't that
many statements that can be made.

N. I've noticed, between the press and a number of
magazines, that you and Sir John Gielgud have been going
around and around about certain aspects of *Tiny Alice.* How
did these come up?

❧ ALBEE : I think this whole thing got started—

N. Not by a press agent—

❧ ALBEE : Oh, God no. I think we have one of the few
press agents who doesn't go around planting false items or
putting things in newspapers just to get attention. He's a fairly
accurate man, and he reports the facts.

However, someone at one point—rather irresponsibly, and I
don't know who it was—suggested in a newspaper that Gielgud
and I were at swords' point about the play, that he didn't
understand it and I refused to explain it to him.

This isn't true.

Now, an actor has to ask a number of questions in order to
play a part, but the answers to those questions must come from
the director. An author can only speak in conceptual terms, and
an actor can't plan conceptions. He's got to play the reality of a
situation, and this reality must be given by the director. It's
dangerous for an author to explain a play to an actor because an
author will talk in totally different terms from those the director
will use, and we all know that in the theater the director will get

what the author wants by using *his* terms, by explaining things in a totally different way.

Thus, if I was reluctant to talk about *Tiny Alice* with John it was only to make sure I didn't intrude. I talked about it with the director, Alan Schneider, at great length, and he seemed to understand the play quite well.

But John and I were never at swords' point or cross-purposes, to my knowledge.

N.   Is it true that you wrote *Tiny Alice* for Sir John Gielgud?

❧   ALBEE: No, I didn't write *Tiny Alice* for John. I told him, when we were together at a party about two and a half years ago, that I would very much like to have him in a play of mine and that I was planning a play that it might be possible for him to be in. When I had gotten three-quarters of the way through *Alice* I knew exactly where the play was going, and I started to think about actors and actresses for the play, and it occurred to me at that point that Gielgud would be fine for it.

I think it would be dangerous to plan a play for a specific actor. (I'm not trying to suggest that John couldn't appear in most any play, because he could. He's a most extraordinary actor, yet it would be dangerous for a writer to write a play or a part for a specific actor.)

It's dangerous because supposing you write very specifically for that actor and he isn't available or he drops dead . . . then, in the future, who's to play the part when that actor isn't around? Also, I think it would inhibit the spontaneity of the writer a bit if he were to write for a specific actor because an actor is really not a three-dimensional character.

N.   Yet I can't imagine anyone else playing that death scene.

❧   ALBEE: I can, but he does an extraordinary job in the play.

N.   Now I'll turn both back and ahead to *Who's Afraid of Virginia Woolf?*—speaking in terms of its transformation to the motion picture medium. I seem to be watching it from all ends, Hollywood and New York, and I find it fascinating. How do you feel about it?

❦ ALBEE: It is fascinating. I may be more fascinated than anyone. I'm a little confused, let's say, by a number of things. Martha, in the play, is a fifty-two-year-old woman. Elizabeth Taylor, who is going to play Martha on the screen is a thirty-two-year-old woman. Mike Nichols, who is going to direct the film version, has never directed a film in his life, and in the theater is coming across as a highly effective director of farce. *Who's Afraid of Virginia Woolf?* is not a farce. So naturally, I'm fascinated to find out what the resemblance is going to be between what I wrote for the stage and what emerges on the screen.

N. Do you have any clearance on the script, anything actually done from this point on?

❦ ALBEE: No. Negotiations for the sale of *Who's Afraid of Virginia Woolf?* went on for about a year and a half, and I spent a lot of time talking to people about retaining control of the play—doing the screenplay myself, having final authority (which is the only authority that counts in the movies; final authority meaning cast approval, director approval, writing the script myself, final cutting approval). I found that it was totally impossible to get these, and that getting part of them would give me only an illusion of control, so I finally shrugged my shoulders and said, "The hell with all that." With the money we got, my partners and I, who have been supporting our playwrights unit in New York, have been able to support our thirty-five playwrights for the past two years.

Frankly, I don't feel as possessive about what's going to happen to any play of mine when it goes into films as I do to what happens when it's done on the stage.

I can only assume that Ernest Lehman—and from the talks I've had with him he does seem to be a sensitive and intelligent man—has figured out some way to do it intelligently.

N. How do you respond to this one aspect of criticism you encounter occasionally—that your work is difficult to understand?

❦   ALBEE: The curious thing is that *Tiny Alice* is really the only play I've written that is theoretically very difficult to understand. The critics—the majority of critics— believed that the audience didn't want to exercise its mind, and informed the audience that the play was too difficult for them to comprehend. Now, the hundreds of letters I've gotten from people since *Tiny Alice* opened run about twenty to one saying, "We understand the play totally; what's wrong with the critics?"

Apparently the critics are the people who don't understand the play.

We've talked, in and out, about the relationship of the author to his audience, the relationship of the critic to the audience and to the author, and on the subject of the responsibility of the audience itself to the theater and the playwright, I'd like to say this.

The theater is only one of the several art forms in existence, in this country and everywhere, but I have discovered, over the years, that you can judge the alertness and the health of a nation's culture more quickly by the way the public treats its theater than its other art forms because there is such an immediacy to theater. The theater exists entirely in the present tense, while the novel, for example, usually exists in the past tense—in the apprehended and reflected.

I think we can truly judge the cultural health of the nation by the approach of the audience to theater, and I worry sometimes about the fact that the audience very often seems to feel that the theater is its possession, and that the duty and responsibility of the playwright is to fashion entertainments for the audience, diversions that will take people out of themselves rather than make them think—perhaps unpleasantly, but clearly—about themselves.

Now, if an audience keeps asking a playwright to be its servant and to serve it badly we'll end up having a very bad theater and we'll end up having a very unimportant and eventually self-defeating culture. All I really ask is a co-existence in the theater between the musicals and comedies and the plays that try to do something a little more serious.

Let me put it this way: Any culture can have any kind of theater it wants, and it gets the kind of theater it deserves, and if the audience looks at the theater and finds that it's usually made up of not-so-good musicals and frivolous escapist entertainments the audience must say to itself, "We don't want anything more than this." They actually *don't* want anything different or better than this. This is the limit of their adventure, and eventually, if this is the only thing an audience wants, a serious artist in this country will have to shrug his shoulders, turn his back, and give up.

The audience does have an enormous responsibility to encourage serious work in the theater because playwrights cannot work in a vacuum, and the responsibility of the author to his audience is to write as well as he possibly can, and the responsibility of the audience to its authors is to listen and pay attention as intelligently as it possibly can.

N. Do you think we've existed long enough, as a nation, to have established a theatrical heritage? Of values to protect?

❦ ALBEE: The American theater, as such, has only existed for the past thirty-five years, starting with O'Neill. We haven't had time to develop a theatrical heritage or a theatrical culture as yet. We're a very young country, and our theater is even younger. We have, however, an extraordinary potential. Theoretically it is the ideal place for any creative artist to work —though I don't know whether this is actually true at the moment.

N. Do you think we've suffered through a lack of repertory or national theater?

ALBEE: It seems to me that the enormous value for repertory theater would be to put on and keep before the public the plays of the past, plays that cannot exist in commercial theater. I'm talking about Aeschylus and Sophocles, Molière and Shakespeare, Sheridan and Strindberg (and many others) because these are the playwrights whose works are so fundamental that no audience can truly be educated in the theater—

can truly understand what is going on in the contemporary theater—without seeing these plays performed. So this would be the enormous value of repertory.

I would imagine that the majority of living playwrights can take care of themselves in one commercial arena or another, so they really don't need repertory theater. But as an education for the audience repertory can be enormously valuable.

N.　　　　I'd like to turn to whatever advice you would like to give the aspiring playwright—most likely in terms of how you would like to see him develop.

❧　　　　ALBEE: God, you make me feel like one hundred and fifty years old—all I've had is seven years' experience in the theater!

N.　　　　Those have been extraordinary years.

❧　　　　ALBEE: Maybe I've been a little fortunate—or more fortunate than most playwrights—in that my career has gone smoothly. My first play, *Zoo Story*, was produced and was successful artistically and commercially. The others have been produced with varying degrees of commercial and artistic success, so I haven't gone through any of the horrors young playwrights are supposed to go through.

There are, however, enormous pressures in the theater. The theory abounds that the theater is not the possession of the playwright. The theater, to be healthy, *must* be the possession of the playwright—*not* the province, the exclusive province, of the actor, the director, the producer, or the audience. Ideally, the theater is the possession of the author, and the author—as long as he does well what he sets out to do—should not be encouraged to change his work or mold it to accommodate to the taste of those who feel ultrapossessive about the medium.

So what advice do you give to a playwright who is starting out? I suppose you could warn him that the theater is a terrible and desperate and cruel and vicious and awful place, that he will be constantly surrounded by people who want to turn him into a servant and seek to destroy his work and to change it.

I suppose you should tell him that he's got to be tough, and as cruel as anybody else in theater, and that he's got to have enormous amounts of self-discipline and an enormous capacity for self-criticism; that he's got to have a strong ego and be able to stand up for what he wants.

Now, if he has and does all this, and fights to the best of his ability, the only other thing he need have is talent. That's the tough one—talent. He can't go to school to learn how to write plays. All he'll learn is how to write somebody else's plays. If he goes to one teacher who's very fond of Ibsen, for example, and is not a playwright, he'll be taught how to write like Ibsen. If he studies with a playwright, he'll be taught how to write like that playwright, which isn't such a good idea, since altogether too much imitation is practiced nowadays anyway. I suppose the young person who wants to be a playwright should study the theater as much as he possibly can. He should know, intimately, every play written from the time of Euripides on up. He should see as many productions as he possibly can, so that he can see the difference between the playwright's intention and what emerges on the stage. He should actually read plays. He should know everything he can possibly know about the theater, but he must have that thing called *talent*—originality, style, genius of one degree or another. And I don't know where he finds this unless it exists within him.

N. Bringing matters of work and study and discipline to the personal level—to you—how do you work?

❦ ALBEE: All playwrights work so differently. When I'm writing I work, more or less, in two parts. I think about a play at least a year before I start writing it down. The actual writing is rather brief—three months for a long play, four hours of work each morning, six days a week. I do some revision in the afternoon. But other playwrights work very differently. Saroyan, for example, used to write a play over the weekend. Lillian Hellman would make twelve different versions of a play before she was satisfied with it. The only awful thing about being any kind of writer is that one is not engaged in a nine to five job working for somebody else. One is one's own boss, and one is quite alone, and one's self-discipline must be enormous.

N.   Have you gone through any heavy revisions on any of your plays after they've opened?

ALBEE: No. I find that I try to rid myself of the play as quickly as I can. The emotional, intellectual experience of seeing the play through rehearsal and opening is so exhausting that I want nothing more to do with the play for months afterward.

N.   How much rewriting goes on during the rehearsal period?

ALBEE: Well, I like to make my own mistakes rather than be saddled with anyone else's errors. If I feel that I've made errors I like to correct them during the rehearsal period. They're usually small corrections, but if I find that rhythms are wrong, or speeches don't sound right to me, I'll make changes. Occasionally I have discovered structural errors, and have had to do a little more serious job of revision, but for the most part revisions are relatively minor—cuts here and there, occasional additions. I've gone through none of this awful business that all movies about playwrights persist in showing— of playwrights putting the third act where the first one was, and rewriting overnight in Boston. (I'd like to see a play in which the first and third acts could be interchanged.)

But the important thing is this: I'd rather make my own mistakes rather than change things according to someone else's suggestion. I've been very fortunate (though some people might argue this point) in working with producers who allow me to make my own mistakes and don't inflict their theories on what I do.

"*I became the British square of all time.*"

JULIE ANDREWS

Few personalities have burst upon the American scene with the blaze and impact that accompanied Julie Andrews. In rapid succession, moving from Broadway to Hollywood, she became Eliza, Emily, Mary Poppins and Maria with a vivid claim to each role that made it her own. Talented, beautiful, charming, poised, versatile, hard-working . . . but the adjectives run on indefinitely. Only with difficulty does the awed, ever-so-mortal man with the tape recorder realize that her perfection, her spontaneity and freshness, weren't created overnight: years of work and grooming are behind it all.

❧   ANDREWS: I was born in a little town called Walton-on-Thames, which is about eighteen miles south of London. It's suburbia, but it was a very pretty little village with a village green and all that vaguely bucolic sort of thing. It isn't absolutely swamped with building projects even now, though it's part of Greater London or Outer London. My mother was born there, all of my family were born there, and the fact that I married a Walton who comes from Walton-on-Thames is sheer coincidence. I was born in Walton, but we didn't stay there long; we moved all about. My father, Edward Wells, Ted

Wells, was a school teacher; in fact, he still is. When I was about three years old my parents were divorced. (I don't remember my exact age at the time because I was kept rather in the dark about it all.) The next thing I knew an Uncle Ted had come into my life—another Ted. This was my stepfather, Ted Andrews. (There was an awful time when I really didn't know who I wanted to be with, and I spent some time with mother and some with father. I guess I mostly wanted to be with mother because she seemed to lead a rather colorful existence, but I missed Daddy very much indeed.)

My stepfather is a Canadian, a vaudeville performer who came to England and married my mother. She was a fine pianist. They teamed up and did a vaudeville act and subsequently became famous. They were a very good second "Top-of-the-bill" in vaudeville, if you know what that is. When I was about eight years old they were beginning to make a name for themselves and they'd let me go on tour with them during school holidays. At the time I thought that was a great treat. Then, with the war raging, my school closed down. (My listing of times and ages is the best I can remember. I've gotten so confused with all the publicity stories that have been printed I honestly don't remember precise details of time and date.) But the gist of this period is the fact that the school closed because of the war. We were all supposed to be evacuated, which we were, for a while. My stepfather—mostly to give me something to do because I was under everyone's feet—decided to give me some singing lessons. Suddenly they discovered, quite out of the blue, that I had a freak voice—an adult larnyx (they checked on this) with a four-octave range including some fierce high notes. This big, belting sound came out of a rather bandy-legged, buck-toothed child and must have shocked half to death everyone within range.

I became a rather weird oddity in the family group. I was made to practice at least a half-hour every day, and I loathed singing and resented my stepfather. I'm sure, now, that one of the reasons he gave me the lessons was an attempt to get closer to me, to win me over, so to speak. Looking back at it all I realize that he did a lot of very sweet things for me.

Anyway, on the odd touring dates when I would join my family they'd give me a chance, occasionally, to appear as a surprise item in their act. (They'd have to get permission from the theater manager to allow me to appear, and some of them wouldn't take a chance on a rather ugly nine- or ten-year-old child. They thought my parents were quite out of their minds, but the ones that did take a chance were very nice indeed.) I stood on beer crates in order to reach the microphone and sang my head off. My mother played the piano—my father sang— I joined him in a duet once in a while. It must have been ghastly. But it seemed to go down all right.

This went on until I was twelve, when my stepfather, who was not only a good tenor, but a good salesman, brought a man named Val Parnell—at that time the head of the Moss Empire Circuit in England, then the largest theater circuit—down to the house to hear me sing. Val said he would like me to be in his review in London. It was very exciting, my very first real engagement. With Val was my present manager—Charles Tucker—who signed me up there and then. I've been with him ever since.

At any rate the opening is the full-color show biz story. The night before the review opened they suddenly decided I was too naïve to be in a sophisticated London show at the Hippodrome so my mother and my agent descended upon them and said, "You've got to give this girl her big break," and all that sort of awful nonsense. The upshot of it was that I sang a song that was ten times more difficult than the one I'd started out with. It was the "Polonaise" from *Mignon*, and stopped the show on opening night and got all the notices the next morning. I really haven't stopped working since, except for an odd holiday once in a while.

After this show I toured all over England—endlessly, it seems. We did a family act for a while; then I branched out on my own and did a vaudeville act. All my background is vaudeville training—plus concerts, radio and television work, still vaudeville, essentially.

I did a lot of English pantomimes—they're epic, and marvelous experience. I was always the principal girl who was rather wet and makes goo-goo eyes at Our Hero and gets him in the end. Most of the time I was kept in short, short dresses, patent leather shoes and ankle socks, trying desperately to look ten years younger than I really was, growing a bosom and feeling wretched about *that*.

Schooling was rather a problem. Until I was ten I went to various schools—no one in particular—except for a type of dramatic-cum-ballet school I attended when I was about eight that offered regular school in the afternoon and dramatic and ballet training in the morning. From ten to twelve I got some of the best schooling in my life; I went to a private girls' school in the town we were then living in, but from twelve on I was working professionally and had a governess travel with me, a combined chaperone and teacher. I had a compulsory three or four hours of lessons every day until I was fifteen, and that was all the education I had. I bitterly regret not having had more.

N.   You mentioned that your intensive early training was in vaudeville. Was that entertainment area a grooming for performers in England as it once was in America?

❦   ANDREWS: Yes. I came on the scene when vaudeville was really on its last legs. Certain towns had already closed their theaters, and there really weren't many good old standards left. Oddly enough, most of the English people I know today, the comedians in particular, stemmed from vaudeville. I can't imagine how they would get a comparable training now. It would have to be in television, but it's an awful thing to ask anyone to be that exposed before he has time to gain some experience elsewhere.

This isn't to say that performers don't work, today. It's fantastic the way people work on Broadway and out in California. When I was on Broadway all the singers and dancers in the show took at least two classes a week and worked hard to improve any area they considered weak. I think the reason competition is so intense over here is because there are literally ten people who can do your job just as well as you can, so you have to pull up your socks and be even better or they'll be in like a shot.

N.   To turn, now, to the key appearances in London that have led so directly to the present. What were they?

❦   ANDREWS: Well, we've covered the London Hippodrome, and though I worked in London in various pantomimes it wasn't until I was eighteen, playing in the Christmas pantomime of *Cinderella* at the Palladium, when a lady named Vida Hope who had directed *The Boyfriend* in London came to see me. She said she was putting together an entirely new company for the American production and wondered if I'd be interested in going. The producers wanted a two-year contract and I was petrified—absolutely panic-stricken. I thought I was much too green to leave England, that I didn't know enough about the business, and simply couldn't stay away from home for two whole years. I said "No," but they came back and said, "Please reconsider," and one thing and another, and—well, everybody was saying "Go," and I didn't especially want to, so finally I went to my father, my real father, and said, "What on earth shall I do?" He was very sweet and said, "Now, listen; it may only run for three weeks and you'll be back. You'll have seen the States, you'll have had a marvelous experience, and we won't be that far away." So I finally said that I would go, but only if it was a one-year contract—if it was a hit I couldn't bear the idea of two years away from home. I wouldn't have earned enough to bring my family over, and they certainly couldn't afford the trip, so one year was it.

I came to America in *The Boyfriend*. I was nineteen the day after we opened, and as you know it was quite a success and ran a year and a bit. The incredible thing about that year's contract was the fact that just about six weeks before my year was up I had a call from a man who represented Lerner and Loewe. He asked me how long a contract I had with *The Boyfriend* and I said, "A year," and he almost fell off the wire. He said, "My God, we all thought you had a two-year contract, like everyone else in the company. We're thinking of you for the musical we're going to do of *Pygmalion*." And I thought, "What *are* these Americans going to do to poor George Bernard Shaw?" I really had grave doubts as to what it was all going to be like.

At any rate, I auditioned for Mr. Lerner and Mr. Loewe and also for Richard Rodgers. Rodgers was doing *Pipe Dream* at the time, so I sang for him and he said he would very much like to have me in his show. My manager said, "We have to tell you that she is being offered another musical, *My Fair Lady* by Lerner and Loewe." Dick was absolutely wonderful about it and said *My Fair Lady* would be the wiser move. Anyway, I got the part, and things went on from there.

N.   What were your reactions to *My Fair Lady?* First of all, during the rehearsal period, then after it opened and it was such a smash hit?

❧   ANDREWS : For a start, the impact of what had happened—what we *had* and the effect on the public—really didn't hit me until about three months after we opened. I was so completely involved with the show, so immersed in it, and so desperately busy trying to catch up with everyone else and to get it under my belt, that I didn't have time to think about what the show was, how very good it was.

We all felt that we had a marvelous show on our hands. There was a great feeling about it out of town, but of course there's always room for improvement. And thanks to Moss Hart's great guiding hand a show that was almost flawless to begin with got better as we neared Broadway. For me *My Fair Lady* was fairly disastrous during rehearsals because I had never done a straight acting job in my life until then. (Oh, yes, I had done one bomb in England, an incredible disaster. This was between *Cinderella* and *The Boyfriend*. I accepted a very limited engagement, thank God, and played a Southern belle from Tennessee. The story was all about Sodom and Gomorrah and bootleg whiskey and Lot's wife turning into a pillar of salt. I can't tell you what went on. It was a disaster. You've never heard a worse Southern accent than mine. I got pregnant by a traveling salesman—in the play, of course—and thank God the miserable thing closed before we got to London.)

So when it came to *My Fair Lady* I found it a monstrous task. I was all right as far as the songs went, I think, but when it came to the acting I was awful. Poor Moss was getting desperate and I'm sure Rex was thinking, "Good Lord, what have we here?" I wouldn't be at all surprised if there weren't times when they all thought of sending me back to London. Anyway, Moss said, "Look, I think I'd better have forty-eight hours alone with her to see what can be done." So then came that dreaded weekend. We rehearsed on the New Amsterdam roof, a marvelous, filthy old theater, a famous place. Moss bullied and pleaded and cajoled and encouraged. He was just wonderful and he did a kind of Svengali thing on me whereby—come Monday, though I probably dropped halfway back again through sheer nerves at facing the company—he had really given me an insight as to how the part should be played. I really did need a strong guiding hand; I had no idea of what they wanted until they told me. It was such a big musical and I had so little courage. I didn't know what Eliza should be—a whiny girl or a gutsy girl, a weak character or a strong one. Moss supplied the route, the direction, the character, and as the nights went by I absorbed Eliza more and more.

I think I learned more about show business during the run of *My Fair Lady* than in anything else I've done. I learned a lot about comedy in *The Boyfriend*—the thrill of getting laughs, the importance of timing, the demands placed upon you. Alan Lerner once said that to play in a long run with as good a part as Eliza is probably better than doing repertory for three years— with a part that had so many changes you could try out every- thing and find out what kind of actress you were or could be.

During the run of *My Fair Lady* I was never really sure, on any given night, that I had enough strength to do the whole thing flat out. It was such an enormous show—the screaming, the singing purely, the singing on the chest, the great dramatic requirements and everything—that I honestly don't think I could do it, today. I was worried about my throat—I wasn't sure that vocally I was going to make it—and I finally learned when I could give and when I couldn't. (I learned an awful lot about my limitations, or just how far I could be pushed when necessary. Playing *Camelot* was just my size and weight, and I enjoyed it enormously—I loved doing that show.)

It wasn't until I did the London run of *My Fair Lady* that I began to examine my feelings about show business. Up until then I had been in the business as a sort of duty—I didn't know what else to do, and it never occurred to me that I could do anything else. I'd never really liked it; I felt it was a chore and I hated the touring. But as I began to feel more secure about it all, I began to love it. It was every exciting. I began to really discipline myself and to practice much harder. I became a less haphazard performer.

N. A departure: *The Americanization of Emily* offered Julie Andrews in a whole new dimension. How did you enjoy that role?

❦ ANDREWS: I loved it. You see, the only bad thing about doing *My Fair Lady*, aside from the incredible hard work, was the fact that I got instantly typed. I don't know whether it was the word "lady" in the title or what, but I became the British square of all time, and it seemed impossible to lick the image. If I wanted to go on television they wanted me to sing something from that or from *The Boyfriend* and I'd say, "Please, let me do something else, something wacky or mad or sexy or whatever." But no. Then came *Emily* and I wanted it, I did it, and I loved it. James Garner was wonderful to work with and I adored him for making some difficult scenes so easy for me.

N. The stock question: How did you feel about missing out on *My Fair Lady* as a movie?

❦ ANDREWS: I didn't feel too badly for two reasons. At the time I was being offered *Mary Poppins*, which is great compensation. And you know, after three and a half years of *My Fair Lady* I didn't mind missing the screen version *that* much. I was disappointed, and I felt that I would have been able to do a lot with the part on film that would have been fun, but I have no "sour grapes" at all about not being cast. I understand the box office reasons, and all, and I'm thrilled that Audrey did it and I think she was marvelous. So apart from the initial, "Oh, well, there—it's gone, I mustn't think about it anymore," I didn't mind too much. Now, of course, it seems like the best thing that could possibly have happened, because I would have forever been typed as that square lady. The danger, now, is that I'll be considered the Nanny of all time, after *The Sound of Music* where I play a governess, and *Mary Poppins*, where I'm a nanny. Thank God for Emily; she saved my life.

N.   I spoke with P. L. Travers recently and we discussed *Mary Poppins* and you at great length. She seemed to think you were a bit lovelier than her Mary Poppins, but she ended up pleased.

☙   ANDREWS : You know, she called me the day after I had my baby. This was between *Camelot* and *Poppins* and I was at the London Clinic when this strange woman's voice came on the phone and said, "Hello, talk to me, P. L. Travers here. I want to hear your voice." And I said, "Oh, dear, what can I say?" "When can we meet?" she said. And I replied, "Well, I'm feeling rather weak at the moment," and asked her if we could leave it for a while. Well, when we met she sort of walked around me—mentally walked around me, at any rate—and we instantly liked each other enormously. I used to send her long letters from Hollywood about how the filming was going. She's a dear.

N.   Now, about *The Sound of Music*. Frankly, I thought the Broadway show was just a bit sticky-sweet, but when I saw the motion picture I was amazed. It isn't gooey.

☙   ANDREWS : I think what happened was that Bob Wise and Saul Chaplin, the producers, decided to get rid of the sugar. No filigree, no carved wood, no Swiss or Austrian chalets, and they stuck to their guns. We felt the same way. All of us agreed that the best thing to do was to take out the saccharin. It helped, of course, that it was a motion picture because they could do such sweeping things visually.

N.   Do you feel any obligation to the role you play? Onstage or in a motion picture? To yourself or the audience?

☙   ANDREWS : Oh, there's an enormous obligation, but it's mostly to the role because if that is done well the rest will follow. In trying to take the saccharin out of some of the things in *The Sound of Music* it occurred to me that Maria *couldn't* be sweetness and light with seven kids on her hands all the time. Seven kids would have to get on one's nerves, at some point or other, so I tried once in a while to show that I might be slightly exhausted by them. For instance, on the bed when they ask me to do this or that, and say, "What kind of things do you mean?" just before I go into "My Favorite Things," I thought, "Oh, my God! Children always *do* ask questions like that." Maria must have had moments when she bordered upon being tired and cross.

N.   Is there ever a moment, though, when you are someone else? An Eliza or a Maria or whomever?

❦   ANDREWS: Well, on Broadway it seems that once you finally get your characterization worked out you can be you for the day and then at performance time you fling yourself into the role. Actually I need an hour or an hour and a half before the performance to think about what I'm going to do. With a movie, however, there is some area of your mind that must constantly retain the role until the picture is completed. The whole thing is such a jigsaw, each shot is hardly ever filmed in sequence, and there are a thousand other things to distract you. You have to hold the whole thing together in your head until the filming's done. I like the challenge.

N.   Did you do any special studying before you tackled Eliza?

❦   ANDREWS: I ran the original movie with Wendy Hiller over and over again and bawled every time. I studied cockney with an American professor of phonetics—here I was English, learning cockney from an American!—but I'm not very good at accents. Most of the work, I frankly confess, happened during performances—I didn't know what I was doing until about three months after we opened. Even with all of Moss Hart's help I had to learn onstage, so to speak, and it's the best way to learn if you can get away with it!

N.   As far as the theater is concerned, does any individual night's performance depend upon the reactions of the house?

ANDREWS: Heavens. It's almost the biggest part of the challenge. Nobody knows you were good last night except the people who were there. So each night is entirely new and must be good. You know, also, the weather makes a great difference. If it's raining everybody seems to cough, and you have to time your lines to get the laugh across. If it's terribly hot the programs are going, and you've got a loud rustle to contend with.

Then again you might have a cold or a headache, or your leading man might have a cold or a headache or even be off and you have to adjust to slightly different circumstances each night. There are the orchestrations to listen to all over again, and there's always one scene you didn't do well the night before and you can't wait to get to do it a little better. Or there's the laugh that disappeared—why? You had it three weeks' running, why did you lose it last night? All these things are maddening, but they're fun.

N.   Have you noticed any fundamental differences between American and British audiences?

ANDREWS: There's very little difference, really. There's a slight variance in sense of humor, but the only comparison I've been able to make is on *My Fair Lady* because I did it both in New York and in London, and obviously some of the jokes would be more understood in England than over here. It seems—just off the cuff—that American audiences follow the book more closely and are apt to be a bit more critical. I think that English audiences are a little more loyal and more willing to just have a great evening's entertainment.

Now, I may be entirely wrong about this because I know that things are changing rapidly—and that the British are becoming much more critical and not accepting everything. But when I did *My Fair Lady* those differences did show up.

N.   What are you scheduled for next? And next after
that?

✿   ANDREWS: Right now I'm working on a television
special of my own which will be shown later—next November, I
think. It's really hard work—terrifying because it's your
baby. In April I start a film called *Hawaii*, and I'm excited
about that because Max von Sydow is going to play my
husband. Oh! Marvelous publicity—can't you see it—"Mary
Poppins marries Jesus." Gorgeous. She must have flown up to
him and said, "Listen, with my magic and your talent we'd
make a great team. I can fly—you can walk on water—what
more do we need?" Actually, come to think of it, who else could
she have married? It's the classic mother and father image for all
children. Anyway, after *Hawaii* I do a wonderful project with
Mike Nichols directing the film of *The Public Eye*, the play
by Peter Shaffer. Then another project with Bob Wise is being
planned although there's no script, but they tentatively plan to
do a sort of documentary musical about Gertrude Lawrence. I
think they're going to try and contrast the real down-to-earth
backstage existence with the glamor that is the performance. I
can't wait to get into all this—her special quality and versatility were phenomenal.

N.   A stock question: Have you had any difficulty
making the transition from your non-celebrity days to the
present?

✿   ANDREWS: Well, the celebrity part of it has sort of
just happened, so I don't know what problems will be presented.
You know it's been ten years since I first came to America.
Although I can recognize the girl who came here in 1954, it's
hard to identify with her. So I suppose I have changed a great
deal over the years.

N.   Assuming a youngster has talent is there any advice you could give an aspiring actor or actress?

✿   ANDREWS: Oh, dear. It makes one sound so pedantic
and superior to give advice. But I suppose there are two things:

first of all, enjoy it—it's a real gift to enjoy the work one does. The other would be to persevere, to work, to refuse to give up, no matter what some people might say. Anyone really dedicated will plow ahead somehow.

N. Have you any idea of the mark—the permanent mark, if anything is written on materials more substantial than water—you'd like to leave as an actress and singer?

ANDREWS : What I suppose I'd like to be, one day, is someone who is fascinating. You know—a person you want to look at or see no matter what they're doing. I think what I'm trying to say is that I'd like to be an original, to be myself and not a pale copy of anyone else. You know, the really marvelous actors and actresses we admire have qualities that can't be pinned down. I suppose I'd like to be that type of performer if I were to leave a mark.

N. A final, simple, corny question : How does it feel to be a star?

ANDREWS : I suck my thumb a lot.

"Finally mother said . . . 'Well, all-a-right, so long as they look and no touch.' "

ANN CORIO

I saw my first burlesque show in Milwaukee when I was sixteen. I went with a girl named Jeanne Kreutzer who cried all the way through it. Then, because she had spent her hard-saved money (we'd gone dutch), she insisted upon staying for another show. I happily complied; the theater was raunchy but I fell in love with burlesque and saw as much of it as I could through its withering years. Oddly enough, Ann Corio was the star of that first show, and over the years I caught her as often as I could, because she was my favorite strip-tease artist. But it was dismaying to interview her, now, and discover that all those years had left marks on me, but none on her.

CORIO: I've got laryngitis so I'm going to have to hold the mike. I don't sound very sexy at the moment do I? You see, we ran for almost four years downtown and I didn't have a vacation, and finally—a week before we opened on Broadway —I went to Florida. The tariff was forty-seven bucks a day and I caught this cold. A big fat bonus I didn't need.

N.   I'd like to start at the beginning, if I might, and ask you where you were born and reared and how you got into burlesque.

❧   CORIO : I was born in Hartford, Connecticut—raised there, went to school; I guess you'd call it a normal girlhood except for the fact that I was always fascinated with show business.

Now, Hartford had no burlesque—I didn't even know what burlesque was. The city specialized in insurance, and I knew *that* wasn't for me. Then a girl friend came to New York and got into the chorus of a burlesque show, wrote to me about it, and got me to come down. So I started in the chorus and graduated to stripping. My whole life centered about stripping, and it had to. I loved show business but I wasn't qualified for anything else. I wasn't trained to be a dancer or a singer, but from burlesque I did go on to legitimate theater, television and movies. However, I don't feel as though I was really accepted in those other mediums. The image of Ann Corio, stripteaser, was always there. But it paid off then, and it's paying off so beautifully now, I really don't mind being from the other side of the theatrical tracks.

Back to childhood—mine was quite normal. My parents were Neapolitan, born and reared in Italy. Childhood was wonderful, the way it can be in small towns. We shook apples off trees and when it rained we ran barefoot in the gutters. When June came around we took off our shoes and ran barefoot all summer and when September came we were shod again.

Family life was typically Italian. My mother had twelve children, of which I'm number six, so when I was home (only six children were there at a time) I was at the end of the litter, but at holidays everyone would come home to Mama and we'd have one of those big Italian dinners with everyone sitting around a big kitchen table. I wonder how she ever did it—but there was always plenty of food, yet my father didn't make very much money. He was a very hard worker, but he was badly paid. Maybe you didn't need much money in those days. Anyway, there'd be so many people around the table you could get your arm broken reaching for a slice of bread.

I went to grammar school in Hartford and I taught Sunday School. This amazes people, but I was raised, and am, a Roman Catholic. The reason we had Sunday School was because we had no parochial school in the neighborhood, and the church was across from the public school I attended. Two nuns came from a nearby convent to teach the children on Sunday—prayers, lessons and all—but they couldn't handle all the Catholic children in the neighborhood so the eighth grade students would volunteer to help them out.

I only stayed one year in high school, however—less than a year, in fact, because that's when I started in show business. Actually, I was in amateur theatrics all my life—in school and church plays—because I was so wrapped up in show business.

N.   How did this come about?

❧   CORIO : I think I must have been an exhibitionist all my life. You have to be, I guess, to want to be in this business. When I was very small a neighborhood lady took me to a vaudeville theater. I'd seen movies, but this was the first time I had seen a live show, and I was flabbergasted. I couldn't have been more than six or seven—I remember that my mother tied a great big ribbon in my hair—and I was so thrilled by that vaudeville show that I'd run to the theater every chance I got. Instead of playing with kids after school I'd walk two or three miles to the downtown section and hang around the stage door just to look at the performers coming out of the theater. Once in a while a very kind actress would come along and let me sit in her dressing room while she'd put on her makeup. I'd be enthralled. And when she let me stand in the wings to watch the show I'd be beside myself.

This early bug for the theater disturbed my mother, who was very pious and very Italian, and thought that I should marry early and have a big family. Show business was the last thing in the world she wanted for any of her children. My father died when I was very young, and perhaps, if he'd lived, it might not have been easy for me to go my way in show business. As it was, when I told my mother that I'd gotten a letter from a friend in New York who was in a show, and that I could possibly get a job in the chorus, she was shocked and horrified. (I might as well have told her I was leaving the Faith.) But I finally talked her into it because she understood that it was what

I wanted to do. So I didn't have to run away from home; she gave her consent.

I was in New York for two weeks when I got so homesick I wrote home for carfare. (I didn't even have sense enough to go to the manager and say I wanted home—and I also had my salary coming to me. $35 a week in those days.) But she was happy to send me the money and back home I came. I didn't stay long, though—the itch to get back to New York and show business returned, and a letter came from the girl friend again. Now she was in another show—she'd gone from Shubert to burlesque. (As I mentioned, I'd never heard of burlesque—we had vaudeville and Sophie Tucker and Katharine Hepburn, but no burlesque.) But off to New York I went again. It frightens me, now, when I look back, because I was only fifteen. In fact, my niece, when she was fifteen or sixteen, thought she'd like to go into show business, and I talked her into going to school instead. I had to say to myself, "After all, *I* was only fifteen when I went away," but I think I must have been more mature at fifteen. Children seem less mature, these days—not all of them. Some fifteen-year-old girls are quite grownup, but most at fifteen are fifteen, period.

So I came to burlesque, into the chorus, but in a very short time I was taken out of the chorus and put into sketches. This allowed me to do a specialty dance which eventually evolved into a strip—when I came into burlesque stripteasing was very much "in." My mother heard about this from some kind friend (and it wasn't explained to her in very nice terms) and she came to New York without letting me know, just as fast as the train could get her there. So I came on one day and there she was, sitting in the front row, and instead of dropping my costume I almost dropped dead. But eventually I got through my routine and she came backstage afterward. She wanted me to go home; she thought I shouldn't pursue this career but should go home and finish school, but I said, "No, this is for me," and I was insistent that I stay and I told her I could go on to other things. (I really never intended to stay in burlesque and continue as a stripteaser.) Finally mother said, in her genuine

Italian accent, "Well, all-a-right, so long as they look and no touch."

That first year in New York was difficult because I always had very expensive tastes. (Even when I was a little girl and mother took us down to get Easter bonnets I'd rather go without a hat if I couldn't have the one with the cherries on it, the one that cost thirty-nine cents more than the others.) The first thing I did was buy a fur coat, which I couldn't afford. I paid so much per week for it that my mother finally had to bail me out. I know she could not afford to do it. And she was sending me CARE packages—it was all very ironic, because it really would have been cheaper to buy the food she sent. But you know how old-fashioned mothers worried, especially Italian mothers. (When I'd go home for a visit she'd spend all her time cooking. All the things that Annie liked. We couldn't open the refriger-ator door because she had it so stuffed with food things came tumbling out. She was a warm, wonderful person—everybody loved her. The late Mike Todd adored her, and dozens of times he'd call from New York and say, "Mom, I'm coming up, put the pad on and the spaghetti," and he'd go up there to visit with her. She came to visit me often, and traveled with me a great deal. She'd never had any of this—she came from a small Italian village, and this was *really* the New World to her. And I don't know how it happened, but *she* developed very expensive tastes, too.)

Anyway, I advanced from a $35-a-week chorus girl to a $300-a-week striptease artist, and each time I threatened to leave burlesque my salary was raised. I was getting offers from producers in New York and they were advising me to go to school and study drama—they thought I should concentrate on becoming an actress. I was touring by this time, of course, and every time I gave my notice the producer thought I was unhappy about my salary and he raised me—"Well, all right, we'll give you $400 a week." And I thought, "Well, I'll stay with it a few more weeks," but then I'd get $500, then $600.

You don't give this money up, especially when you've never had it and when you come from a big family and there are so many things you can do for them. This is how I got hemmed in, until eventually I reached the point where I was working on percentage and my income reached a very high figure and I realized that I couldn't give up all this money and security and start all over again.

Also, of course, the image had been created. I had become known all over the country as "Ann Corio, Burlesque Queen." People couldn't think of Ann Corio without thinking of a strip-teaser or a burlesque queen, so it became rather impossible to turn around and start in as a dramatic actress.

Eventually I did do a good deal of summer stock, and legit shows and movies, but every time I was cast in a role (and it took me a while to get wise to this) it was a part that called for very little clothing. When I received a phone call in California —this was in 1958—offering me the stock company lead in "Cat on a Hot Tin Roof" I thought, "Oh, I've arrived at last, they're accepting me as an actress." But after I read the first act, and realized that Maggie wears nothing but a very flimsy slip throughout, I realized why I was being cast in this role. That play was so depressing; I always take on the characters I play. . . .

But for so many years I wanted the chance to appear before the public in clothes I could keep on.

N. Has the "look but no touch" business given you any problems?

❧ CORIO: No, not really. I think the one thing that has helped me all through my career is that I had such a wonderful family life. I wasn't one of the girls that ran away from home because of problems. My family was (and still is) very close-knit; there was a great deal of love. My mother was with me a great deal of the time, and I had so much respect for her (and this will sound strange, coming from a stripteaser) that I never learned to smoke because my mother didn't think that ladies should smoke. I think my father left a lasting impression on me, too, even though he died when I was very young. He only made about $15 a week, yet he managed to buy a house in a middle-class Irish neighborhood, and he moved my mother into it and raised his family there. We had an old-fashioned

back yard and a grape arbor and there was such a constant
warmth and closeness . . . we could only speak Italian when
we ate, because he didn't want us to forget our origins, and
somehow that, too, kept us a closely-knit family.

I think all this helped me avoid the "look but no touch"
menace. I also have the theory that a girl will be treated the
way she wants to be treated. A woman is never made; she makes
the man. A man will always treat you the way you want to be
treated. If you act like a lady he will treat you accordingly—
he takes his cue from the girl.

N. I remember you well as a stripper because I saw
you often. I was always impressed with the fact that there was
something different about your performance, and for some
reason you fascinated me more than any other stripper I saw.

❦ CORIO: Well, I never did a bump or grind. (I'll bet
most young men nowadays don't even know what a bump and
grind is.) You know, suggestive movements. I always wore
very beautiful costumes. I think that being very feminine was
part of the trick, and the use of semi-classical music. I liked to
appeal to everyone in the audience.

I always believed that to be successful in burlesque—you
know, a *real* star—I had to appeal not only to the men but to
women. I had a great following among women because of my
beautiful gowns. Did you see my final number tonight? I
recreated it exactly as I used to do it. The same music, the same
costume—a replica, that is. There's nothing offensive about it.
Husbands could always bring their wives to see me, and they
did, very often. The funny thing is this: I was out of burlesque
for twenty years until we opened *This Was Burlesque* four
years ago in New York. The very first night, when I went on
the stage I hadn't rehearsed my number, but I fell into the
routine at the very first beat as though I hadn't been away
from burlesque at all. It was like being right back at the Empress
in Milwaukee or the Alvin in Minneapolis or the Apollo on 42nd
Street.

N. You may always have been feminine but you can't
deny that you have sex appeal.

✿   CORIO: Being a woman myself I wouldn't know about that. But when a woman is terribly feminine I think she exudes a great deal of sex appeal. Twenty, twenty-five years ago I'd get letters from people who'd seen me perform that told me I was like a little girl taking her clothes off, not really realizing what she was doing. Of course I knew damned well I was taking my clothes off, and what went off when.

At first I didn't want to do this number, but I was told by Mike Iannucci, our producer, that I had to do it—if I didn't we wouldn't be honest in presenting the show. Now I enjoy it.

N.   What impact do you get from the show, knowing it's the only burlesque in existence?

✿   CORIO: I'm absolutely thrilled. This was a great challenge—the idea was Mr. Iannucci's, the title was mine. (Not that I'm so clever; I just happened to think of it.)

While I was playing in *Cat on a Hot Tin Roof* for him at his theaters in Pennsylvania he would mingle with the audiences during intermission, when they were out in the lobby, and he'd hear people say, "Wouldn't it be wonderful to see Ann in a real burlesque show again." So Mike came to me and said, "Have you ever thought of doing an all-out authentic burlesque show?" and I admitted that I hadn't. It took him about three years to pry me loose from Malibu, but finally I came East. It took us a full year to get the show on because people didn't believe that it could be done. They said, "Burlesque is banned from New York, you can't do it. We couldn't raise the money." We'd talk to people and they'd say, "Oh, this is a wonderful idea! Don't talk to anyone else—I'll put up all the money." Two days later we'd get that inevitable phone call saying, "Well, I changed my mind. You'll be closed in a day."

But I knew what I was doing. I knew that the type of show I was going to produce and direct (I never meant to direct the show, either; this was an accident) was a show that would be accepted. I wanted to put the emphasis on the comedy, the wonderful comedy sketches, the classic bits that were disappearing from the American scene. (The emphasis had gone the other way, you see, to the nudity and stripping which was not really burlesque.)

N.　　　　That's right; the great comedians—

CORIO: We reared most of the great ones. Red Skelton is still a burlesque comedian. It's no accident that he goes on year after year in television, and that his program was increased from a half hour to a full hour. He's got the stamina and versatility burlesque gave him. He's still the slapstick burlesque comedian, and every Christmas Eve he recreates his specialty, the trying-to-get-arrested scene that he made a burlesque classic.

Jackie Gleason graduated from burlesque, too. His greatest success on television was "The Honeymooners." Well, in burlesque we called it "The Newlyweds"—it's a basic burlesque sketch that he turned into a whole series.

The movies, but especially television, raided burlesque of our great talent and our classic sketches. Yet they never accepted us, wouldn't even give us credit for what we gave them. Not too long ago Danny Thomas put on a show called "The Wonderful World of Burlesque" which gave us some sort of recognition, but it really wasn't for real—it was, shall we say, "burlesque with sponsors." We got along very well without soap commercials, thank you.

But this show is great. It's pure nostalgia—it's burlesque as it was in the old days, with the chorus girls dancing on the steps, singing off key, and the comedians with the baggy pants. No stand-up "sick" jokes. We haven't a single message and we're not knocking anything. People come in for two and a half hours and forget their problems as they sit there and laugh themselves silly.

How authentic are we? Well, Steve Mills, who is our top banana, the mainstay of our show, is (to me) the funniest man in show business. He was the star, the top banana of the burlesque show when I made my debut (not quite the right word, perhaps, but leave it in) in burlesque when I was fifteen years old. Steve has been in this show since we opened and he'll be with me as long as we run.

N.   Why did you move from downtown to uptown?

☙   CORIO : We were in the very famous old Phoenix Theatre downtown—the name had been changed to the Casino East—and we were there for three years and did very well. But then came the race riots that hurt our business, so we figured we had to come into a location that would be safe and where people could find us more easily, especially tourists. (Our weekend business held up, but Tuesday, Wednesday and Thursday were off.) Now we're packing them in again, and it's wonderful —wonderful to hear people really laugh.

Another thing in our favor, perhaps, is the way Broadway is overpricing its shows. The going rate for a musical on Broadway is nearly ten bucks. We're not too popular with the Broadway Theatre League because we maintained our off-Broadway prices after we moved. Our top price is $3.95 the first part of the week, $4.95 weekends. And anyone can come to any performance and get a seat for $2.00.

N.   Do you think burlesque will ever come back?

☙   CORIO : No, it will never come back. Our show is the very last of burlesque. This is it. And it's really very sad, because when we close this is the end of so much. First of all, the sketches aren't recorded anywhere—the comics have these sketches in their heads but they've never written scripts.

The main reason burlesque can't come back is because of the astronomical costs of producing the shows. In the old days you could put on a top-rated burlesque show with almost nothing. (A pun is not intended.) Today everything is furiously expensive. Also, I wonder if anyone else would have the heart and the knowledge and the driving nostalgia to put into a show; I loved burlesque, and with my colleagues we wanted to bring it back to respectability, to restore comedians to their dignity. This is the last of burlesque, unfortunately.

N.   And all those lovely girls won't be shown as nicely—

☙   CORIO : There's no place for them to go. There's no place for them to learn the burlesque routines. I coach these girls every week in the sketches, and they've gotten very good. Tonight, when I had a difficult time speaking because of my laryngitis, the chorus girls were ready to pinch-hit for me, and they got an opportunity to do speaking parts that aren't as simple as they might appear. (Timing is a very tricky thing.) Also, in the show, they've been able to sing and do specialty dances and production numbers they'd never get near on Broadway.

And they're intelligent girls, and talented. One of them is a Phi Beta Kappa—she graduated this past summer from the University of Denver. All the girls still go to school—drama, ballet, voice. This is a great show for them because they make enough money to support themselves and to pay for their lessons.

N. Will you take *This Was. Burlesque* on the road?

CORIO: It's my great ambition, after we close in New York. I get so much mail from fans all over the country— people who saw me 20 years ago—saying, "Won't you please bring the show to Chicago," or St. Louis or wherever? They remember me, they remember burlesque, and they want one last fond look at it. I'd love to be able to bring the show to the people who won't have an opportunity to see it in New York. As I mentioned, this is the last stand of an art that shouldn't have gone. Burlesque is funny and human and lovely and provocative—there's nothing else like it.

N. Could you explain what you think we'll miss by the death of burlesque?

CORIO: Well, there are two things we'll miss—actually, aside from this show, they're gone already. First, burlesque was always the poor man's musical comedy. We no longer have low-priced theater; we've already covered the cost aspects, and it's frightening.

Second, I think that going to the theater to be able to forget problems, to relax and laugh through an evening's entertainment, is a thing of the past. Burlesque is natural, earthy, normal man-and-woman sex with laughs and beauty and fun. Today theater is wrapped up in the avant garde—the four-letter words, the problems, the prostitutes, the homosexuals. You can't go into a theater now without sitting and thinking and trying to get the message and trying to figure out the problem and many times you come out depressed.

I think you should be able to come out of a theater happy— to be able to say, "I had a good time." We all have enough problems without bathing ourselves in someone else's woe for two and a half hours.

N.   The final question : How do you manage to look the same as you did twenty years ago?

❧   CORIO : It's luck. Plain luck. Perhaps not really, because I do lead a very healthy life. I'm not a heavy eater—I love food, and love to eat, but I don't care for starches, candies, that sort of thing. I take good care of myself—I get enough exercise, and don't overindulge in any way.

For someone who takes good care of herself I sound great, don't I? Forty-seven bucks a day in Florida and I come away with laryngitis.

"I do a lot of preparatory work before I go on the stage, and as the years have gone by I do more of it, not less."

HUME CRONYN

If you were to observe only three of Hume Cronyn's performances—considering, for example, the power and depth brought to *The Seventh Cross*, the playful sensitivity displayed in *The Fourposter*, and the impassioned neuroticism breathed into *Richard III*—you would have three Hume Cronyns. He is, in short, a great actor, totally in control of whatever role he assumes. But since he has played many more than the three parts mentioned there are actually scores of Hume Cronyns, of which at least a few are known to virtually everyone in the English-speaking world.

CRONYN: I was born in London, Ontario, in 1911. For anybody whose arithmetic is uncertain, I'll be fifty-four in July. I went to one of those Canadian boarding schools which are modeled after the English public schools—Ridley College, where my brothers and uncles had gone before me. I spent nine years there, then went to the University of McGill for two years, and left there to go to the American Academy of Dramatic Arts, which about takes care of my so-called formal education. I did study abroad at the Mozarteum in Salzburg, but this was a matter of only a few months during two successive summers.

I don't know how I became interested in the theater. Certainly nobody in my family had anything to do with it. In fact, I'd have to go back generations to find any relative who was in the theater, but somehow or other Mrs. Pritchard, one of David Garrick's leading ladies, was related. I was already an actor before I discovered that she was a family connection, even though in the dining room at home there were two marvelous old steel engravings (the only theatrical touch in the whole house), one of Garrick and one of Mrs. Pritchard as Hermione in *A Winter's Tale*.

My parents went to the theater a great deal, and they traveled a lot, and since I was much the youngest member of the family (there was thirteen years between me and the next eldest child) I often traveled with them and when they went to the theater they took me.

I think my father would have been a marvelous actor. He read beautifully and he spoke extremely well. He was in political life for a while, so I often heard him speak, and he was very good at it.

Except for these remote connections I don't know why the theater attracted me. I was seven or eight years old when I started playing theatrical games with my cousin, Robert Whitehead, who is a few years younger. We used to make up plays and perform them on the staircase. He refers to it rather amusingly, now—he says I always chose the best parts, and he always had to play the villians and ended up locked in the fruit cellar.

I think part of my interest in the theater sprang from the fact that it seemed adventurous and romantic, and while it certainly was not a conscious choice, as a child, it offered a lovely alternative to the life around me, which was extremely conservative, ordered, and rather intimidating. This is apt to sound a trifle Freudian, and I'm not sure that it's accurate, but when you grow up and you've got two brothers who are over six feet tall and a father who is extremely well known and respected and who reigned like a god over the household, and you've been brought up in an Edwardian (if not Victorian) atmosphere, it's easy to long to escape from the standards and measures which are applied to the rest of an enormous family, and which have been filled satisfactorily over and over again. If you feel that you might not be able to live up to them you say, "Let me out of here."

That may have had something to do with it, but it's pure speculation. I hadn't reached my teens before I announced that I was going to become an actor—yet when I started at the University I was going through for Law. I had been persuaded by example and inference, rather than having the law laid down as "This is what you must do." To go into the theater was a bit of nonsense I would outgrow—as a child might outgrow the idea that he wanted to drive a fire engine.

But it all came back to me later on, and I realized that I did not want to go into Law, and I did not want to go into the world of business, and that I *did* want to go into the theater. When this happened I went to my mother. (My father, by this time, was very ill, and one couldn't discuss problems of this sort with him.) I told her that I wanted to forego training in the Law and wished to go into the theater instead, and that I would like to have some proper training for it. My mother, who was an extraordinarily sweet and understanding woman was, I think, somewhat mystified by this interest, but she said, "Well, this is what you want now, but go back to the University for another year and if, twelve months from now, you still want it, I'll see to it that you go to either the American Academy of Dramatic Arts in New York or the Royal Academy in London, England." With that offer I went back to complete another year at the University, during which time I completed very little work but appeared in seven different amateur productions in Montreal. Some with the McGill Players Club, some with the Montreal Repertory Theatre, some with the English Department at the University. From there I went to the Academy. I got out at the height of the Depression and started scrambling for jobs. This wasn't easy. Among the early ones were jobs with the Jitney Players. We traveled around doing one-night stands of the old comedies like *She Stoops to Conquer*, and *The Rivals* and melodramas like *The Streets of New York* in which I played Gideon Bloodgood. I drove a truck and changed the scenery and earned $25 a week. But this was my second professional job; the first I got while I was still in school.

While at McGill I got a job for a few weeks at the National Theatre in Washington, D.C., at fifteen dollars a week playing a one line walk-on. Then I joined Bob Porterfield at the Barter Theatre in Abingdon, Virginia. It was the second year of that operation. I was his partner. I had some sort of title—I can't remember what it was—Director of Productions, something like that—and Bob was the Administrative Director. In those days it was really a barter theater. We received more vegetables at the box office in exchange for tickets than we received cash. (Now it is quite·changed. Very few people bring barter to the box office any more.)

From the Jitney days on I wangled jobs somehow or other. Yet I've never overcome the feeling of anxiety that I had in those years. They left me with sort of a terrible greed to play, and at times I work harder than necessary and perhaps more often than I should. When I finish this season I hope I have enough strength of character to stop for a while.

During the last four and one-half years I've done nearly 200 weeks of work. It would have been lovely to have that happen at twenty-three or even thirty-three, but now I'm feeling the effort in the marrow of my bones. But it depends when you catch me. Give me about ten days off and the whole tune will change.

N. What were the first parts you played that began to impress public and press?

❧ CRONYN : I have George Abbott to thank for a great deal. He gave me my first really big part, in *Three Men and a Horse*, which I played for the best part of two seasons. I was twenty-three then, and had come in to read for an understudy, and by virtue of one of those theatrical stories dear to the movies I ended up playing the leading role. This was very exciting, but I didn't realize at the time (I'd had so little experience) what a break it was. In quick succession for George, I did *Three Men on a Horse, Room Service* and *Boy Meets Girl*. Working for him was a marvelous experience. I couldn't wish any young actor

better luck, because he is an expert director, was an actor himself; he's a great disciplinarian, has a great sense of character,
and is the foremost authority in this country on the playing of
farce. Farce is a very special undertaking. I think that if training could be comprised of alternate doses of the classics (particularly Shakespeare) and farce the actor might turn out very
well.

*N.*â€ƒYou've spent a great deal of time in Hollywood.
How much have you enjoyed your work out there? What are
the basic differences between motion picture and theater acting?

🌺â€ƒCRONYN: I'll answer the second question first. I
think too much, far too much, is made of the differences. There
are differences in degree. Work in the theater—well, that's
mother. If you can do that well you should be able to do the other
things well, and I think I've had enough experience in film and
television to be able to speak with some authority. To be persuasive on the stage is the most difficult, the most challenging,
and consequently the most stimulating and interesting work the
actor can do. I'm not trying to minimize the skill that's required
to give a good performance on the screen, but to me it is easier
and less interesting. It offers rewards if you're successful;—it
can be very remunerative of course—and if you have an expert
and stimulating director and a man who understands the camera
you may be pleased with the result. Alfred Hitchcock gave me
my first opportunities and I hold him in the same reverence I
hold Abbott. But the film is essentially a director's medium,
whereas the stage is essentially the actor's. The same is true of
television. Television and film are now very closely related.

I would rather work in the theater than in either of the other
two, but I'm delighted to work in the other two as well.

I can't tell you that I have a favorite medium or that I have a
favorite part. But I do have a small prayer: "Please, God, let me
not do the same thing all the time." I like to switch from one to
another. Of course, one learns quickly, with film or television,
that everything has to be pulled down and done on a different
scale. A look in the eye, the slightest movement of the mouth,
the turn of the head, the sagging of facial muscles which

wouldn't be seen in the front row of the theater register with a camera. The person who has worked almost exclusively in the theater is apt to go before the camera and have two things happen. They overplay on the one hand and on the other generally bring a greater emotional intensity (which is marvelous) than the actor whose background and training has been film only.

N.   A departure: I wanted to ask your wife this same question, but I'll let you answer it on behalf of both. What are the advantages and disadvantages of being man and wife in private life and in appearing together, as really a Lunt-and-Fontanne duo, in the theater?

❦   CRONYN: There are advantages and disadvantages. The advantages lie in the familiarities that come with marriage, so that when you work together as actors (or as actor and director; we've done that too, since I've directed Jess in four or five plays) you have a kind of shorthand between you, so that certain things can be accomplished infinitely more quickly than they could be with a stranger.

As for the disadvantages, in playing any part or directing any play you draw upon your own emotional knowledge and background, and when you perform in certain situations with your wife or husband and you're conscious that you have lived through a circumstance related to the one which exists in the play or the film, it's possible that your reactions to these circumstances are so sensitive (indeed, almost abrasive) that there springs up a conflict or exaggeration in attitude toward the problem which the playwright states, a problem which could be solved with a stranger in nothing flat. But with one's wife you've opened a can of peas you wish to God you hadn't opened.

I'm not sure this is clear. Let me invent a situation. You're playing husband and wife, and the situation is one in which the husband drinks far too much and there's a violent quarrel about the drinking. Now, if on the night before a performance you've tied on a beaut and behaved like an idiot, and you come to this scene and play it out, what happens is that reality enters and takes over in a bad sense, and discharges, through this fictional situation, a kind of violence the playwright never intended. Again, this is not well said, but roughly, where one's mutual emotional experiences may allow you to solve an acting problem very simply on the stage, it also happens that these very same experiences, the same familiarity and mutuality, may also create problems.

There can be ego problems, too. If you're working with a strange actress and you use certain terminology she may find it perfectly acceptable and see, immediately, what you're striking at. If you use the precise terminology to your wife, and her reaction is "Don't use that tone of voice to me, I know it too well and hate it," one finds that there are problems which have nothing to do with the theater but have only to do with your personal life.

Jess and I work together a lot because we like one another, because we have children, and because we like some sort of family life. Marriage is difficult and not much fun when one of you is in California and the other in New York, or one in England and one in—well, you name it.

"Togetherness" can have disadvantages. In the present case, for ten whole months, we not only share the same house, the same table, the same bedroom, but also the same dressing-room, and for the best part of twenty-four hours a day there is no respite from each other. We're also on the stage together. Married life and the theater are not easy to combine even under more normal circumstances.

But I've got a remarkable wife—she is extraordinarily talented, tolerant, and understanding.

N.   To turn to your roles. They have varied enormously, from *The Fourposter*, for example, to *Richard III*. I realize that each must vary in method of preparation, but what actual preparation and homework precedes your presentation? How conscientiously do you assume the identity of the part you play?

❧   CRONYN: This business of "What is your approach to a role?" is frightfully difficult to answer. I'm not sure that I've even read any explanation from other actors who have really made a research of their own particular attack that appeals to me. When we go and talk at schools the question is inevitable—and I take a tremendous gulp, then there's a long silence, followed by an inadequate answer.

Obviously I have my own method. Equally obviously, I don't think it's very original. But it's mine, and I would hesitate, in fact I would very carefully avoid, trying to define it for any student or young actor in terms of "This is the way *you* must go at it," because every actor has to find his own means.

I get irritated by those books and those instructors that try to lay down a law as though they have found the only true path to glory. One must find one's own means. (In this sort of discussion I'm bound to use certain maxims, perhaps even clichés, but they sum up what I think I've learned.

People have said to me, from time to time, that they admire my "technique," or I can read in print that I have "unusual technical capabilities." These comments aren't always complimentary because so often what people mean by "technique" is some sort of artificial or mechanical approach to a role.

The best definition of technique I know is this: that means by which the actor can get the best out of himself. It's as simple and as broad as that—and as personal and private. How do you make use of that instrument which is your voice, that which is your body, all the components of yourself, and that emotional reservoir of experience that must be brought to bear on everything you play? Speaking generally there are two broad approaches.

You must become so facile in the use of your physical equipment that it will respond instantly and do what you want it to do. Obviously this means that you must exercise your voice and train it and get it to respond, and understand it almost as one would a musical instrument. Precisely the same is true of your body. This is why I would urge any young actor to work very carefully, if he can, as a dancer, and to sing, and to do really quite exhaustive and frightfully dull vocal exercises. All this has to do with form. It is external. Because—and this the second approach—one can have a superb voice, marvelous control, a body trained like Nureyev, and still be a bloody awful actor.

Without the inner things—without being able to call on qualities of emotion or spirit—you're stuck with only a husk, a frame, a case. How do you go about developing what should be inside? How can you exercise that inner person, enrich it, make it immediately responsive? This is much more difficult because it's infinitely more subtle.

If I can digress for a moment.

When I did that television show with Olivier some years ago (an exhausting undertaking) we were under great pressure. It was a long show, and a difficult one. He had an enormous part, and it seemed to me our rehearsal periods spanned ten hours. There were meal breaks, but that was all, and sometimes I would go uptown from where we were rehearsing, with Larry, and he'd go to the gym—not to take a steam bath, but to work out. He was right to do that. It wasn't masochism. And I've been pretty good about doing that, too; if I hadn't I couldn't play what you saw me play last night, and I certainly couldn't play *The Miser*, since that role requires tumbling and a kind of expertise in footwork someone my age normally wouldn't be expected to have.

To go to another maxim, this time back to schoolboy physics. There's a physical law called Kirchoff's Law of Radiation, which states that the best absorbers are the best emitters. Actors are in the business of emitting, of giving out, but they can only give out what they've managed to take in and absorb. How one charges the batteries, how one learns and grows in the sense of total artistic appreciation and an understanding of the world we live in and our particular society, is a much more subtle and complex thing. One can't awake in the morning and say, "From now on I'm going to be aware, aware, aware. I'm going to be like a sponge and soak life up." You can't do it mechanically, yet without one's emotional antennae constantly aware of how people behave, respond, and react; without some degree of analysis of your own surging emotions—particularly in moments when they're ungoverned; you're not growing. You have to find out these things because that's the grist of your mill. All this must be, in turn, lent to the author by being brought to bear on the given emotional conflicts of a play or motion picture. I think we are poverty-stricken where well-trained actors are concerned. We've got a great wealth of talent, but how often do you find an actor of middle years (you can't expect it of a very young actor) who has a well-trained voice, excellent speech, a marvelously trained body, and a full emotional range, combined with intelligence, imagination and discipline?

As a matter of fact, some of the things I just mentioned are presently considered boring and old-fashioned. A whole crop of actors has grown up in the dirty sneakers and dungarees school, exhibiting a kind of militant bohemianism that says "Ah, who needs discipline? So they didn't hear me—Well, I didn't feel like it tonight." I don't say that it's conscious, but a terror seems to have developed about learning to be able to do a thing over and over again and do it well each time. The fear is that the requirements of a formal discipline in the theater will destroy spontaneity.

That just isn't true. It takes a great deal of perseverance to learn real discipline and not have it strangle you, not to fall back on stereotype forms. But the whole struggle which any artist has (and actors can be artists; it's rare, but they can be) is this struggle to keep form and content in balance. Very often he doesn't succeed. In some cases one understands the content but has never been able to give it proper form, so what comes out is a vomiting of emotion, of hysteria, of laughter or tears without reason, of an inability to involve the audience. The actor cannot play both his role and enjoy the audience's privilege at the same time.

I'm not sure how clear this will be to someone whose work isn't year by year in the theater. And I realize I haven't managed to tell you how I approach a role. Still, these things may be worth mentioning. The usual disappointment is to see actors who have some understanding of form, who know precisely how to move and use their voices, but who are hollow men. Nothing really goes on inside them. Intellectually you can appreciate that their work is skillfully done, well read, tasteful, but inside you don't give a damn. And just occasionally you see that absolute marriage of form and content, of technical application, emotion and discipline. When you see this you are so transported by what's going on up on that stage that the audience simply suspends its critical faculty. It's only after you go away that you say, "My God, how was that accomplished? How incredible that was!"

Then the actor's life becomes justified and worthwhile, and only then.

I don't have a very high opinion of acting, by the way, or of the actor's contribution to society. The only excuse for doing it is to attempt to do it bloody well. Much of it is (in my opinion—and perhaps I say this now only because I'm exhausted) a shabby life and a struggle against what seems to be unequal odds and one's own lack of responsiveness.

But you hold out some light for yourself. This is what I want, this is what I envisage, this is what I reach for—and then you discover that you can't do it at all. This is why, long ago, I gave up looking at films that I made or television shows I made—the results are always so depressing in terms of what I'd hoped to achieve, and it's too late to do anything about it. An artist can look at a canvas and say, "I loathe that," and tear it up, or put it away in the attic. The actor can't do that. You can rewrite something, or decide, in the end, that you don't want to submit it for publication.

But what the actor does has a very short life, no overwhelming importance; and compared to most of the other arts I think we are of little significance.

But back to your question. Finally.

I read extensively in preparing for Richard. I do a lot of preparatory work before I go on the stage, and as the years have gone by I do more of it, not less. And I've learned, over the years, how to go about finding my own technical approaches. I dare say I waste quite a lot of time—it would be much easier to give oneself over to a kind of academic study of the background of a classical role, and read about other performances, and the various scholarly treatises. This would be very interesting, but I'm not sure it would do a damned thing for you once you got up on the stage.

You've got to wrestle with your own unwilling creative spirit, "the slow dead heave of the will," and make your imagination function, discover within your own experience, and reawaken areas of emotion and feeling that in some way relate to the situation given you by the playwright.

And then there's that terrible business of editing. If you do become very stimulated and rich in ideas, the chances are you find six things to do where only one can be employed effectively, so your performance becomes cluttered by cleverness. The whole business of marshaling one's energies becomes more and more important as one grows older. Where to use it, where not to waste it, how to cover the fact that it may be forced, how always to leave an audience feeling that there's more there. How to lead an audience to a point where the smallest nudge can push them over a precipice of feeling instead of trundling them downhill.

N. You mentioned the fact that we see so few "total" actors. Isn't it true that England produces more of them than we do?

CRONYN: We have had total actors here, you know. I would say Alfred Lunt is a total actor. And Freddie March. And Osgood Perkins was. You probably don't remember him, but as a young actor he was my idol. He never had the standing of Lunt or March but he shared billing with them. He was an actor of equal importance if not as much public acclaim, and he could play a marvelous variety of roles. I saw him play in Molière, Shakespeare, contemporary comedies like *Once in a Lifetime*, comedy-dramas like *The Front Page*. Then he'd go off and make a film. He had a great knowledge of how to use both body and voice. He was Tony Perkins' father.

Osgood was a wonderful actor; he died when he was about fifty. But I don't know the answer to your question. There are certain obvious answers that are given over and over again, but I'm not sure that they really carry the truth.

My daughter is just going into the theater, and we're sending her over to England to go to school. I could hope for nothing better than—if she has talent and if she develops—that she go to work in repertory and start in on the classics. Here I am at my age coming to the great and important roles I've been playing here, with rather a slim background of experience to support them. I cut my teeth on endless variations of *Getting Gertie's Garter*. I worked in lots of shallow comedies, some of them terrible, playing enormous parts. They obviously taught me something, but the accent was generally on externals. The things one can learn from having to try to bring to light the work of really great writers, first-rate dramatists, these are the things that make actor-artists.

It's been said (so often that it's become tiresome) that the difference between an American and an English actor is that the English actor is better prepared for his job. Whether the formal training offered in English drama schools is necessarily better than that offered by the best American schools is something I don't know, but there is something about English theater life that pays dividends. For instance, an actor working in the theater in London can still make a film, still do television. He's got a broad potential spectrum of employment. He doesn't have to elect to do one thing or the other. Here, if you have to pay some bills and you've done a series of plays that have been failures, it means you pick up and go to California, and one does not do that for the weekend. One has to stay there for a while. People must know that you're there, and immediately available, and you work on television or in films, and if you're successful it takes a great deal of courage to turn your back on that to come back to the often unrewarding theater where you may prepare and rehearse for two or three months, play out of town for three weeks, come into New York and close inside of seven days.

You can't blame actors for becoming jaundiced with this continuing sort of experience. It's only within the latter half of the last decade that theaters such as the Guthrie and the one in Seattle and Lincoln Center are beginning to offer actors a genuine repertory experience and genuine repertory employment. When I was a young actor I tried desperately to get into Eva LeGallienne's company down on 14th Street. I knew I should be there but they wouldn't have me. And when Shakespeare was done in America it was, for the most part, done by touring English companies. Broadway theater was taken up, for the most part, by the same sort of thing that takes up its theaters today—musicals, light comedies, and their equivalent. In the 1930's and '40's more serious plays were done successfully, but the preponderance of stuff that appeared even then was rather lightweight. This may be a fine way to develop technical facility, but an actor must have more than that.

N. To turn, now, to the Guthrie Theatre. You've been here for two of its three seasons. How have you found the total experience, both from the standpoint of the theater as a part of the community and the response from the community? What do you think you've gained from it? And what do you think of the role of repertory in the American theater?

❧ CRONYN: I'll take the easiest question first—my own experience. I think I've taken a great deal out of it. No one ever had to persuade me to come here. I had written to Tony Guthrie a few years before this theater was built, saying, "If you ever again do the sort of thing you did at Stratford, Ontario, please bear me in mind because I'd like to be part of it." Tony's got a long memory, and he remembered, and about fifteen months before this theater opened he wrote to Jess and me and asked if we would become part of the company. We wrote back immediately and said, "Yes!"

I didn't want to do the same thing two years in succession, so I skipped the second season, but told him that if they wanted us back for a third, and we could agree on roles, we would come back. And here we are.

I think this is now the end of it for me. It isn't, or I hope it isn't, the end of my repertory, but I like to change. I have a horror of being caught doing the same thing over and over again. I don't like to play exclusively in movies, or exclusively in the theater; I like to switch. I also like to do other jobs within the theater. That's why I sometimes produce, sometimes direct, and sometimes even try to write. I'm often criticized by friends who think I attempt to do too many things. They're probably right, but at least the effort is made to keep involved. (I think I would probably rather write than do anything else, but it takes a kind of dedication I am incapable of giving. I've done enough of it to know. I made a living on occasions by writing, but it's lonely work, it takes enormous discipline, a tremendous investment of time, and I've learned that I'm generally better on short-range projects than something that may require a commitment of years. I can bring lots of energy to bear on something that will take three or four months, but I get rather frightened of something that stretches into unknown time. (This is why, although I've been offered opportunities to undertake the artistic directorship of repertory companies, I've always said "No." I don't trust myself to do through with it. I'm afraid I'd get halfway through, then become disenchanted and find I wasn't up to it.)

Back to the Guthrie Theatre—I think that it now trembles in the balance. One of two things can happen. It can, under the very best kind of artistic direction, with the most carefully chosen company, and by exposing itself to theatrical centers other than Minneapolis and St. Paul, develop into a National Repertory Company of considerable reputation and prestige. Or it can become a glorified local stock company playing on a repertory basis.

If this company is to attract the most gifted directors, designers and actors, it will do so only by achieving a reputation for artistic excellence which will make individuals say, "I would like to become a part of that total effort." It won't do it through the salaries it offers. It won't do it—despite the fact that Minneapolis is a charming and comfortable city—by saying, "Come and live in Minneapolis," because most actors are based either in New York, or Hollywood, and are sometimes indulgent enough to get married and have children and apartments to pay rent on elsewhere.

It's a great thing for the younger actors, of course, but you can't make a company up of just the younger actors. And you shouldn't. You need people of experience and weight to lend some sort of leadership to the company and to serve as examples. It's very hard to learn from your contemporaries alone. It's good to be exposed to people who have presumably developed to a degree beyond what is possible at twenty-five or thirty.

Now, this is Tony Guthrie's last year here as Artistic Director. He'll come back to direct a play again next season, and perhaps the season following that, but now the mantle of Artistic Director falls on Douglas Campbell, who is very gifted indeed. (I've done two plays with him, and I know.) He's got to find other directors to work here, and he's got to hold onto those elements in this company he considers most valuable, and he's got to be fairly ruthless in eliminating those he finds inferior and replacing them with the first-rate. It's an enormous job, and one has to be fairly expert as an administrator as well as the director of an individual play. One must have an understanding of all those elements that give the company a sense of purpose, to form artistic policies which are good not only for the particular season but over the long run.

Fortunately, they have Peter Zeisler and Oliver Rea. I think that the combination of talents that have made this theater outstanding under Guthrie's direction has been a very happy one. Peter knows a hell of a lot about running a theater. Oliver has been expert, I think, in maintaining the theater's relationship with the community, the University and the Foundations.

I hope this theater will go forward to an enormous success. I suppose it has already enjoyed a considerable degree of success, but I hope it goes on to an even broader one.

There are, of course, a number of these new theaters being built, and that is rather troubling because if a community is persuaded to spend X millions of dollars on this kind of creation, and it fails, it gives a terrible black eye to the whole movement. It's difficult, in America, to find people capable of undertaking the job of artistic direction. We have produced relatively few directors with a broad knowledge of the classics and an ability to execute them; and that, in itself, would not be enough. One must lend leadership to an entire company, one must become familiar with administrative problems, and there's the entire relationship with the local community which is most important.

Many of the cities that are building theaters don't know very much about the theater or its operation or the makeup of a company. In some instances I dare say they're in for surprises. (None of that matters if the results are satisfactory.) But at the moment we seem to be going through a period where people think that once the building is erected—that's it. Unfortunately, that's only the barest beginning. It isn't how you build a company. (I'm requoting something I used elsewhere by calling it "the edifice complex.") The welding of a company is a long-range program that takes perception, determination, and an absence of Auld Lang Synism. (The phrase doesn't turn out right, but I think you know what I mean.) Now, one does need the nucleus of a company to hold it together and to continue its ideal and found its tradition, but the effort has to be made continually to upgrade it, to demand more of it, and to infuse it with new blood, new ideas. You can't just repeat. Admiration for Guthrie's talents have been expressed too often to need repetition from me. What is unique about them is that rare combination which made this theater and others possible, as well as a challenge and adventure for all concerned.

The very nature of this theater, with its open stage, demands of the director a knowledge of theatrical choreography that fills the apron with life and color which is *per se* exciting. You have very few aids of any other nature—such as conventional scenery, and one requires a company that is particularly trained. One needs an expert designer—I'm thinking of costumes, really, and God knows they have one here in Tanya Moiseiwitsch. But there are certain dangers in this kind of presentation in that you may begin to give too much emphasis to the external flourish, the theatrical effect, the brilliance of groupings, color, dramatic lighting effect—and somehow the emotional essence, the content of the play, escapes you. Then the perceptive theater-goer may come out and say "Most interesting" and then wonder why the hell he was never moved.

Fortunately there have been productions here in which (and again we come back to the old business of form and content) there was an interesting and exciting form, and there was also emotional content and life.

These have been more than brilliant charades.

N. How do you find the audiences here in terms of comprehension and response?

❦ CRONYN: I don't think you can safely generalize about audiences. The audiences one plays to here are very different from the general audience one plays to in New York. I would not say that they are less sophisticated, or less knowledgeable, but they are less jaded. This audience is prepared to follow, to concentrate and listen to a degree you are less likely to find in New York. This in itself is encouraging. (When you came in this morning you said that you felt, last night, that people were making a real effort to follow what is a difficult plot—not one person in a hundred is acquainted with all that family history—by waiting until intermission to do their coughing. This is what one hoped for.)

In New York I don't think you get that degree of tolerance, and you get very quick judgment and superficial opinion. A lot of theater-going in New York is done by a sort of professional audience. I don't mean that the people in the audience are from the theatrical profession, I mean that they make a business of going to the theater. Consequently they are superficially astute about it, but their theater-going is a fashionable rite, and this becomes dreadfully dull.

I have heard it argued here that one has a duty and an obligation in a classical theater to re-educate the audience, to make them listen, to bring back to them, by force as it were, the appreciation of the spoken word, of lyric writing, and redevelop their powers of concentration even at the expense of entertainment (which word has a kind of shabby connotation associated with Broadway).

I disagree with this. I think "entertainment" is a perfectly sound word and a desirable reason for going to the theater. I don't believe, for instance, that if you take a play by Congreve—a play that runs three and one-half hours, employing imagery, language and syntax which, to our ears, is archaic and do it less than brilliantly—you really encourage an audience to come back for more Congreve, or, indeed, for more Restoration Comedy. I think that *Richard III* is a much better presentation today, quite severely cut. For a total understanding of what is going on one must know the Henry's, particularly *Henry VI*, part III, and the background of the Wars of the Roses. Tony Guthrie uses a very good analogy. Richard was written as long after the facts it dramatized took place as we are now removed from the Civil War. Now, if we go today and see a play in which there are references to Generals Grant and Lee, and to Richmond, Appomattox, and Cemetery Ridge, and in which they play "Dixie," the probability is that anyone with even a grade-school education knows that it's about the war between the North and the South, knows what the issue was, knows who won, etc., even though they have no particular interest in American History.

But when you go back to the Wars of the Roses and start with what Margaret has to say about Henry VI, her husband, and young Edward, and what happened at Tewksbury, the audience is lost. So there are great passages in the play which—for the audience for which the play was written would be easily understandable to say nothing of the fact that the language (while very often exercising a vocabulary far beyond that of the man on the street) was infinitely more familiar to them than to the audience of today—are better omitted. (Fight your way out of that sentence.) Now, scholars and purists cluck at us for cutting the classics, but they are batting a very sticky wicket because we are, at the outset, demanding more of today's audience than Shakespeare demanded in his time. Today the whole business of entertainment communication has become a sort of visual shorthand. The best of contemporary movies are a compression of imagery. Take Fellini or a half-dozen others; in their pictures one emotional impact follows another, one impression follows another, so quickly that a total awareness takes place in the fraction of a second. An equivalent emotional impact in a verse play of Elizabethan times might demand a page-long soliloquy. We grow more impatient, now, with words, and it's a pity. There is less appreciation of them because we employ them less. I'm exposed to people who talk a lot—writers, directors, actors (who are always talking)—but I don't really hear much first-class conversation. If anything there must be less inclination toward good conversation in other professions. Perhaps, by now, engineers are using mathematical formulae as speech. But to sit around a room and hear discussions about fundamentals, contemporary mores, broad political philosophies—never. Or hardly ever. I have a feeling that there was a time when fundamentals were discussed more easily—certainly there must have been such times because they were reflected in the theater. Today there is a very thin market for the exchange of serious ideas in the theater (at least in New York) or for language, and even wit—better not stray too far from Joe Miller's Joke Book. And I also have a feeling that we're all too exhausted to be required to think or listen—or is this only a reflection of my own attitude at the moment?

N.   The final question : Are you conscious of an obligation to any quarter in your portrayal of a character?

❧   CRONYN: You have a sense of obligation to the author, the playwright. He's the wellspring of what you're doing, and one has to do justice to his work and avoid perverting it. There is an equal obligation, of a different kind, to the audience. This is a relatively simple one to discharge. It means that you come to the theater prepared to work, trained to be heard, sympathetic to the audience's needs, and able to vary the playing as one senses the different requirements of an audience. And they do vary—often the variations are subtle, but there is a difference between an audience of students or University people and a matinee audience of middle-aged ladies. Emphasis, pace, speech patterns—all may be altered a bit to get to the audience, hold it.

But the great obligation is to the playwright, who has (or should have) created interesting things to move and provoke people, to share or suggest experiences beyond the daily round, to illuminate something either forgotten or never experienced. This is when theater is at its best and when the audience can take most from it. It doesn't often reach that level. I'm not terribly enthusiastic about the contemporary theater. It's an uphill course. I think that the theater's palmiest day was in Shakespeare's time and again in the 18th century and in the late

1800's and the early 1900's, when the theater provided a kind of entertainment that could be found nowhere else. There was no competition from films, television, or mass publication. The only really equivalent delight was in reading and in conversation.

Theater, at least in this country, has become a minor art which caters to a very small luxury audience, most of whom are escapists. People often go to the theater now with a kind of intolerant deafness. Living at the pitch and pace we do, battered continuously by oral and visual images, a man comes home to rest and escapes either into his newspaper or looks at television, or goes to a film where he can be amused and say, "Please don't make me think and please don't make me listen, really listen."

With the best playwrights—certainly with the lyric ones— one must listen and want to listen, and want to be stimulated and disturbed and provoked. Marvelous things happen in the theater when one can say, "I hate it," or, "I don't believe it and I must tell you why." The playwright has accomplished something again, in a converse way, when one comes out and says, "He's right, I'd forgotten that is true."

But to use the theater to pass the time, to fill a vacant evening—no. Go to the film, turn on television, sleep. But the harassed, image-bombarded, rushed, shouted at, pressured public should recognize the theater for the encouragement and stimulation it offers, the chance to get the hell away from contemporary social pressures. We all need individual Waldens—not for the peace of the pond alone but to rediscover our own lives.

"*If you can swing . . . nothing else matters . . .*"

SAMMY DAVIS, JR.

In the course of a casual conversation, just before his death, Ian Fleming paid what I consider to be the perfect tribute to Sammy Davis, Jr. We were talking about reincarnation when he said, "Next time I'd like to be born as Sammy Davis, Jr. He's the most incredibly gifted man I've ever seen—and to think of being able to take an audience and hold it and actually reshape it to make it *your* audience must be the most thrilling thing that can happen within *any* lifetime."

After seeing Mr. Davis in nightclubs, on television, and in *Golden Boy* I can only concur with Ian. But if there *is* such a thing as reincarnation, and we have a choice of identities, how many Sammy Davis, Jr.'s will there be?

DAVIS: I was born in New York City, into a theatrical family. I was in show business by the time I was two years old. My interest, therefore, was something I inherited—I had no choice in the matter. Most kids have a choice of what they want to be—I guess you could call it a misery of choice. Not me. No chance to be bricklayer or dentist, dockworker or preacher—I guess I was meant for show business even before I was born.

Now, I'm not complaining. I am very pleased and happy about the association I have with show business, my whole life in the business, not because I am—in quotes—successful—but because it's great to perform. I was as happy when I was in the opening act at the Strand Theatre in New York or the Royal in Baltimore. Show business is a love affair, as far as I'm concerned, and I can't imagine doing anything else.

N.   How were your talents—and they can only be called extraordinary—discovered?

❦   DAVIS: They weren't discovered. Nobody discovered them, I never discovered them. They became a matter of awareness.

Actually, I don't think anyone has discovered them yet. I would like to think that whatever—again, in quotes—is a Sammy Davis—and every performer, every artist, would like to know—has not been touched yet. Let me put it this way: If I had to look back on my life and think, "Hey, I didn't grow any that year!" I'd be a very unhappy man because you can't survive without growing. I suppose it starts out as a point of view, and in a way it's a very commercial thing, but you must, in our country, progress. Grow, improve, develop.

The one thing about America as contrasted to any European country is the way we've got to make headway. The cats in Europe can stand still. Take Gerry Mulligan, who's sitting here with us: he could go to Europe right now and live for the rest of his life like a king, and he could live like a king based on what he did ten years ago. You dig? Because all the cats over there are blowing what they blew ten years ago. They don't progress. I've never seen it to fail that any expatriate, whether he's an artist in terms of being a writer or an artist as a musician or an actor, they go over there and stay and when they come back— man, they're ten years behind even if they've only been gone a year.

Our country motivates artists, it's a wheel that runs and runs fast. You don't know what's going to happen next week in America, who's going to be top dog. And just when you have it all figured out—just when you decide it's all Beatle-rama—up comes Louis Armstrong with "Hello, Dolly." Louis Armstrong never had a million-seller in his life, and all of a sudden he's top dog with "Hello, Dolly."

There's no telling. No predicting. Nothing for sure. You can't sell a big band—suddenly a big band starts to go. You can't sell jazz, they just won't dig it, and all of a sudden in one little town way out in left field jazz starts swinging. But you go to Paris and you see the cats they're blowing the same things that went on long, long ago.

Now, the same thing applies to our business—we can't stand still. Not for a minute. I don't want the audience to second-guess me—not ever. I don't care what I open up with, but I don't want them knowing beforehand. I can't afford to have them say, "Well, he sings and he dances, then does the impressions, and then he plays the drums." In Vegas, for a long while I didn't play any instruments and I didn't dance. Then I cut out the impressions for three or four visits, and people would begin to ask for them. I keep switching.

Golden Boy surprised and bugged a lot of people. They said, "Why does he want to do a Broadway show?" I did it because I want to grow. Sure, the money is marvelous, but if I can't live with myself after I've made the money then the money is no good. I know, when I leave *Golden Boy*, that I'll be a better performer than I was when I went into it because of the exposure to fellow-actors, the regimentation, the sort of confinement that a Broadway show has upon an individual in terms of what he must do onstage. I'll be better, that's all.

The same goes with television. I did one special, and it came off great, and I was very happy about the reaction to it, but if I can't make the next show better—if I can't top it—then I don't want to do it. I want to get out of it, because if it isn't better I'm no good to anybody.

The cat that makes it in America, the cat that's talked about, the cat that survives, he can change the world around him because everybody wants to copy him. You dig? The Mulligan sound went around the world. Ever hear of a Japanese sound coming this way, or a German sound, or an English sound? Take Beatle-rama, the whole fantastic thing. It's a throw-out from us. The other day I was doing "Hullabaloo" and I said to somebody, "We've got guys in prison, guys who can't get a job, who can sing a hell of a lot better than these English cats." They come over here and do Negro music—they finally learned the blues. Or maybe they just learned to write the chords. We bounced it over there ten, twenty, thirty, forty years ago, and now we're getting it back.

N.   I'd like to ask you about *Golden Boy*—from the standpoint of your night-after-night performance. Do you vary, at all, or is the audience consistent in its reactions?

❧   DAVIS: The audience reaction changes every night, and I have to play the role according to my audience. Some nights, for instance, the love scene can be played in a very tender manner, the way you'd do it in a serial love story, and other nights it's got to be a blood-and-guts love story. But that's an actor's problem he has to work out. Therefore the night club experience pays off. In a night club you've got to size up your audience quickly—do they want to hear you sing, do they want jokes and gags? Do they just want to laugh or do they want the artist? Hell, you find out what they want and go the whole route.

This is paying off for me in terms of the theater. There's enough give in the performance to shift the emphasis, slow it up or play it fast.

But I love doing *Golden Boy*. It's a great show, it's tremendous exercise. I don't mean in terms of physical exercise but in terms of mental. Not to be second-guessed, as I mentioned before, giving them what they want and a little bit more. I want to learn.

Most of the trouble with most people in America who become successful is that they can really and truly get by on bullshit alone. They can survive on it. You know, you can live on a good record for months. You can live on any one thing for months if you pick and choose your spot. One good TV show can make some people last longer than they have a right to last. They milk it and get everything out of it they can without putting in a new nickel's worth. I know a singer who lives on one

hit every five years—and every five years it's the same record
in a different tempo. In between times he does nothing. But I'm
trying to achieve another level, and another one after that.

Do you mind if we get back to discussing Richard Burton—
the conversation we had before we started taping?

N.   No. I said that I wished Burton had stayed with
Shakespeare repertory a little longer because I thought he
needed the discipline.

❦   DAVIS: Well, you know of course, the Olivier and
O'Toole and Albert Finney and Paul Scofield—all the brilliant
Shakespearean actors who epitomize the British classical actor—
say that as a Shakespearean actor Richard played, without
doubt, the definitive Hamlet of all time. I'm not talking about
the exercise he did here in New York, because all that was was an
exercise. In which he said, "I want to go and do it now as an
exercise and have some fun with it," because he already had
done the definitive Hamlet. Because of age he couldn't go onto
the deeper, older Shakespearean roles, but he did so magnifi-
cently with all the Shakespearean roles he performed that I
don't know what he could garner by staying in repertory for a
few more years. To me the discipline Burton has—or the lack of
discipline—is a marvelous thing because it adds excitement. It
makes Burton what Olivier ain't. (I love Olivier, I relish everything he does; he's a genius. Don't mistake me. If you had to
worship something mortal here on earth I would go and bow
twice a day to wherever Olivier was standing.) But Olivier, who
is a technical genius, works from the outside in and has a
magnificent quality for this. Consequently, in *Othello* the
whole thing he manufactured—playing Othello as a combination of a Jamaican and American Negro—was incredible. All
sensuality, all cliché—he grabbed every cliché he had ever been
exposed to in terms of Negroes; everything he read or heard or
knew, and everything he could borrow from every Negro actor
who'd played *Othello* was in those scenes.

But when I think in terms of Burton I find more excitement,
more fluidity. Actually, I think he's finally growing into a
splendid motion picture actor. Magnificent, in fact. But I think

that on the stage he has all of the things most of our guys lack
and most of the things the British cats lack. Now, both O'Toole
and Finney are buddies of mine—I know them and I know their
work very well. Each is marvelous in an individual way. For
instance, O'Toole was great in one big Shakespearean play in
London; he was superlative. He came back and did *Hamlet* and it
was a fiasco. It was like "forget it." Yet he'll go back again,
maybe in ten or fifteen years, and he'll be brilliant at it. But the
first time out that Burton did for an important audience and the
important London critics he was classified as *the* definitive
Hamlet.

So as I said I don't know what he'd garner by going back to
repertory. He got the discipline, maybe we should call it the
foundation, he needs, and from now on he should develop as
Richard Burton. He has taste, he has selectivity, he has timbre,
richness of voice. He certainly has the gait of Shakespeare—it
rolls off his tongue so beautifully that the guy from Altoona
who came to see *Hamlet* to see the guy who'd married Elizabeth
Taylor stayed to see Burton the actor. I feel pretty strongly
about this because I think Burton is unique. You can't compare
him to anybody.

Before you came Gerry Mulligan and I were talking about
jazz and what it is today as opposed to what jazz was when we
first met. I was struggling, then, and he was doing the things
that meant something.

Gerry's a cat who's vastly underrated. He's an underrated
musician, an underrated arranger. He took and polished and
really made the whole form of music they later labeled "West
Coast Jazz." It wasn't West Coast Jazz—it was Gerry Mulligan.
The cool sound. Everybody cashed in on it, but he never did
cash in on it because he was the guy who never varied from his
original point of view.

So what you're saying is that you would have loved Richard
Burton to have assumed and kept the same posture dramatically
that Gerry assumed and kept musically. But Richard did give
in to the commercial in terms of motion pictures. But he did not
give in artistically because he's taken all his repertory training,

and his definitive *Hamlet*, and gone to the top in another art form. In other words, he's going to do a lot more than another *Hamlet*.

Watered-down Burton—even tricky Burton—is a better actor than most other actors could be in three lifetimes.

N.   I surrender. I'd like to get back to you, now : Could you state your objectives as an entertainer? (And I have to use the word "entertainer" because you're so many things—actor, singer, dancer, etc.)

DAVIS : I want only one thing, and don't let anybody ever kid you. If you've worked as hard as I've worked for what I've gotten today; if you've paid as many dues in thirty-five years as I've paid, in one business (and this is the only business I know) ; then you want everything that's coming to you.

By the same token, however, rather than lie back and wait for it to come, I want to work for it. When I signed that contract with a motion-picture studio to produce my films you'd better know that I have worked for that contract in every area there is to work in, and I'm entitled to the contract. When I get a contract with a network I have paid my dues and I have worked to get it, and they know that they're going to get, for their dollar, the best that I have to offer. I'll give it the best. No "Catch you later."

Whether these shows will be successful or not nobody knows, but if you give your best you can hold up your head and say, "Well, hell, man, I swung at the ball. I swung at it so hard I twisted around three or four times." But if you just let the ball go past you can't hold up your head.

Before we did *Golden Boy* people said, "It's a bomb, it will never open up." We came in—we all worked hard (not just me). Everybody worked, contributed, knocked themselves out. Now the same people come back and say, "Well, I knew you'd make it—you've got Sammy Davis and this and that and how can you fold." It's very easy, how you can fold. Frank Loesser just folded for a million dollars—*Pleasures and Palaces* died in

Detroit. So what I want is everything that's coming to me as long as it really is coming to me.

N.   How has the fact that you are a Negro affected your career?

❧   DAVIS: It's helped me. Enormously. It helped me in the beginning by making me mad—mad that I was colored. I saw cats around me who couldn't shine my shoes, as far as talent was concerned, getting all the breaks. This doesn't make for happiness. Then one marvelous day I woke up and said, "What the hell are you bitching about? Being colored isn't stopping you. Nothing is stopping you. Work, learn—if you want to be as good as they are learn to be as good as they are. Learn the things Donald O'Connor learned. Learn how to dance, how to sing, how to act, how to play an instrument, how to work in motion pictures, how to work in television. You want to be that good, then be that good. Work at it."

Being a Negro gave me this as a starter—made me determined to be the best. So being a Negro really hasn't hurt me in my profession.

Tomorrow I should know whether or not I sign a deal with a major network for television. Well, it's been a long uphill climb, and how sweet it will be because when I meet the three big cats at eleven o'clock tomorrow morning, when they have the figures and everything, how sweet it will be to know that it's happening. That once I thought, "Hey, I made it, and I never thought I'd make it because I'm colored."

I don't know if this makes any sense to you, but if it doesn't I can't explain it. What I'm really saying in essence is that life is what you make it. Being white can be a burden, too—you dig? Would you want to go through what Gerry Mulligan went through? As a white jazz musician? With every colored cat putting him down, and all the publications coming out saying, "His music's synthetic, it isn't real jazz," and going through all the pros and cons and analytical drivel that didn't add.

This, when the only thing he knew was what he was playing, and he knew better than the dopesters that what he was playing was good.

White, black, it doesn't make much difference—not if you're really out to prove something, because anybody who's really trying to prove something has a rough time of it. But if you can swing, if you've got the rhythm which in essence is the key to life, nothing else matters.

"Rodeo, *of course, changed my life.*"

AGNES DE MILLE

Oklahoma! stands as a landmark in the history of our theater. It introduced the team of Rodgers and Hammerstein, proved that music in the theater can bring to vivid life a show with more substance than musical comedy, more popular appeal than opera. It also established what we might call the semi-classical dance, and the American folk ballet, as valid and integral parts of our theater. Credit for the latter goes, of course, to the determined and ingenious Agnes de Mille—who's been tied to a star ever since.

DE MILLE: I was born in New York City, on 118th Street in Harlem, in a house where rats now seem to eat the babies. Conditions were a bit different, then, however, and I was not eaten. I started growing up in New York, but at an early age we moved to Hollywood, and it was my great good luck to see Hollywood change from a little country town—a beautiful town, really, with orchards and groves and big garden areas—into the world center of the film industry. It was an exciting transition, particularly since with it came the growth of all the Universities and the music centers and the other bits and pieces of culture in the Los Angeles area.

My mother was instrumental in establishing the Hollywood

Bowl, actually launching its first two seasons. This was most fortunate for me, because at a very crucial, formative time of my life I heard a symphony concert every summer night for three months straight. I would lie flat on my back in the sage and listen, and it was lovely.

I went to college there, at U.C.L.A., at a time when it was expanding from a small college into a giant, and the director of the college (he was called the director because the President was in Berkeley) came East and raided the colleges for their top graduate doctors. In one year he nabbed something like ninety-three of them, which was an enormous and valuable addition. I got these doctors when they were hot off the griddle, frantic with ambition and filled with idealism. They took us over the hurdles in a most thorough way, and it was a wonderful education. For example, Lily B. Campbell, a professor of English literature and English drama, was a perfectly remarkable woman. (She is now retired.) I had the good sense to keep the notes I took from her courses through all these years, and when I was working on my new book I went back over them and found a lot of very good material. They gave me a doctorate two years ago at California, and I said I would be very honored and delighted to receive it if Lily was in the room. She was there, and I threw my arms around her and said, "I had no idea of what a good course this was!" and she said, "My dear, it was the best in America, there's never been anything like it," and this is absolutely true. It was a phenomenal course, and I actually had several of the same caliber. In philosophy I had a professor Charles Reiley who was a pupil of William James, and he used to give talks on comparative religion which were so extraordinary they had to be held in the college auditorium, a vast place, and at the end of the season (my jargon has changed over the years; we used to call it "term") the kids just sat there and clapped and clapped and clapped until we were half-way through the next hour. Nobody cared. I've never forgotten it, because the entire university was filled with the same vivid enthusiasm. I think that if I really have a talent it's a talent for being in the right place at the right time—when things are happening. (I don't plan this; I generally position myself reluctantly. I had planned to go to another college, but my mother didn't want me to go out of town; she wanted me near home because I was very young. I wasn't really too young— mothers have a way of thinking a girl is too young if she's below fifty—but I went along with her, to my great good fortune.)

I came to New York because my parents divorced, and for a long, anguished time I couldn't find a job here. I broke my heart over that, and kicked around with a lot of experimenters and failures, people like Martha Graham, so that I saw the renaissance of dance actually happening on 9th and 10th Streets. I was (unwillingly) a witness to it and a participant in it, but I myself felt a total failure. Then I went to London and failed there with a group of kids that included Frederic Ashton, Antony Tudor, etc. Collectively we failed for years. I came back to America when the war threw me out of England and got in with a group that included Josephy Anthony (now one of the finest directors of American theater). We always seemed to be on the edge of real achievement, yet we always failed. But I was with them at the moment they perceived what they were going to do— an exciting time to be with anybody. What they envisioned for the dance, particularly the dance as associated with theater, was truly remarkable.

Shortly after we got into the war I got my first big break, which I can only call a very happy accident. The Russians decided that it would be politic and patriotic if they added an American ballet by an American instead of a Russian to the repertoire of the Ballet Russe, so they asked me to do one—I think they thought that the novelty of it all would balance any lack of quality that might show up. Well, I didn't care *why* I was asked, I just bloody well did it, and I did the best I could. It was a smash. We had twenty-two curtain calls opening night— *Rodeo* really was "in." I was even asked to be on the faculty of the School of American Ballet—they had no Americans on the staff, but now that we were at war they figured it would be a good idea if they had. However, I declined—I had been sheltered and protected and nurtured by the Ballet Arts school at Carnegie, and I reasoned that since they had seen me through the bad years I was more or less obligated to stay. Also I was pleased to.

At any rate, the people who were to do *Oklahoma!* (the show was as yet unnamed) attended the opening night of *Rodeo,* and they decided I'd be a good risk. They didn't decide this right away, however—Richard Rodgers was reluctant. He saw that there was talent, but he thought that the conditions of Broadway were totally different from the conditions of the Russian ballet, and he doubted whether or not I could handle a bunch of tough Broadway people. But he finally agreed to try me.

As it turned out I didn't handle a tough bunch of Broadway people because I brought in my own students. That's what *really* changed things—well-trained dancers and acting dancers were used in a Broadway musical. Bambi Lynn was in that first chorus, and so was Diana Adams, now a bone fide ballerina, one of the world's great ballerinas (now retired). Marc Platt was in it—he now runs all the shows at Radio City. It was a Who's Who.

N.   Didn't *Oklahoma!* really establish the dance as a medium in Broadway musicals?

❧   DE MILLE: That would be a pretty broad statement to make. There had been predecessors. In Balanchine's biography, the newest one (he seems to have one a year written by one person or another), it is stated that he introduced ballet to the American theater, but that isn't true. Charles Weidman and Doris Humphrey (and she was a woman of really notable achievement) were doing ballets in musical reviews in the early 1930's. They made quite a success of them, too. Balanchine came on a bit later and began producing ballets using his wife, Vera Zorina, as his star. It is claimed in this book that he did the first dream ballet—he probably didn't, but he did precede me with one by years. (I don't think this matters at all; there have always been dream ballets.)

The thing that mattered most with *Oklahoma!* as far as the dance was concerned was the absolutely overwhelming success of the play as a whole, which was historic, and the way that ballet was so enmeshed with the characters and the plot development that it could not be deleted. Everyone in the ballet was a character in the play, so that the style of the ballet was the style of the play. It was of a piece, so to speak, and the dancers were of the texture of the play and in style and in content with the rest of the play. This was new, as was the caliber of the dancers, all the dancers, not just the leads.

I didn't particularly intend to break with tradition. You see, I hadn't seen many musicals because I couldn't afford to go to them, so I didn't know enough about traditions to break any purposely. It just seemed to me to be the right way to do things. And it was my marvelous good fortune to be with people like Rodgers and Hammerstein, who were ready for innovations and extremely sensitive to all types of suggestions. For example, Oscar had written out the scenario of the ballet, the dream ballet that was to end Act I, and I didn't think it was any good. (It was a ballet about the surrey with diamond wheels and gold fringe and Aunt Ella dressed as a circus queen and the cast was actually transferred to the circus.) And I said "Mr. Hammerstein, this isn't the way dreams are. Dreams are generally dreadful, and I think we should do anything we can to introduce suspense at the end of Act I to help swing us into Act II. The play is so slender in its meaning that whether the girl would go to the party with one boy or with the other boy is hardly earthshaking." At the moment we were losing every island in the Pacific, and I couldn't imagine an audience getting excited about boys dating girls. And I said "There's no sex in the play. If we could introduce the post cards . . ." and he was enchanted. So we got our Post Card Girls in short skirts with feathers in their hair and went on from there. But I was talking to people who were sensitive and responsive. . . .

It's a wonderful thing when you can work this way. I've done nineteen shows, now, but I don't always talk to collaborators. It's a great thing when you can speak up, and their eyes light up and they say, "Go on with your suggestion." When they neither try to block you or take over, but truly collaborate. That's when you have successful shows. It doesn't have to be a great general collaboration of *everyone*, but when you get three or four people you've got an enormous collaboration.

N.   Can you pick out individual evenings and events that stand out? That are significant for you and the work you've done?

❧   DE MILLE: *Rodeo*, of course, changed my life—it just bloomed from one night to the next. I don't think our opening night production was a great performance, frankly—we did many better ones as time went along. But I was a success right then, and everything changed. (Of course, you're only as much of a success in New York as your last production; that isn't true in Europe, but it is true here. Reputations accrue, over there; here only your latest work determines your rank.)

A better performance of *Rodeo*—truly a beautiful one—came on our first night in Los Angeles when my father and my uncle were present. We'd had time enough to smooth out all of our problems, and we danced fit to kill. Another great night came in *Oklahoma!* the first night I brought my husband to see the play. He'd married me without ever seeing anything I'd done. The cast did an extraordinary job out of pure love for me. My husband went to war the next day; he never told me if he liked the show or not, but he said that he had an awful lot on his mind. Obviously, he had; he shipped overseas forty-eight hours later. Yes, there've been extraordinary performances. The first night that Nora Kaye did *Fall River Legend*. (Not the opening; she was ill on opening night and Alicia Alonso jumped into the role and learned it. She had never danced a dramatic performance in her life. Yet she learned this very difficult role—at that point it ran fifty-three minutes, nonstop: she was never off the stage. Morton Gould's music was difficult, too. Alonso is a very great dancer, but she's not very musical, so the role was hard for her, but she was successful. It had been designed for Nora, and Nora was lying in bed in a hospital, so I sent her a duplicate of the bouquet I'd sent Alonso with a note that said, "We're waiting!" She came back when she could and danced it. Her performance was miraculous. I remember that my husband and I walked home from the Met arm-in-arm just saying "Oh, boy!") Others—oh, there are so many. The opening night of *Brigadoon* was spectacular. But if the dancers are good it isn't just the opening nights that stand out; it's all the performances that talented, professional people give.

N. How has the dance fared on Broadway since *Oklahoma?*

DE MILLE : The dance is not as important this decade as it was in the late 1940's and the early 1950's. There are two reasons for this. One is the fact that the best choreographers, men like Jerome Robbins and Michael Kidd, have become directors and producers. They've done this very deliberately because they realize that they have enough power, by fulfilling other functions, to protect their own work—it isn't cut to pieces and destroyed. Also, there's a great deal more money in these other functions. A choreographer who is just a choreographer doesn't get very much money, and he cannot get royalties unless he can command them by individual power. The major producers, composers and writers will not grant royalties to a choreographer beyond the New York run, so the choreographer loses out on subsidiary rights—the stock performances and the amateur performances which actually aggregate (surprisingly) a bigger business than New York City. We do not participate even when our dancers are used—and mine have been used many times, almost universally in *Oklahoma!*, *Brigadoon* and *Carousel*, for example. These dancers are built into the integral plan of the show, but yet I get no money at all after the initial engagement. Jerome Robbins didn't like this any better than I did, but he's more energetic, and he's now gotten himself into the producer's role, thereby getting his full rights and maintaining them. Now, the other reason is that writers and composers realize that they now have to divvy up with us on the Broadway run, so they bypass us. The dancing in contemporary plays on Broadway consequently tends to be less and less, except in a show like *West Side Story*—a show which, in the full sense, points the way toward what will be American lyric drama. (To date we have not written a good American opera, unless we count *Amahl and the Night Visitors*, which was written by an Italian who has become an American citizen but writes in the Italian operatic tradition. Since then *Vanessa* and several others. I don't know why we haven't written a good opera—we have good composers, good musicians, but they don't work in that medium. We have, however, an extraordinary lyric drama through movement. I think that Martha Graham's work must be considered as more than just dancing. She has produced a theater, and it's a valid and complete theater, as *integral* as the Kabuki, let us say, or any of the Indian classic drama. Jerome Robbins, in *West Side Story*, began to produce lyric theater, expressing drama through movement and singing, which opens the door to the future. I really believe that our way of lyric expression is going to involve movement to a greater extent than music per se.)

N.   Could you evaluate what we might call "the state of the dance" in both the theatrical and classical areas?

❦   DE MILLE: Some of what is being done is very good—and some is very bad, as always. I think Graham is a genius. I think Balanchine is a genius. (His work isn't uniformly good, but whose is? He does an awful lot of work—four or five ballets a year. He has done more than any other person in the history of dancing; he's turned out two dozen masterpieces, an incredible achievement since it is so very hard to do these things. You're always dependent on living bodies.)

I think Frederic Ashton is a first-class choreographer whose works will live, and I think MacMillan is another. I think that Jerome Robbins is starting to find new ways and means of making the dance more vivid and immediately important.

Then there are the great folk troups of the world, like the Moiseyev Dancers of Russia, The Bahanyhan of the Philippines, and IMBAL in Israel. The caliber of their work—the seriousness, drama and humor—is extraordinary. These things we always have with us.

I don't think that dancing has yet been discovered by the films. It's a new art, a separate art. Jerry did the best job of all in filming the dancers of *West Side Story*. He almost caught the dancers on camera and transferred them to film to give us the sense of presence we get in theater. But these techniques have to be learned. A good choreographer is not necessarily the person to handle a camera.

They haven't touched dancing on television. The production numbers are atrocious. They just start the camera and let the dancers dance. Unfortunately, once again new techniques are called for.

John Butler has done a great many good, interesting things with the dance on television, but he doesn't get the best hours. He does them on Sunday morning. But he's made enormous strides in the handling of a camera. Dancers are going to have to be composed especially for television and filmed with time and care. The limitations are not only spatial, or involved with the distortions the camera affects (which can be used to advantage, after all), but get terribly involved with time. Television studio time costs enormous amounts of money, astronomical sums, really. So those who want to compose for television are prevented on this practical basis. You need the time on camera for experimentation, for development, for taping, but costs are such that it can't be taken.

In the grand old days in Hollywood they'd film scenes over and over again—in Shearer's glamorous era at MGM they'd make thirty-five and forty takes of one scene. I'm not sure they needed to take all that footage, but they did it, with a full lighting crew and a full camera crew. In the end they'd have an Irving Thalberg masterpiece that would pay off in the millions. But there's no possibility of this kind of heyday on television. An exception was a trip up into Canada to do a Canadian telecast using the Royal Winnipeg company. This was a government station, and we were treated much more liberally with production time and camera time and expenses, but it's an example of what can be done. (I did a Scottish piece for them because the Scotch technique of the dance lies very close to ballet. It isn't the same, but it was suitable, and we did a ballet called *The Bitter Wierd* which my husband says is a vile name. "Wierd" means "fate," you know, in Celtic, and he said, "If you mean fate why don't you say fate?" But I like the sound of "Bitter Wierd." It was a hit, so I did it on CBC, went up to spend a whole week with them in Toronto. I didn't get great amounts of money, though I did get a very good fee, and I was treated like Madam Queen. When I was in Manitoba I felt as though they'd given me Manitoba. It was a lovely feeling; I've never had it here.)

N.   I'd like to turn to your writings, now, because whether you're dealing with autobiography or the dance you write as well as you choreograph (if that's a word. If it isn't, it should be) . What are your objectives as a writer?

❦   DE MILLE : Primarily I think I write for myself, as a person and as a dancer. I don't know—I never know—who the public is. I could never guess what the public wants; I do what pleases me, and it's all I can do. I know my taste isn't the best, but it's my taste. Perhaps my strength is that I'm fairly commonplace, thus what pleases me pleases others.

As to my material, I try to tell the truth as much as I possibly can. I'm a little careless with facts, however. When I did my history of the dance I turned the whole section on classic dancing over to Rudolph Wittkower, the head of the Department of Art History at Columbia University. I said, "Will you please review Greece and Rome for me because I don't know much about them." He phoned back and said, "Well, it's all quite charming. You went at it with a style all your own. Facts don't bother you, do they?" Well, we cleaned up the facts. (I don't think facts matter except in a dictionary or an encyclopedia.)

I do try to be as fair as possible, always remembering that I am me, violently opinionated and quite angry most of the time about one thing or another, but I think that opinion has its values.

N.   What advice would you give a youngster who wants to enter the field of dancing, either as dancer or choreographer?

❦   DE MILLE : I've written about everything I know on that subject in a little book called *Advice to the Young Dancer*. It's in paperback, and I don't want to repeat.

Girls go into the medium with a great deal of dedication—so do boys, except that the trade is considered onerous for a man in this country and most men are shamed out of it, which is too bad. But as things stand now, there isn't a great opportunity to make a comfortable living as a dancer, and this is tragic, because when girls get to be about twenty-five or twenty-six they think that they'd better have a husband and children. This would be all right if we had permanent ballet companies—most of our top ballerinas have children. Tallchief has two, I think, and Melissa Hayden has two, and it doesn't slow them down a bit—they go on whirling with the greatest of ease.

For men it's more difficult. One of my boys has a wife and four children, but he's hard put to make a living. He can't go off on one-night stands all over the country, and he has to dance with automobiles. This is heart-breaking because he's a really first-class dancer. He spent his entire youth in the rehearsal hall learning how to dance.

We're not set up, here, to groom and protect our young artists. I'm not talking about the student artist; the foundations give them rather large grants. I'm talking about the young mature artist who is gloriously trained and then left with nothing. I think the foundations had better look to their business more closely; once they've educated people in the arts (and this goes for musicians, too) they should see to it that there is a place for them to function. There are very few places for them, now. Doing television commercials isn't one of them—it isn't for *that* that you give up all your games and childhood fun.

We joke about television commercial work for the serious dancer—the silly gyrations around new cars and toothpaste tubes and bottles of nauseating soft drinks—but it's demoralizing.

Then, too, I've seen people who are ballerina stylists and men who've had positions with the Russian companies forced to teach youngsters in floating classes that sort of come and go without definite goals. They would have goals if there were an opportunity, but there's no place for them to aim. Washington, D.C., now has a ballet company, a resident company under Frederick Franklin, so they've got something. We have City Center, but we should have three of four in a city this size. Chicago has the Chicago Opera Company, San Francisco has one, but there ought to be many, many more. And they ought to have absolutely top-grade choreographers. (This is a great failing because a company is only as good as its choreographers. There are never too many top ones, just as there are never too many top composers, but we're not giving opportunities to those we have.)

N.   Recently, in both London and Paris, I saw Nureyev and Margot Fonteyn perform. And I saw all the excitement, the almost feverish adoration, they inspired. Does this sort of thing happen very often in ballet? In Europe or here or anywhere?

❧   DE MILLE: It happens very rarely, and when it does it is always monumentally exciting. It happened when the Diaghilev ballet hit Paris in (I think) 1908, and when they went on to London in 1910. Anna Pavlova didn't make front pages, though she was the toast of New York—she was the eighth wonder of the world.

I'm always glad when it happens because it's marvelous for everybody. I've seen Nureyev and Fonteyn in "Giselle" and I thought they were staggeringly wonderful. I adore her. I don't like her equally well as a performer in everything she does, but she is the best Sleeping Princess I've ever seen, and her Ondine is heavenly. She's also a very lovely woman who is adored by her company, literally worshiped as a person and a ballerina. I'm not acquainted with Nureyev, but he is also marvelous, and has a bit of magic. A lot of people say he doesn't jump any better than many other Russians who came over with the Bolshoi, and maybe he doesn't, but he has the pure magic that for instance Maria Callas has—she really doesn't sing very well, when you come right down to it, but who cares? She bewitches you. But the comparison is unfair to Nureyev, who really does dance extraordinarily well.

N.   I'd like to turn back to your *Book of the Dance*. In assembling a history of this proportion, what objectives did you have?

❧   DE MILLE: They were confused. We had several objectives, in fact. You know, the origin of the book is odd. Someone at Golden Press called me and said, "Would you like to make a little compendium of your Omnibus lectures?" Well, Joseph Welsh had published his Omnibus lectures, and Leonard Bernstein was publishing his, so I said, "Why not? I'll turn in a buck or two with no effort." I didn't have many Omnibus lectures—just a few, in fact—so I threw in some extra pieces that had never been used. They put it all together and it was a mess.

They sat down with me, and M. Dwplaix, the head of the Hachette Frères for Europe and a perfectly charming gentleman, said, "We can publish this. It's a perfectly nice book, but you could rewrite it and we could do a good book." I looked at him and said, "I'd be happy to, but I'll have to take my time. Will you give me the kind of pictures and production I'll need?" and he said, "Yes." I said, "It's going to be very expensive for you," but that didn't phase him. So we took what we had, tossed it out, and started over.

I wrote the book four times, cover to cover, because I started with what I knew about the dance and what I'd experienced, but as I began to examine and read and research I realized that I didn't know much about anything, so I was working from the middle out, so to speak, to the absolute dismay of the editorial staff. We spent three years assembling the pictures. (All my life I've been marking books for pictures, but a great many of those weren't available—some were copyrighted, some were in prints that couldn't be reproduced, some were in museums and were unobtainable. We had some bad luck that way, but on the whole I think the picture coverage is excellent. Now that it's done several people are outraged because they didn't get half-pages, but since I covered the Orient in three pages I don't think any individual in the West has a right to get upset.) Factually it's correct. As far as emphasis is concerned, and areas where editorial opinion enters, it represents my opinions about things.

I thought of the book as a volume that should be of interest to the average adult who isn't an absolute addict when it comes to dancing. The book begins with a definition of terms, because if I don't define them the average Kiwanis member won't know what I'm talking about much of the time. If I use "distortion" I'm using it in my terms, not his, and the same goes for "form." It seems very elementary, but it wasn't so easy to do.

Then, when we got into anthropology and so forth I had a meeting and said, "Could we introduce the word 'prostitution' because it is very hard to write a history of dancing and never approach that subject," and they told me I could. With that the book went up to the college level immediately.

There's also a great deal of material in it that most practicing dancers don't know and that I thought they'd find interesting. I read in only two languages, French and English, and there's a great amount of material in other languages I wish I could have gone through. But I wanted to write a book that would not just repeat what I read, and would fill in gaps and summarize with a jolly point of view. I hope there's some humor in it, too—there never is in dance books. Whenever possible I let the dancers speak for themselves. That makes things come alive, because really they're so droll, so amusing, so human.

"I don't like to have the audience running away with the play."

DAME EDITH EVANS

Edith Evans is the First Lady of English Theater. "Why?" is something we don't ask, after succumbing to her spirited, controlled performances in movies like *Tom Jones*. "Why?" we would never think of asking after observing the sweep and grandeur with which she makes an uneven play like *The Chinese Prime Minister* seem great. She speaks, in and out of interview, with warmth and profound respect for two of her esteemed compatriots, Sir John Gielgud and Sir Laurence Olivier, both of whom have added shadows of brilliance and the substance of genius to today's theater.

Dame Edith makes the grouping a trinity.

EVANS: I was born in London. I went to a very ordinary school—a church school that isn't there anymore. It was bombed during the war. Then, when I was fifteen, I became an apprentice. I had my indentures. I was apprenticed for two years to the millinery—I always liked beautiful things, beautiful materials, and I thought I should like to be a milliner.

Then William Poel—he was a very famous old director, the originator of this straight moving without curtains, the sort of Shakespeare productions we get now (in the old days people

used to drop curtains for every blessed scene; the thing never
went along, and Poel originated this unbroken flow, so to speak,
which brought it to life marvelously)—saw me play for a
friend who used to do Shakespeare productions in an amateur
way. She was rather an exceptional amateur—she had very
high standards, and she didn't want to play the leading parts
herself. At any rate, Mr. Poel saw me play in *Much Ado About
Nothing* one evening after my millinery, and he thought I
looked all right so he asked me to play Cressida in *Troilus and
Cressida* at one of his special performances for the Elizabethan
Stage Society. George Moore wrote about it considerably, and
asked me to play a leading part in a play he had written titled
Elizabeth Cooper. Of course, the Stage Society prevented it.
They couldn't possibly have a milliner play the leading part.
It wouldn't have done at all. It wasn't a question of equity, it
was a question of nonsense, so I played the very small part of a
housekeeper and got my first contract from playing that little
part.

Two managers sent for me, actually, and one gave me a
contract. And that's how I got on the stage. I was put on, I didn't
try to go on, but when I got there I knew it was where I
belonged. I knew at once it was the life I wanted, and it's gone
that way ever since.

At first, of course, I understudied and played little character
parts. It was for the Vendrenne-Eadie management in the old
Royalty, at that time on Deane Street. I played in *My Lady's
Dress* in which we had Lynn Fontanne, Gladys Cooper, Beryl
Mercer, and a man named Golding. All these I know now except
Berryl—I rather think she's dead. But we were all young
together in those days, during my first engagements at the
Royalty. Then all the men went to war, you know, went off to
France. And so many of them, especially the best of them,
didn't come back.

As time went on my parts got bigger, of course, but I'm not
going to rattle them off; it would just be a collection of titles that
can be found in *Who's Who*. It's impossible, too, to say what
my favorite roles were—it would be easier to name my un-
favorite parts, but I don't particularly want to do that.

Essentially, I like to play people who are alive. I don't care what age they are. I adored playing Rosalind twenty years ago—I fortunately got a fresh look at the part, and it made a sort of history in a way. Of my later parts I like Daphne Lorinda very much because I played a really live woman, *such* a woman. It was written by a doctor who was a playwright in the Chekhov style. Being a doctor as well as a playwright he knew all about women. He had seen them with their hair down, all the façades stripped away. Since then I've enjoyed *Hay Fever*. And I enjoy *The Chinese Prime Minister* now, but it's a very long, difficult part.

I think it all comes down to the fact that I like parts with life. And with as many facets of life as possible.

N. What sort of preparation—homework, so to speak— do you undergo for a part?

❦ EVANS: When I first read the play I usually see the woman in it—often I see her in bits and pieces, and then I have to join them up. There are always little bridges you have to keep crossing until they come.

But I don't think I work like an actor. I said the other day, in an interview, that I'm a born artist. I work like a painter. I throw away and throw away until I come to the truth, to what I want. But I do brush on, and then discard, as I'm rehearsing, until suddenly it comes.

I don't like all the goings-on around the theater. I don't like any of the fuss and bother. I just like acting the part; once it's made I try to remake it each performance.

But isn't that like painting? I can't paint. I can't draw one single line, but I do know that my technique is like that of a painter's. It would be lovely to be a painter because you could do it wherever you wanted, whereas we have to go down to the place where they've got the play. And I should like to do things as I felt like doing them, but I have a very lazy streak. Perhaps it's just as well that I have to be at a certain place at a certain time. Otherwise I might keep putting it off, and I don't think that the patience of the cast or the audience would be infinite.

N.   Have you enjoyed your work in motion pictures?

❦   EVANS: Yes, I've enjoyed them very much. I've only done about a half-dozen altogether, though lately there's been one a year. *Tom Jones* and then *The Chalk Garden* and then a little part in *Johnny Cassidy* which I enjoyed very much. I play Lady Gregory. It's an American picture with Rod Taylor playing the leading part.

I'd like to do more movies, in fact. I'm impatient with this eight performances a week. No life, no homelife, and I need that. Anyway, I do what comes and I don't fuss too much about the future.

N.   Sir John Gielgud complained about the lack of continuity or "line" as being disturbing in making movies. Has this bothered you? Shooting the middle first, the beginning last, etc.?

❦   EVANS: At times. I think sometimes you wish you had really known what happened in the whole of a film before you do one scene, but I haven't let that worry me very much. I was fortunate in that I'd played the part in *The Chalk Garden* in London for quite a long time, so I knew the play thoroughly and the shooting sequence didn't matter. I knew what she was like all the way through. In *Tom Jones*, too, everything seemed to fit in the right way.

I think John has done more films than I have, so he probably has come across some awkward moments. I don't worry as long as I have a sensitive director, and up to now I have had that. Wonderful men who help me a lot, who watch to see that I don't do too much. In the theater, you see, you have to do so much more because it has to go such an enormous distance—all the way to the back of the auditorium, you see. But my directors have helped re-shape, me, so to speak—Tony Richardson, Ronnie Veame, and in the last one, where I have only a very small part, Jack Cardiff.

I wanted to play Lady Gregory in this film because she was very famous, a historical character. She was a very prominent person in the Irish National Theatre, and though the part in the film is small she's a good person to portray. And Jack Cardiff was very nice to work with.

If I had an insensitive director—and I should try to find that out before I signed my contract—I couldn't work with him. I couldn't work with a man who is mechanically minded. I have to work from my heart, and then they must see to it that I don't make it too big, as I would in theater. But I must do what seems true. I can't do trick things. I never used a trick in my life and I never will.

N.   What would you say the notable changes in theater —particularly in the plays written and presented—have been during your career?

EVANS: It's extraordinary. They say that Shaw, in a way, started breaking rules, and then Bridie followed, breaking *all* the rules (he never wrote a real last act, but he wrote divinely about people and humanity). But now it seems that we're going through a psychoanalytical age where we have to dig up everybody's inhibitions and lay them all out on display, and I'm rather waiting for the time when *some* things become sacred, or at least covered, again. Once Princess Bibesco said to me that "vitality precedes beauty." I'm waiting for the beauty, because we're getting a lot of vitality lately. I haven't seen anything since *The Royal Hunt of the Sun* and *Virginia Woolf* because we began to rehearse this play, and I started to study it at least four months ago, so the very new ones I haven't seen, though I shall see them as soon as I'm free. Whether I shall like them or not is another matter.

It seems everyone has to say everything, now. I only hope, when they think they've finally said it all, that we shall go back to something with a little more form and graciousness and gentleness. Life isn't lived entirely at the lower levels, you know. I know that the world of animals and gardens and things have got their frightfully rough sides, but they've got a lot of grace and beauty as well.

When I went to see *Virginia Woolf* my friends told me I shouldn't like it—that it was nothing more than a lot of drunken people shouting at each other—but I didn't feel it was *just* that. I think they all go on too long. They make their statement and then they won't let go of it.

The Royal Hunt of the Sun goes on too much, too. You want to say, "Well, I've taken your point, now let me think about it. Don't keep ramming it home."

The Killing of Sister George—a great friend of mine is in that—is a tremendous success. A very good play. It's serious and frightfully funny at the same time. We're looking on that young man as one of our new playwrights.

I haven't seen the O'Toole, yet—I haven't seen *so many* of the new ones—but I shall go to see them all as soon as I'm free because I believe in having opinions about them, too.

Actually, this is quite a bad time in the theater with the exception of a few. We're none of us doing much business. I don't think mine is going to do a great deal of business—it does attract a special public, however. It ran (in a somewhat different version) for about twelve weeks in New York.

But I'm looking forward to seeing all these new plays, and then I shall know what I think, without people telling me. I dare say I won't understand some of them at all. Even those on television. Where do they *get* those people?

I've got a country home and I live among country people who work in the fields, on the farms and all, but I seldom see anything of them, of their lives, in what is going on on the stage. I don't know where they find these people, with their strange complexes and inhibitions. Do you know anyone like the people in the Aldwych's *The Homecoming?* I rather hope not. It's a world completely apart from me, and I had always thought myself—in my relationships with friends and people generally—very cosmopolitan. I know people of every sort of weight and age and class, but I have yet to meet any like these characters on the stage. I suppose they've got to be dug up, the way Tennessee Williams digs them up, but it's reassuring to know that the world itself isn't populated with them.

N.   You've worked mostly in London, haven't you?

🌑   EVANS: Yes, I was born here and I've done most of my acting in my home town. I'm like the Parisians, you know—they always act in Paris. If I had been an American actress I should naturally have gone all over America, just as your actresses do. Not so long ago I went down to Malvern for the Shaw plays, and I went to the National. Long ago I went out, mostly with new plays, for a few weeks at a time. But I've got no touring public at all. Most of my films have been made here, in and near London. Actually, we don't have much to tour for, anymore—it's a small country, there aren't many towns and there aren't many theaters; besides, they're beginning to find their own entertainment, and there's always television. And there are pubs, and even clubs, where they can have drinks and sandwiches and a sort of music hall entertainment. The Music Hall itself is almost gone. And the actual straight theater is filled with all these violent people.

I suppose it will sort itself out. "Vitality precedes beauty," you know, and the beauty will come later on.

N.   Are you conscious, as an actress, of an obligation to the role you play?

EVANS: Oh, tremendously. I wouldn't take on the part if I were not. I wouldn't dream of being in a play I didn't like (though I have, upon occasion) or playing a part I detested (though I've done this, too, I fear). But these have been accidents and I've been wretched all the time they played. There was a play called *Tiger Cats*, years ago. Such a dreadful business, yet I was supposed to be an enormous success in it. She was such a frightful woman to play . . . it nearly killed me.

I've been lucky in my authors. I've worked in plays that were good to work in. I've enjoyed them. The parts have had life; the women were important, or at least had life, and it's been my obligation to make the audience feel it.

N.   Why does England consistently produce so many fine actors?

EVANS: I suppose, in a way, it's a sort of perverseness. We've got a tradition in our country, handed down from the Puritans, of not liking the theater. *They* banned theater. And from the time beginning a little after Elizabeth, actors were disreputable people, not nice people at all. I think there's something in this: we've had to fight. We haven't been encouraged.

Things have changed, rather. Now we have two state subsidized theaters. The Stratford, and just this last year, the National. One might say that we are now respectable.

Then, too, we're acting in our native language, and when you start with our good native playwrights, beginning with Shakespeare and Sheridan, we're acting our own blood, as it were. Just as the Welsh sing all the time—in the streets, everywhere, and sing divinely—I think the English are inherently good actors.

I think the commercial situation has been good for the English actor, too. In America it seems this word "success" is hung about the neck. I don't think it's quite so forceful over here. If you make a failure here you don't hide, you don't run away; you don't have to sort of avoid people or not mention the thing. It's like that in New York. But over here we can have failures and still go on. Johnny's had them, I've had them, we all have—and we've still gone on, we've still been the same people.

We want success, but we aren't ostracized if we don't have it. I think this makes us more patient, more willing to try things that might not succeed, more willing to take our time. All these things are important to the development of good actors, and it may be—tradition and natural inclination aside—the reason why we have so many good ones.

N.   How does it feel to be in a play that fails?

❦   EVANS: Oh, it's very sad. If it's had a really bad press you feel miserable. I don't read reviews because I can't take very bad criticism or very good criticism immediately. Having done the thing it's over, you know; it's like having a baby, then someone comes in and says it's wonderful, too wonderful, or (if something's wrong) it's awful. It's too much! I can hardly play the second night! I feel I've done it, I've exhausted it.

I'm never rabid to get back to the theater the second night. I've exhausted myself on the first night. I don't like first nights, to be frank. I always say to myself, "You've got to do it tomorrow, you've got to do it next week," and this is a most unhappy feeling.

Whether the play is or is not a success, you're almost never perfectly suited, perfectly happy. You've tried to make something and you've pushed yourself too far in some direction, and it isn't right for you and you know it . . . if it's a failure you *really* know it. That's what's so awful. You've done what you could, but there's always somebody who will rub it in. And then, any strong personality calls for both commendation and disapproval, and the stronger they are the higher the praise can be and the more wretched the condemnation.

It's bad enough being in a success. Being a failure is a very personal but nonetheless real hell. But we get over it.

N.　　　　How influential are critics in England? How accurate do you think they are?

EVANS: As I said, I never read my notices, not until the play is well along in its run or even over. I haven't read the criticisms of this play, yet. One or two people have sent me bits, or told me what was said, but if I wait until the play is over before I read them I can get something from them. Yet once you begin to know the personality of the critic you know exactly what he will say.

Each critic has his own private human standpoint, you see. Some of the established ones love the theater, and know about the theater, but this does not prevent their personal feelings from coming between. It seems impossible for any of them to criticize objectively—to stand apart from what they themselves happen to like. That seems to be asking too much.

This is why I set my face against meeting any of them. I won't meet them. I never would, even when I was a young actress. I remember that when St. John Ervine's wife asked me to lunch one day I said, "Will he be there?" and she said, "Yes," and I said, "Then I won't come." So he went out. (He's made quite a joke of this.) Someone introduced me to one of the critics in the foyer of the Old Vic the other day; if they'd asked me beforehand I would have said, "No, I don't want to meet him." Don't let them get to know you. Let them be surprised, because you're always trying to do something fresh, to discover something in yourself that will give a fresh look.

This is why I'll play no more retired actresses. I've done two of them, and that's enough. I must play something with future, something that's going to be different. This is why I never, or rarely ever, plan ahead. I like that open door. I like not to know what's coming. It's exciting, that way. Something marvelous usually comes around the corner.

N.   Could you pick out some of the actors you've played with you have deeply respected . . . and why?

❦   EVANS: I'd have to start with John Gielgud and Laurence Olivier because those two have greatness in them. Larry possesses a tremendous physical vitality which makes him able to rise up and do whatever he wants to do. One doesn't always agree with him, but one always has to notice him. Johnny's the other way. He has a marvelous strain of beauty as well as greatness. He's a real actor, you see—the inspiration, the spirit, the passion. He's right to be in theater because it's his heart and soul, it's his life. He's not like Larry at all because he doesn't give you a physical impression. With Johnny it's a terrific beauty that comes from the voice and the heart and the spirit. Larry is like a dynamo, a human dynamo.

And they both have tremendous impact on the audience.

Now, Ralph Richardson I don't know quite so well. I think his is more from the head, if you know what I mean. I've seen him, in moments of his plays, come across with moments of absolute genius. But I don't know the general layout of his work too well.

Paul Scofield is the slightly younger one coming on. I haven't played with him, but he must be remarkable. But I have played with both Larry and Johnny, and I suppose they really are the two greatest actors I've played with. In the old days, when I was very young, I was directed by Charles Hawley, but I never played with him. He was a great comedian, like your top comedians of a generation or two back, like Otis Skinner and people like that. And then, Gerald du Maurier was undoubtedly a great comedian. In a way he was before his time because he did it all so easily and so naturally. Nobody knew the effort that went behind it. He started this easy, natural style, but the public didn't grasp what he had behind his performance.

N. All the actors you've mentioned are the product of repertory theater. What do you think the actor gains from repertory experience?

EVANS: I think the most important thing they gain is an ability to cope—to cope with virtually anything. They do this much better than I, who've had no repertory. (Although I have managed when things have gone wrong. Playing at the Old Vic, my string of beads broke and they were all over the place. One just had to carry on with the play, and sweep them up as gracefully as possible, but it was a great throw for me. I don't do it easily.)

Yet the actor shouldn't be in repertory too long because he learns to do things the quick way. He doesn't go down into the part; he's apt to adopt the quick, showcase way. Patterns and lovely tableaux. But—and this is the word I wanted—it does give them resource. Especially if they're in a good one, where they have style and good taste.

N. Getting back to you, you have appeared frequently on Broadway?

EVANS: Not terribly frequently; I haven't played outside London enough to call my departures anywhere near frequent. But I've never had a hit on Broadway. I've always been fortunate enough to do well personally, but I've never been in a play that was an outright hit.

I played the nurse with Kit Cornell—oh, a long time ago. I had to come back to London because my husband died. I played a television a few years back, *Time Remembered*, for George Schaeffer, which I enjoyed very much. (Margaret Rutherford played it on the stage here.) I wish I could have played that part in the theater—I enjoyed that old countess so much. She was enchanting, a delicious person, and gave the actress an opportunity to do all sorts of human things.

N.   If you were to give advice to the young, aspiring actress, what would that advice be?

❦   EVANS: First I would suggest, in this day of our Lord, that they went to one of the two or three good schools. To begin with, they meet professional people. They get into the atmosphere of the theater before they get into a real theater. They're trained well. And I'd keep an eye on them, if I had someone that was of particular interest to me. I would probably go to watch their lessons to see that they weren't being taught any tricks. But this is the proper gateway, and after this they must follow their hearts.

I should also try to tell them never to do anything that was in bad taste. Vulgar they sometimes might have to be—you have to be vulgar if the part calls for vulgarity, but you should never stoop to vulgarity to get an effect.

And never any tricks. I don't believe in tricks, I don't do tricks. It's cheating.

As far as the part is concerned you have the responsibility of thinking and being the person you're playing. And then that fiercely important thing—you have to learn audience reaction and how to control it.

I'm a great one for controlling an audience, you see. I don't like to have audiences running away with the play. I know the play and I know what's coming and I know how they'll enjoy it best. No jockey lets his horse run away—*he* tells the horse what to do. And that's what we should do. We should tell the audience what to do. This is the art of the theater, the fact that we are responsible to the audience for their having a good evening. We dare not let them take the bit in their teeth and scream themselves hoarse, unless that is what we want them to do.

No chef would serve up three or four things that mitigated against each other, with the first so delicious that people ate too much of it and consequently couldn't enjoy the next. I think cooking and riding are exactly the same as acting, once you get down to basic procedures.

I do not like an audience to run away. I never let them run

away. I tell them when they can have a good laugh and sit back and enjoy. That's when I catch my breath and have a rest. And if they don't laugh, if it's a quiet house, I must catch my breath somehow, so I must go on and force them. (But not with tricks.) Woo them, cozy them, but make them come up and have a nice evening. It takes a lot out of me, but I couldn't act at all if I didn't do it like that.

N. Do you find any appreciable difference between audiences?

❦ EVANS: Oh yes. Temperature, world happenings, sensational happenings, a disaster, the weather (when it's very hot or very cold)—all these things have an effect. They're just like us. We have to try to make an effort to be as gay as we should be.

I was at a military meeting once when a horse started out, then bolted back to the stable. When the race was over the rider brought him out and made him go around the course. Couldn't let him get away with that; nobody was watching, but he had to go around.

I'm this way with an audience. I won't let them bolt, no matter what the prevailing mood may be. I may be unpopular because of this, but I don't think so. Audiences and young people don't know why they respect me, but they do. Or seem to. I don't think they call me an "old trout" yet. But if I stooped to tricks then I *would* be an old trout, and they wouldn't come to watch. I think one gets one's payment.

N. Now, looking at theater as a whole, what are your hopes for it? What are the goals you would set for it?

❦ EVANS: I don't quite know what to say. I would like the theater to be lively and I would like it to have a great deal of beauty. I think we have some extraordinary directors. Although people may not all agree with Peter Hall and his policy he's just done something at Covent Garden—a production of *Moses and Aaron*—which has apparently made history. In fact it was in the *Times*, a steady paper if ever there was one, that I read it was absolutely operatic history.

Now, when I say "beauty" in the theater I mean the sort of beauty that you see when you look around in the country, lovely, growing beauty, each thing a bit different, precious and unique because of its difference. . . .

(I don't see beauty in most modern architecture. It looks like barren utility to me. When I look at a lot of the new buildings I think, "Oh, yes, done for cheapness." It never occurs to me that they were done for comfort, and certainly they weren't done for beauty. They're probably very comfortable inside, but you don't know one room from another. A friend of mine who is the head of the Westminster Home Helps said she'd moved to the new occupancies in Victoria Street, and went into somebody else's place because one floor looks just like another.)

I think I'm fighting a little bit against uniformity. In plants and animals there is so much that is alive and beautiful, and infinite variety. I'm holding on to that vase of roses—the poor things are nearly gone. I brought them up from the country on Monday. (The roses this year are absolutely glorious.) They're nearly gone, now, and I can't bear to let them go. But they aren't all of the same shape and same size and same coloration, are they?

I think I would like to see, in the theater, less uniformity and great beauty. Beauty of design, beauty of speech, beauty of humor. I'm waiting for the time when the inhibitions have all been dug up, put out, dried out, as you would treat weeds, then swept and away and burned so that we can start with nice green grass again. That's what I should like. I'm really tired of all these tedious inner people being brought to the surface. They're only weeds.

"We were essences, you see . . . I was the essence of first love."

JANET GAYNOR

I came of movie-going age at the time when Holly-wood stars were brighter than any in the sky, a day when *Photoplay* occupied newsstand space now given to *Life*. Garbo, Dietrich and Shearer lured us into theaters with siren calls, but so did the dulcet voice of Janet Gaynor, who symbolized not so much the un-attainable as the ultimately desirable. In fact, roles in such films as *Seventh Heaven, State Fair* and *A Star is Born* are forever projected upon the very secret area of permanent visual recall.

❦   GAYNOR: I was born in Philadelphia but moved to Chicago when I was seven and lived there until I was fifteen. Then my mother remarried, a man from California, and we went to San Francisco where I finished high school. It was my stepfather, really, who was that guiding light who said I should be an actress. I don't know why he felt this way because I was a very ordinary simple school girl, but he had lived in Holly-wood, he knew people in pictures, and he felt that I had the spark (or whatever it can be called) that could make me succeed as an actress. I wasn't a bit stagestruck, and really wanted to go to college, but he said "No." He felt that movies should be my life so we moved to Hollywood. I started working as an extra, and from then on things happened very rapidly. I wasn't even a typical extra—you know, the dress extra who would be in a ball or in a society background. I was young and very tiny and I looked so childish I didn't get very many jobs that called for an evening gown. Then the casting director at Universal called me and said he had a lead in a two-reeler. (At that time they made two-reel Westerns, and the lead consisted of three days' work, but still it *was* the lead.) William Wyler was making two-reelers at the same time. My Western wasn't for him, but then I was asked to come to Fox to make a test for *The Johnstown Flood*. I tested and they sort of rushed me off the set before they'd even seen the test and they signed me to a five-year contract. The extraordinary thing was that the studio gave me *Seventh Heaven* when I was absolutely unknown.

A splendid German director, Frederick Murnau, who'd directed *The Last Laugh* with Emil Jannings (an all-silent picture in the total sense; it didn't even have subtitles and it was so well done it created a sensation) was brought over here by Winnie Sheehan, the head of Fox, to direct *Sunrise*. Murnau wanted Lois Moran for the part—she was very prominent, then, in those very young, very fresh, girl parts, and Mr. Sheehan said, "Well, we have a little girl that can do anything Lois can do. Why don't you come over and test her?" So he took a test and I got *Sunrise*. (This sounds wrong, chronologically, but I actually made *Sunrise* before I made *Seventh Heaven*. They were released the other way around.) Anyway, I finished *Sunrise* after six months of work, took off my blonde wig at lunchtime, let my hair hang down and started *Seventh Heaven* after lunch.

N.   Could we discuss some of your other movies?

❧   GAYNOR: Well, I adored doing *Sunrise* because it was my first really big step, and I learned a great deal from Murnau, who was an absolute perfectionist. (And the fact that it was a silent film made pantomime—gestures and expressions—vitally important because it was the only way the camera captured your thoughts and reactions. Even now the camera has to catch what you're thinking and feeling more than what you're saying; the dialogue can only be supplemental.)

Back then, of course, the director had the time to really let you know what you were doing—I understand it goes faster, now. Or perhaps the actors are much better trained. After all, I was absolutely untrained as an actress, and he'd take twenty or even thirty takes of the smallest scene. I must say this wasn't because of me but because there'd be a glimmer of light on the wrong bulrush or something equally small. But it was wonderful training.

From there, to go to Frank Borzage, the director of *Seventh Heaven*, was almost enough contrast for a lifetime. Murnau was all mental, Borzage totally romantic—all heart. It was another lovely and valuable experience.

I think I had a wonderful career; I enjoyed it all, and have no sad tales to tell you.

As for other movies—I loved *A Star Is Born*. It was such a strong part. And in between there was *Sunny Side Up*—it was gay and fun and I had a chance to sing. I didn't sing much, but they called it singing, and I loved to dance. I hadn't been trained for dancing, either, and I had to take a few lessons, and even that was fun.

Then—*State Fair*, with Will Rogers and Lew Ayres. It was such a good picture, such a genuine American one, and Will Rogers was great.

What else did I make? Well, I made three a year for ten years, thirty in all. A lot of them were films I enjoyed making—they were good, as entertainment, but not like those I've mentioned, the ones that will hold, will stand up.

N.   Can you think of any you disliked?

❧   GAYNOR: Yes. I very much disliked the picture we made right after *Sunny Side Up*. It was called *High Society Blues* and it was concocted just to cash in on the great success of *Sunny*. I didn't feel as though it was right for Charlie Farrell and me to do at all, but I must say that the studio was usually wise about selecting my pictures.

Once in a while I put my foot down and didn't want to do this or that. I remember once that I reached the point where I felt I had been going into too many light roles; after all, I had been a success with my first three pictures, *Sunrise, Seventh Heaven* and *Street Angel*, and from that time on they got lighter and lighter. So I went to Mr. Sheehan and said, "I want something dramatic," and we had quite a do about it. I went off to Hawaii in something of a huff, and when I came back they said all right, I could have a dramatic role. It was *The Man Who Came Back* and it was positively the worst picture I made. I don't think it was invented just to show me I didn't know everything, but it was a role I was simply not at all equipped to do.

N.   When you played a role were you conscious of an obligation? In the sense that you felt obliged to satisfy yourself, the director, writer, public—

❧   GAYNOR : It's difficult to pin down the sense of obligation. Outwardly you have to satisfy all of the people you mentioned, perhaps primarily the director (the writer's work has been done before). The director must tell you what to do, he must clarify your role if there's any misunderstanding or confusion. Fortunately I had approval of my scripts and didn't have to make anything I didn't like, which was wonderful. It was also a great responsibility—I certainly can't say that every picture I made was one I would always be proud of, but the good ones were extraordinary. It's a marvelous thing to have a role you like, to be able to say wonderful lines that have been written for you, lines you'd be much too inarticulate to say on your own. A good role is greater than you. It's an adventure, an expression of emotion you perhaps will never experience. When a part is right, and you really feel it—well, it's hard to explain. When you paint there are times when you become part of your subject. A really great role gives you this feeling, this identity.

N.   How strong is the influence of the director?

❧   GAYNOR : It would be hard to find a good picture that isn't well directed. It's the director who has to understand what the writer put on paper and it's up to the director to put it on film with the most effective images to dramatize the words. Then he must interpret again through the actors to make sure they fulfill their roles. His stamp simply must be on the picture, and he must really be given the overall credit for success or failure.

N. What primary changes came to Hollywood during your career?

GAYNOR: I went through the big change of talkies— that was the time when everyone trembled. Many careers were simply cut off, not because performers couldn't speak but because the voice simply didn't go with the personality. That was true of John Gilbert, who was a great star; his voice didn't sound the way people expected it to. (Remember, too, that the recording equipment was frightful. I recall that when Charlie and I were making a picture, and they decided to put in two reels of talking at the end of it—they did this with many pictures at the time to compete with the full talking pictures—that we had to go back to the studio at night. The whole set was draped with a sort of horsehair padding. We did our little scene, our bits of dialogue, and the next morning we went over to the studio to see and hear our takes. They felt I sounded the way I should, fortunately. But that was the beginning of our talking career.)

I must say that I didn't like my voice at all. I thought it sounded flat, so I decided to do something about it. I had a few lessons and immediately I was called in and asked what I was doing to my voice. I said, "I'm trying to improve it." They said, "We don't want you to improve it. We want you just the way you are. The voice goes with you."

That—the coming of sound—was the big change for me. I missed all the fuss that came with television.

N. How much attention did you pay to reviews and criticism?

GAYNOR: Not very much. Remember, I'd make a picture, then have to wait at least two weeks while it was cut. Sometimes I'd go away—subject, of course, to being called back to re-shoot—and then I'd go to Hawaii or out to the desert. By the time the picture was released (six months later, quite often) you were deep in another movie and you couldn't break your heart over something made that long ago. It has nothing to do with what the critics can do to you in the theater, where a show can be closed overnight. It was quite removed.

Naturally, I adored reading lovely things about myself, but I was in that unique position (and this sounds filled with ego but I hope not) of having all my pictures make money. So the studio didn't care about critical reactions, either, as long as those lines were out in front of the theaters. Actually, most of my criticism was on the positive side. Once in a while a reviewer would say, "'Well, this is a Janet Gaynor picture, and if you like Janet Gaynor you'll like it"—that's about as bad as they got. They never tore me or the picture apart.

N.   How about fan mail? I had the impression, during those years, that stars were literally inundated.

❧   GAYNOR: Oh, we were. We got such loads of fan mail we couldn't possibly have read it, overselves. It was all taken care of. The thing we got down to, in answering mail, was that anyone who sent money or stamps got a photograph. But you couldn't possibly have sent out pictures in answer to all the "free" requests. Most were routine: "You are my favorite actress, will you please send me an autographed photograph." Some were personal letters, and they'd always be taken out for me to read . . . often they were very touching.

I know I got some crank letters, too, and they were frightening. A man in India claimed he was married to me and that he was on his way over to claim me. *That* I didn't like. The studio only let me in on these things, though, when they felt I should know. Another time a man was on his way to see me, and he kept sending letters, each time a little closer to California. He'd started from somewhere in the East, but I'm not sure I appreciated his ardor.

N.   During your career the publicity departments seemed to be working overtime. Did you find anything annoying in the image of the Janet Gaynor they created?

❧   GAYNOR: Yes. So often I felt they would paint me as such a little darling it was all sort of revolting. My roles were not *that* saccharine. (Some were, but I'd always be able to say "Remember how I started? I wasn't gooey in *Seventh Heaven*.") But they always wanted to paint me as though I was too sweet for words, and I felt that I really wasn't such a ninny. I hoped I had some sort of a mind, and I felt as though I was intelligent. (Not that they thought I was stupid; they seemed naturally to assume that I was naïve.)

Now, the roles I played were naïve, but that was different; the roles were an essence. In my career, because I didn't have to go on too long and change an image, my roles were almost the essence of young first love. I think first love can be interesting— it can be romantic, full of sorrow, or tragic. It can bear the full sway of emotions because it *is* young love, first love. But I would object to the way publicity people seemed to confuse first love with insipidity. Of course, publicity had changed terrifically. When I worked the publicity department handled everything, all the photographs and interviews. Then the candid camera came in and fulltime glamor went by the boards. No longer did the public see the stars only in lavish dress, stepping in and out of limousines. The veil between the star and the public was torn away.

N. It is true—as was so often rumored—that temperament reigned supreme in Hollywood?

GAYNOR: There was very little temperament. We were professional people, you know, and we worked as hard as we could to make our movies good ones. We had fun, but not the fun of irresponsibility, and we couldn't really be self-indulgent.

Most of our tantrums were manufactured by press agents. I never saw any that were real. Occasionally if I really wanted something, or didn't want to do something, I'd say, "All right, I'm going home," and I would. But it wasn't in a temper. It was because I knew it was the only way I could get what I wanted. This happened rarely, however, because almost everyone concerned with making a particular picture was more concerned with making it well than with puffing ego all over the place.

N. What did you—and do you—think of the Star System?

❧   GAYNOR : I think that stars brought people to the box office, and I think that, to a certain extent, they still do. In my day people went to see a Garbo picture, a Joan Crawford picture, a Norma Shearer picture, a Janet Gaynor picture. It isn't like that now. I still think that people might go to see Elizabeth Taylor, but the public now wants the picture to be good, first, and feature a personality, second. They usually don't go to see a personality, now.

N.   But all of you had such sharply delineated personalities—

❧   GAYNOR : That's the point. We were essences, you see; we didn't overlap. We couldn't have played each others' roles. Garbo was the essence of glamor and tragedy, and Dietrich was the essence of glamor-that-would-lead-a-man-to-destruction-without-her-being-hurt. Norma was the essence of the matron, the faithful wife. Joan was the five-and-dime girl that made good by marrying the rich boy. I was the essence of first love. Who are these essences now?

Of course, after we went by the men took over. In my era women were the stars. Then Gable, Cooper, Grant, Tracy—for years the men were the really big stars. Now it may be evening up again.

N.   How does it feel to see remakes of your top films—like the musical versions of *State Fair* and *A Star Is Born?*

❧   GAYNOR : Well, they've made several musical versions of *State Fair* and I thought the films had a great deal of charm. But I don't think they were as touching as the *State Fair* I did. The minute the music comes in it's another sort of thing entirely; it may be as entertaining or more so but the reality, the identification, suffers. About *A Star Is Born* I have to be honest; I don't think it was as good a picture as ours.

N.   Do you notice any drastic change between the movies of your day and those made at the present?

❧   GAYNOR : They've changed, of course, just as everything—interior décor, women's fashions, and lighting—

has changed. I really don't hold myself up as any sort of critic, and when I go to see a movie now I enjoy it. I don't really tear it apart or compare it, and I see a marvelous performance without being aware of any performance, any technique. The subjects seem more free-flowing, now; we made pictures that had a beginning, a middle and an end. But I love many of these new films. I think that any era has its share of good motion pictures, and I don't think you can compare them in terms of style or concept. Today's films are simply "of now."

N.   Now, Janet Gaynor was a star for ten years and she made thirty pictures. At the peak of her career she abruptly quit. Why?

GAYNOR : I really felt that I had had it all. I had all the pleasure and excitement of being at the top and I wanted to know other things about life. I felt I didn't want to spend my whole life being an actress.

Remember, I told you at the beginning that I had never been stagestruck. I'll never forget a night when I was talking to Frances Goldwyn, Sam Goldwyn's wife, and she said, "Now, Janet, I want to know exactly why you stopped making pictures," and I said, "Frances, I'd made them for ten years. I had a wonderful time, but I simply wanted to know another side of life. I don't want to stay in that particular corridor all the time."

I'd made up my mind to quit before I married Adrian. I might not have stuck to the decision if my marriage had been an unhappy one, but Adrian took me into a whole new world, a world of art and fashion. I hadn't known anything about this world, and I found it fascinating.

N.   Then you bought a ranch in Brazil.

GAYNOR : We got it, actually, because Adrian had a heart attack and had to give up his business. We were invited to go on one of those junkets to Rio, and since we'd never been to South America we decided to go. We loved Rio and São Paulo but we wanted to go into the interior, so we arranged to fly in on an old DC-3 with crates of parrots and heaven-knows-what.

We went up to the state of Goias and were absolutely smitten. So we bought a ranch and Adrian designed a lovely house and we went back every year afterward to spend eight or nine months. (We came back to California in between, of course, because our son Robin was in school.)

I don't spend too much time there, now, but it is a magnificent place. We're up about 1800 feet, but we're quite near the equator. The sun is higher but because of the altitude it's cool, and in the months of June, July and August it's almost cold. It's tropical, yet we have fires at night. It's a cross, really, between Palm Springs and Hawaii. The air is soft but we have ninety inches of rainfall a year, so you can imagine how green it is.

We raise a little bit of everything. Cattle, of course, and coffee (though the market's gone) and superb vegetables. I took the seeds down from here and they flourish unbelievably. (We fill two stalls in the market place.) We have thousands of banana trees, seven different varieties.

Mary Martin and Richard Halliday have a place next to ours. They came to spend a very short weekend with us and fell as madly in love with the area as we had, so they bought a place next to us where they seem to be spending most of their time.

N.   A final question, and a very personal one. Most women are lucky if they succeed in finding one very happy marriage, but you've had two. And both of your husbands have been forceful, accomplished, highly creative men of consequence. Could you describe life with Adrian and with Paul Gregory?

❧   GAYNOR: You're right; I have been most fortunate. Both men have been extraordinarily talented and exciting to live with. Adrian was an artist, and he saw everything through the eyes of the artist. He was a fine painter, and had two exhibitions in New York. Everybody knows, of course, about his fashions, and how he dressed all the ladies at Metro—Garbo, Shearer, Crawford, Macdonald—and how he costumed the lavish musicals they made. Then he went into business for himself. (It's hard to describe your husband; you know him so well.) Adrian had a fine mind as well as this striking creative talent. That's what was so exciting—living with someone who, each day, regards each day as a new day for creation. Not necessarily fashions but the painting or simply seeing and planning.

Paul, of course, is just as creative, but in different ways. Paul isn't the artist with the pencil put to pure white paper; he's creative with people, and I think the way he produced *John Brown's Body* with Tyrone Power, and then his magnificent *Don Juan in Hell*—

That was an innovation, you know; bringing four stars out on the stage with scripts to read. Now it's done, but it hadn't been done until Paul staged it. Then Paul did a superb job with *The Caine Mutiny Court Martial*. Paul has flawless taste in knowing what to put together, then puts it together in a way that produces a maximum of art and excitement. And he, too, sees each day as a new opportunity.

I think creative people see much more than others begin to see. They are simply more aware of everything—of light on a leaf or the play of expression on the face of a person walking by. Their curiosity, their range of interests, their wonderfully complex personalities—all these things make them infinitely more alive than ordinary people. I feel extremely fortunate to be able to have a second experience like this.

"The actor tackling Hamlet *simply has to stay the course."*

SIR JOHN GIELGUD

I am not alone in regarding Sir John Gielgud as the greatest actor of our time. Who else can so sublimely command a role and grip an audience in a spectrum of plays authored by playwrights as diverse as Shakespeare and Albee?

Within one week, this spring, I listened to the Gielgud *Hamlet* on record, then, on a late night television show, caught him in *Julius Caesar*, and on the following night saw him in *Tiny Alice*. The audio gaps involved in the changing of records couldn't diminish him, the frequency of inane television commercials failed to daunt him, and the complexity of his very modern stage role fell easily within his grasp.

There is no other actor of this caliber, and I am exceptionally pleased that he seems in such great form in this interview.

GIELGUD: I was born in 1904 in London of a theatrical family. My mother's family was the Terrys—the famous Ellen Terry and her sisters, many of whom were stars in English theater. My father was the son of Polish parents who had lived in England since the 1850's. My grandfather was a correspondent in the War Office when he first came to England.

He also had theatrical ancestors. His mother had been a famous Polish actress, and there was a bust of her in the hall of the Opera House at Lwow, though I supposed it vanished during the second war.

At any rate, there was a great deal of theater in the blood of my parents, though neither of them felt that the theater was a good profession for me to enter. So I went to a private school, then to a public school (Westminster) and they assumed that I would go on to Oxford, where my two elder brothers had attended different colleges.

But I said, "No, I want to go on the stage." I was already beginning to design scenery and was crazy about going to the theater. Then I discovered that in order to become a scene designer I would have to learn architecture, which would involve a great deal of máthematics. I was very bad at mathematics and knew I'd have rather too bad a time of it, so I said rather desperately, "Well, then I'll try to be an actor," although acting was rather far from my mind. So they said, "All right, you needn't go to Oxford. You can try your luck on the stage till you are twenty-five." I went to a dramatic school for a year, then got a job with a kind second cousin, a Terry who was touring a play. I stage-managed for her, played very small parts and understudied. Then I began to get quite a little work in London—partly through influence, I'm afraid. Yet I did plunge through these early years playing small parts, and earned very little money, but I was lucky enough to go into a repertory theater at Oxford which was run by a man named James Bernard Fagan, an Irishman who had run a Shakespeare theater after the war—in London—with very little success but with a good deal of prestige. So he went to Oxford and founded a little repertory theater in a very humble building and I was there with Tyrone Guthrie and Flora Robson (among others) —actors he'd chosen as young hopefuls. I played in repertory there through sixteen or seventeen plays. I also acted in several Chekhov plays in an outlying London theater directed by Theodore Komisarjevsky, who had a great influence on my career. Then, because I played the piano by ear, I was lucky enough to understudy Noel Coward, who had been a huge success in his first drama, *The Vortex*. This was in 1924. (Meanwhile I had played Romeo unsuccessfully in an outlying theater, as you play off-Broadway here, with an actress named Gwen Françon Davies as Juliet. I was nineteen and made rather a mess of it, and that put me very much out of conceit with myself. It was a very good thing. So I went back to Oxford for another term, and it was during my second Oxford season that I was offered this understudy of Coward.)

I subsequently followed Coward again in *The Constant Nymph* which also called for piano playing—so my impromptu ability at the piano (which I must have inherited from my father; I've never been able to read music) stood me in good stead in my early days of theater. It's odd, the way things happen, the bits of good and bad luck that eventually mold a career. I wonder what would have become of me if I hadn't been able to play a bit of piano. Bit by·bit during the 1920's I began to get better parts in the West End of London, trying to learn my business. I followed Leslie Banks in a play titled *The Lady with the Lamp*, about Florence Nightingale, which starred Edith Evans. She had just completed an exciting season at the Old Vic Theatre—she'd gone to the Old Vic for almost no money, although she was already established as a very reputable West End actress, simply because she wanted to learn how to play Shakespeare. (She thought she had been a failure in a West End production of *A Midsummer Night's Dream* so she went to the Old Vic and worked there for almost two years, playing all the big parts for virtually no money and surrounded with a second-rate production.) So, when I got an offer to go to the Old Vic the following year, under the same conditions, she strongly advised me to give up the West End and go—just as she had done. So I went, and there I met Martita Hunt, who was the leading lady that first season, and Ralph Richardson during the second season. I played—during 1929 and 1930—about sixteen Shakespearean parts, including Hamlet, Macbeth, Romeo, Richard II, Antony, Prospero and King Lear. So when I left the Old Vic I felt I had really obtained a good grounding, the opportunity to try my spurs in a great many different types of role. I had sustained great long, demanding, classical parts at a rather early age when I had plenty of energy and enthusiasm and learned lines very quickly and was very adaptable and excitable. (This didn't mean that I had also acquired any degree of selectivity. I had actually acquired only a great deal of experience and a certain amount of what might be called bravura and perhaps a great many bad tricks as well.)

Then in the early 1930's, I was offered a contract by a West End management, and found two new plays. One was titled *Musical Chairs* and the other *Richard of Bordeaux*. One was a modern play, the other a costume play written by a woman, and they came along at a wonderful time for me, just as I felt I was capable of handling two big parts of totally different style. In the case of *Richard of Bordeaux* I directed for the first time as well as acted in a play with a big cast and a great number of scenes. I was lucky again—it was a big success and it really started me off. I even became a sort of matinee idol in those years. A little later in the 1930's came the Shakespeare productions—*Hamlet*, which I directed and in which I played Hamlet, and *Romeo and Juliet* with Laurence Olivier, Edith Evans and Peggy Ashcroft. Olivier and I alternated the parts of Romeo and Mercutio. I also around that time played Noah in Andre Obey's play (the part of a very old man, of course) and Trigorin in Chekhov's *The Seagull*. Then Guthrie McClintic brought me to this country to play Hamlet with Judith Anderson and Lillian Gish in 1936 and 1937. So the 1930's were a wonderful time for me.

After that, and up until the Second World War came along, I was in a number of plays and in management for a year. I did four productions in 1937, and had a very big say in every play that I did—casting it and often directing it and playing very good parts with wonderful companies. When the war came everything changed of course. Though I still was able to work in various exciting productions in London. I was also fortunate in being sent on some very big trips abroad to entertain the troops in Gibraltar and afterwards in the Middle and Far East. In 1944 I did another season in London under my own management, in which I played Hamlet for the last time; also Ferdinand in Webster's *Duchess of Malfi*; and in Congreve's *Love for*

Love which I had done with enormous success the year before and was put into the repertory; and Arnold in *The Circle* by Somerset Maugham; and Oberon in *A Midsummer Night's Dream*. Then some new plays began to arrive, but I've never seemed to be very fortunate with modern authors, except in the early days of Coward's play *The Vortex* and the 20's and early 30's in *The Constant Nymph* and *Musical Chairs*. In later years I've played only one very successful modern play, *A Day by the Sea*, by N. C. Hunter, a pastiche Chekhov study of English family life which I also directed. (We had a marvelous cast. My part was that of a priggish young diplomat, not a very interesting person, but difficult to bring to life. I enjoyed playing it because of the quality of the whole production.) To bring me up to the present, Graham Greene's *The Potting Shed*, and now *Tiny Alice* (a complete departure from anything I've ever done before) make me feel that I'm at last steeped in the avant garde to the very lips.

N.   How does it feel to play in *Tiny Alice?*

❦   GIELGUD : It's a little hard to describe. I'm thankful to have done so many things, so many different things, during my career. You see, I'm sure that my training in Shakespeare and Chekhov gave me the best lessons I could possibly have had in acting. With the Shakespeare parts I learned how to project a performance, and with Chekhov I learned how *not* to project it. In Chekhov you feel you're more or less part of a novel. You play as though the fourth wall is down—for the other characters in an inner world which the audience is really only permitted to observe. Their response, of course, is valuable, but in the Chekhov plays you really don't care if there are laughs or applause or any other discernible reaction from the audience, whereas in Shakespeare it seems much more necessary to involve yourself with the audience, to carry them along with the strangeness of the language and the poetic content. You don't exactly throw it at them, but you're at least aware of them and of their reactions. Certainly in the soliloquies, and in many of the big scenes, you have to frankly play at the audience, whereas in the average modern play (particularly in Chekhov) there is an intimacy in the acting, a give-and-take between the people on the stage. (This is very useful when you go back to Shakespeare, just as Shakespeare is very useful when you go back to Chekhov.) You seem to need a skill in presentation in which you can use different stops, just as a painter would use his color or a musician would use his instrument. You learn with experience to know what kind of play you are in, what particular kind of voice to use for it, what kind of speed to employ, how the phrasing and balance of speech belong with the particular author you're trying to act.

Now, *Tiny Alice* is in many ways not realistic. For example, in the last act I have a very stylized death scene (which is almost like a death scene in a Shakespeare play) in which the hero is supposed to have been shot dead and still talks for ten minutes afterward. This is very difficult to accomplish unless you're trained to a certain kind of unreality in the way you act. A completely realistic style would not be possible because the audience wouldn't listen, they wouldn't hear you, so you need what can only be called "a style." (I don't really know what "style" is, but an acting style to go with the writing style is tremendously important in a play like this because the play itself is a new form.) We had difficulty at rehearsals finding a style—but after playing it over a hundred times we began to be confident enough to know where to play in an intimate, realistic way, and where to suddenly broaden out and play in a more stylized manner. One hopes the audience doesn't notice the joins.

What is interesting is that I find *Tiny Alice* a play with wonderful theatrical situations and points of emphasis, but a play in which the links for the actor seem to be rather weak. Whether the weaknesses are deliberate or not I can't tell you, but it's the actor's job to cement them over. The author has not always given the actor exactly the words he needs, in a modern play, to join two episodes or situations together. So the actor must use his imagination to invent links and one finds, after a few experiments, that one can fill in the cracks, at least for oneself. Reading Albee's play on the printed page is an impressive experience; in fact, I found it more impressive to read than to act, but that's because there are many technical difficulties I have to face every night in putting over certain lines and scenes and situations. They must be tackled at each performance with equal regard, so to speak, yet they must fluctuate with the demands of the audience. The more an audience is with you—the more they respond, the less you need to do; so you try to find, when you're playing to your best audiences, how to select the simplest methods. When the audience is not with you, you apply the same methods but tighten them, as it were, like an elastic. This makes for a better audience by virtue of the way you hold and handle them. But you learn your most rewarding lessons from the good audiences.

N. In line with this, is there a difference in an audience that attends the theater on, say, Tuesday night, and an audience you might have on Thursday? Do they vary greatly in responses?

GIELGUD: I am always impressed by the fact that the best actors of my acquaintance refuse to acknowledge that audiences differ at all. If you say to Dame Edith Evans, "It's a bad house tonight," she is apt to ignore your remark and walk away.

I have always been much too inclined to depend on the good will of the audience. I suppose it's vanity—one wants to be liked or sympathized with, or even hated (as the role demands). One wants to feel that one is moving and interesting and fascinating. I get angry when I catch sight of people falling asleep in the front row or hear them rustling programs or fidgeting, but I try very hard not to be aware of these things, because if you allow them to disturb your concentration you find that you're playing solely to wake someone up, or stop someone else from rattling a program, and ignoring the hundred or five hundred people who are listening with great intent.

Of course, it's very difficult to give an absolutely regular performance, and there are pitfalls in regularity because you can become over-accurate too and time everything to perfection and still be very empty and mechanical. The challenge is to keep a spontaneity, to provide a certain flexibility (the other actors help you in this to some extent) so as to offer a certain variety but not to destroy the pattern and shape of what has been originally arranged in the rehearsals with the author and director.

But you really must not be tempted to change everything because somebody told you last night that this scene wasn't good or that line wasn't right. There's a danger in listening to too many people and even in observing oneself too closely, though at the same time one must observe oneself coldly every night, and mark all the things that seem to be good or better and the things that seem to be less good. But if you make this too much of an obsession you also begin to destroy your own impetus.

I often find if I go on bad-temperedly (at the beginning of a matinee, or on a night when the house is very unresponsive) that if I relax and refuse to worry about it, my own performance begins to spring to life and I gradually take the audience with me. But if I allow myself to go on and become put off by something (either in my personal life or in the response of the audience) I can destroy my performance for an entire evening, and though I may rant and rave and say what a vile performance it was, that is no excuse to the audience that paid to see me. Thus the actor must really keep himself always tremendously in check even in a profession that is notoriously explosive and dynamic and prone to temperament.

Temperament, I think, is something you can very seldom indulge in excepting at rehearsals, when you're trying things out and you dare make a fool of yourself, if necessary, in order to express yourself or experiment with some emotional scene. Then, of course, you're trying to establish and mark down (as best you can) what is really good, what really works, throwing away what is really bad.

Now, an absolute reproduction of emotion on the stage never really works. It's very nice to shed real tears (which I've always been rather proud of being able to do) but I've acted like that and seen other actors—expecially women—who shed boundless tears, and tear themselves to pieces, who have not always been effective in performance. It's far more important to

make the audience cry than to cry yourself (as I've learned to
my cost) and if you are very emotional by nature (a useful
attribute in creating a part) your performance can become
endangered if you allow yourself to become enraged just because you can no longer feel the emotion every night. So,
instead of presenting it in the impulsive, true way you found at
the beginning, you're apt to get corny, phony, and overact.
This is one of the greatest difficulties with long runs—but as I've
had a great many of them I've always been able to work with a
great deal of experiment and concentration. In fact, the only
thing that keeps you going in an eight-times-per-week long run
is the proper control and selectivity you learn from your
betters and from yourself. This knowledge, gained over the
years, is your ultimate consolation when you tackle a new
part—otherwise you're just as apt to despair in middle age as
when you are a youngster. A new role is always exciting, but
you're also terrified that you won't—this time—find the key.

N.   I'd like to turn to Hamlet. I've seen the role played
by you, Olivier, Burton and Grizzard, and I've seen vastly
different interpretations. Why is Hamlet so subject to both overt
and suble differences?

✿   GIELGUD : Hamlet is always the actor, really—the
actor who plays Hamlet. It seems that every actor who plays
the part successfully must identify himself with the role in an
absolute sense, and find he will amplify those things in himself
which he thinks belong in Hamlet's character. And the audience
finds this fascinating.

Before I ever played Hamlet (I had always wanted to do the
part, of course) I thought that "acting" Hamlet would be a
very put-on affair, that I would invent a very strange and
poetic personality and be very distant and aloof. But when I
came to play it I was fortunate because I played it first in the
absolutely full five-hour version at the Old Vic. This is a
tremendous feat both for the actor, and for the audience. The
other parts, of course, were left intact, giving Hamlet a little
more rest than he has in the "star" version (as we call it).
Therefore the play as a whole supported me better than it does

when you have to play in the cut version, in which all the limelight is thrown on Hamlet. I suddenly found, in early performances, that out of necessity I had to be myself (I think that until that time I had dreaded audiences seeing what I really was because I thought they wouldn't like it; I didn't very much like it myself). The odd thing is, if you use your bad qualities (and you get to know these better and better as you grow older) as much as your good ones, acting ceases to become showing off. (And I think that in his early stages there is a vast streak of exhibitionism in a successful young man of the theater.) This is almost inevitable when you play great parts, wear beautiful costumes, command sympathy and heroic respect—you can't help enjoying those things and being thrilled by the response you get from an audience. This spoils you, and if you're conceited and vain Hamlet can give you many opportunities to emphasize those qualities. It's part of the game, really, the exhibitionism of any young man who has to play love scenes and kings and heroes. But when you strip the kings and heroes to show the real man underneath (and Shakespeare continually does this) you must take something from yourself, whether the quality itself is good or bad. You find this part of yourself in a scene or in the part, but you must insert it cunningly, like the best dressing in a salad, without destroying the conception of the character but granting insight into your own actor's comment on the character. For instance, Olivier— the most marvelous actor, particularly in *Macbeth* and *Othello*, an incredible actor whether or not you fall in love with his completely original conception of a character—found such a complete physical and mental approach to the two parts I just mentioned that while (in my opinion) neither of these performances was completely true to the text of Shakespeare, he was so great that he could for instance show his Macbeth and convince us as a black-souled villain from the moment he came onto the stage. (In my opinion Shakespeare meant him to be a fairly good man in the opening of the play, a man only tempted from nobility later by his wife and by the witches and by growing ambition to murder Duncan and become King.)

In the same way Olivier's idea of playing Othello as a

Jamaican Negro is a very odd one. He succeeded marvelously —there was something striking and intensely original about his appearance, in his walk, his gestures, his voice, his movement, his whole conception—not a bit of the old-fashioned trappings of costumes and earrings and barbaric splendor. (He got the "barbaric" all right but he got rid of the "splendor.") You got the feeling that his Othello could be a soldier and a civilian at the same time, yet never a stage figure. Not being a huge, mighty man like Robeson, for instance, he couldn't play the part along those massive lines. (I played *Othello* with disastrous results a few years ago at Stratford-on-Avon; I know the part well and in some ways I tried to do the same thing Olivier did, to avoid the conventional trappings yet make myself exotic and interesting. Unfortunately I only succeeded in looking like an Indian colonial civil servant, which wasn't quite the right thing.) But it is extraordinary that if you take your own strongly felt view about a character and really play him all-out, you not only live up to your potential by acting as well as you can (by using what is in you as well as what comes from without) but you actually enlarge the character, especially if the great figures of Shakespeare are to be your goal.

N.   One thing that has always bothered me about *Hamlet* is the movie version, Olivier's, when at the beginning, we see the statement, "This is the story of a man who cannot make up his mind." What do you think of those words?

GIELGUD : I don't agree with that statement at all. I never did. I thought it was the greatest possible mistake. I don't think Hamlet's problem is that he can't make up his mind. I think he *can* make up his mind, but is so surrounded by circumstances, by predicaments, that he cannot adapt to his own conscience. The world about him is continually disillusioning him. He cannot find anything to give him a point to work from; everything comes in on him and destroys his ideas and ideals as quickly as he forms them, so he's continuously delayed and thwarted and baffled by the circumstances of every scene in the play.

That's why I think it is such an exciting play to watch. What makes it so difficult to act is that—considering all the bravura connotations of the part, and the quotations and the famous lines—it's terribly difficult, unless a very young man plays it who is not afraid of all this tradition. It's very difficult to avoid chopping the play up into a number of operatic arias, which are very good in themselves but do not make a progressive line. This happens to Hamlets very often.

This is why I kept saying to Richard Burton, "You must experience this scene and not know what's going to happen next."

Of all Shakespeare's plays *Hamlet* is the most difficult because the audience knows it far too well. When I played it for the troops at the end of the war I found it wonderful to play, in the Middle East, for example, to an utterly inexperienced audience, to men who'd wandered in simply to get the weight off their feet. When the sentries saw the ghost in the first scene, the audiences were so staggered by the excitement of that scene that they seemed to follow the rest of the play with absolute ease. They had never seen it before, hadn't read it, didn't know the plot, but they gave you a spontaneous reaction you rarely get in a West End or Broadway theater where everybody is looking at your points and comparing your performance with the one given by B, C, and D.

Personally, I think Olivier's *Hamlet* was the least successful of any of his other fine films (though I never saw it on the stage), and his performance one of his least effective despite his vitality and electricity. I didn't find him an ideal Hamlet, whereas I think his Macbeth and Othello and some of his Lear were wonderful.

N.   George Grizzard surprised me; I don't know what quality—

❦   GIELGUD: He and I once had a long talk about the part. I had directed him in a play here in New York two years ago, and got along very well with him. I didn't see his Hamlet but I would think he might be excellent. I'd be afraid he might be just a bit lightweight for the actual physical grind of the part.

Burton, physically, could stand up to *Hamlet,* and that's where he was enormously lucky and clever to choose to do it. Although I think Burton now has more the physique for a Coriolanus or Macbeth, he is still young and handsome enough to look superb, expecially in the clothes he wore in the New York production, and he certainly has the stamina and energy so essential to a part like Hamlet. The actor tackling Hamlet simply has to stay the course. (Of course, Olivier too, is a tremendously strong man who does athletics all the time and will leave no stone unturned to be physically perfect; he has infinitely more vitality than I have.) But Burton has a different kind of energy. He could play Hamlet fifteen different ways, almost in the same rehearsal, and I would give him notes before he went on, propping them on his dressing-room table, and he would act on every note at that same performance without even rehearsing at all. He is enormously skilled in that way but he is also apt to be rather undisciplined. Sometimes he plays for himself and has fun with the part. I don't think he really knew how to study the line of the part. That's what I tried to help him with, fearing that filming has encouraged that tendency in him. (Film experience can be bad for a young actor; he becomes used to the cutter and the director being responsible for the continuity, and everything is done in bits and pieces, whereas a theater performance takes place in a definite progressive form which the actor must follow every night.)

The continuity of a part is extremely important in all the big plays like *Hamlet* and *Antony and Cleopatra* and *King Lear.* You see, you can be off the stage for a few minutes or even twenty minutes, but while you're off a varying amount of time passes on the stage—a few minutes or hours or even twenty years. You've got to know where the play went while you were offstage. I remember Granville Barker saying to me, "It's frightfully important, in Lear, in each of the three mad scenes on the heath" (which are divided by scenes in Gloucester's Castle, between Lear and the Fool and Edgar), "it's frightfully important to know at each re-entrance exactly what point of madness you have reached. The line of the madness must progress with absolute certainty, and it's the actor's job to

convince the audience of the progress." (On film, of course, it's
perfectly easy, because all three mad scenes can be shot in
whatever order the director chooses, and no one will be the
wiser.) One reason I didn't think Orson Welles' Macbeth and
Othello were successful on the screen (powerful and exciting as
they were) was that he is also, I think, apt to lose the arc, the
line, the line you get in the stage version. If you haven't
played the stage version you don't know where the line is. I
think the same is true about Marlon Brando's performance of
Antony, which had so many brilliant facets, but still fell short.
He didn't know the line of the forum scene, and Mankiewicz
thought that by cutting it cleverly he could avoid Brando's
having to know it, but his lack of the knowledge of the line
destroyed the power of the scene for me. Brando lost his voice
two or three times during production and filming was delayed
until he got it back. He played every speech almost full out.
The crowd was put in as close-ups and cuts to give reactions and
variety but Brando didn't know (as I did with Cassius, having
played the part on stage) exactly where the climaxes came that
Shakespeare intended, where the scene went up and where it
came down. And though the play had been changed in parts for
the screen (its strong passages had to be toned down somewhat
for the microphones) I still managed, I think, to maintain
everything I had learned in the theater about the shape of
scenes. Without that stage knowledge I'd have been lost. I
couldn't—with Shakespeare, particularly—play a stage part on
the screen without playing it first on the stage; I think that the
author who writes for the stage knows precisely the shape of the
scene and writes it purposely for that particular form. (I have
just played King Henry IV, in Shakespeare's play, for Orson
Welles, in his new film *The Chimes at Midnight*. Having never
acted this part in the theater, I shall be apprehensive of the result
for the reasons I mentioned above.) As you play it you find
the line, and even if you don't find it in rehearsals you find it
during the performance. Once you've found it, it's much easier
to play it on the screen—not the same way, but unless you
know where you're going (particularly in blank verse) the

audience finds it difficult to follow. The speeches have a certain shape and curve.

During my recital *Ages of Man*—the thing that helped me so much was to find a complete arc for every speech, even though the speeches chosen out of context are merely snippets. (This sounds very inartistic and perhaps Shakespeare would kill me for doing it.) But it's very important, when you do sonnets and speeches alone on the stage for a couple of hours, to make each one in its own way as complete as possible, like a lied by Schubert or Schumann. When I was preparing that recital I used to study the records of singers, Souzay, Schwartzkopf, Fischer-Dieskau, because it seemed important to make each particular speech in some way a total statement in itself, and also to lead, with a sense of progression, to the speech that followed in my program, which I carefully chose for contrast or climax. The whole program had to be invented and bent into a certain form—once I found the form I never really changed it. (Sometimes the speeches were not complete in themselves, so this gave me a new problem, of studying them solo just for their individual beauty and content. Then, when I acted in the whole play again afterward, I found that I had gained a new feeling about some of the speeches, and this feeling remained even though, of course, it was far easier to do them when I had other people around to support me and to fit in with me.)

But the speaking of verse—which is the thing I'm supposed to be good at—is, to me, merely a question of controlling your tendency to make beautiful sounds. I have a horrible tendency to sing and to be rather romantic and poetic because I was too-much praised for good verse speaking and diction for some years and it rather went to my head. Now I try awfully hard not to deliberately use so-called beautiful sounds. I learn to do a thing as perfectly as I can, correctly, then try to smooth it out so that the audience won't see that it is in any way an exhibition. I must try to make it seem so spontaneous and natural that I might be speaking ordinary colloquial prose, although I'm speaking a most important and beautiful verse.

Really, it's a continual struggle to find the perfection in acting, then to conceal the method by which you found it, not exhibiting the tricks or the devices by which you arrive at a certain understanding of a scene or of a character. In most other arts, in painting and in music, you have simply to use the material you know and turn out a finished product that is permanent.

N.   I'd like to turn, now, to the contrast in the development of young actors in England and in America. You seem, decade after decade, to turn out a much greater number of accomplished actors than we do. What causes this?

❧   GIELGUD: We get much more experience—there's no denying that. England is a much smaller country, and we've got an extraordinary tradition of theater. I don't know about the educational aspects—I did not attend college, but I was blessed in having parents who took me to museums and made me listen to music and read fairly good books before I really wanted to look or listen or read. I've found, over the years, that the greatest contribution to my feeling about the theater is the reading I did when I was young and the appreciation of fine things I've acquired over all these years. Such actual talent as I may have is another matter. I suppose I inherited some of it, but it took a long time for me to channel it into any decent sort of shape. You are never sure of what you have achieved even if people tell you you've been a success; you immediately become a bit suspicious of your own powers.

There probably are as many good actors in this country as there are in England. It's just that the classics provide the best training, and most of us there do them earlier than they do here. (I think, too, that television and films are dangerous financial advantages to the performer; even in England we're finding it very hard to keep our young actors in the theater. They all go off into other fields and make much more money and have much more success.) It so happens that my contemporaries—there were about eight of us, Olivier, Redgrave, Richardson, Guinness, Peggy Ashcroft, (Edith Evans and Sybil Thorndike of the older generation too)—worked a lot together over the years with the same kind of enthusiasm for Shakespeare (especially) and for Chekhov and Ibsen and the classics which were somewhat out of fashion. (One forgets that those plays were not played much in the years after the first war.) Between the wars there was a great deal of classical experiment in London, a lot of Sunday societies that were equivalent to the off-Broadway theaters here. We young actors had an enthusiasm to learn our business because the older fine actors at that time were so greatly venerated by us. (Some of them I never even saw on the stage but the great figues in London, when I was a young man, were Tree and Alexander and Bancroft. Irving was dead but a few years.) My own heroes were Matheson Lang, Leslie Faber, Gerald du Maurier, Mrs. Patrick Campbell. These people had a great tradition as actors and actor-managers, and we thought that to become an actor-manager was the very greatest thing. Those of us who were ambitious pictured the authority and excitement of presenting big productions ourselves with fine casts and beautiful mountings.

I don't think this "total" aspect of theater enters the actors' imagination here. They want to get jobs. There are hardly any leading actors who are managers in this country, whereas when I was young in London there were a great many. I didn't work for many of them, but they were there and they created the kind of aristocracy in the theater which we all hoped to emulate. The First World War destroyed all of that, but there still remained in England (perhaps it's a class-conscious snobbishness) a feeling that the West End was the elite of the theater.

You had it here too—this sense of an aristocracy—when I first came here in the 1930's. There were the Lunts, and Helen Hayes, and Katherine Cornell, and figures like McClintic and Jed Harris and Max Gordon, figures who commanded the theater and who commanded respect from the young actors and actresses. Now it's a hurly-burly of showmen and a certain number of ambitious and sincere managers who haven't got the glamor to stand as examples to the young.

We were also—Edith Evans, Peggy Ashcroft, Maurice Evans, Ralph Richardson, Olivier, myself, and others who've done wonderfully well—willing to both give and give up a good deal in order to develop. All of us gave up the West End to go to the Old Vic, where we played for ten pounds a week, had

wretched dressing rooms, no billing, stock scenery and costumes, and we did this for a year or more with great willingness
and great excitement. We had a feeling of undergoing some sort
of sacrifice to improve our talents. It was a mixture of a certain
amount of self-sacrifice and a great deal of ambition and enthusiasm, and this is an awfully good mixture for a young actor. I
don't think there's the same sort of opportunity offered the actor
now. It's true that actors can go to Connecticut, or Ontario, or
Minneapolis; it seems that Guthrie (who was trained very
much in the same school as I was) has inculcated the feeling
here that to belong to a small repertory company is an admirable thing, much more exciting than getting odd jobs on Broadway or playing very big parts off Broadway. And they're
playing for smaller money than on Broadway, on the chance
that they will suddenly get wonderful notices and be brought
to New York, perhaps. But the whole thing is such a rat race
now. I think that agents are the great menace on both sides of
the Atlantic. They handle their clients (particularly the successful ones, who are easy money for them) in one way only:
to tempt them with more and more financial gain. They don't
care so much about the young people, except on the outside
chance that they may find a swan amongst the geese; if they
do find a very successful young person they will exploit him to
the full, push him on, then feel that they're responsible for any
degree of success that he may achieve. The between-man is so
all-prevailing that you don't even go to meet your manager
when you're engaged for a play. At auditions they bring their
agents with them. This was unheard of when I was first on the
stage, and it has destroyed the personal relationships that are so
important between managers and performers. Then the unions
—they've done good in destroying bad conditions and piracy,
but they also stand in the way. Not having props at rehearsals,
no tape recorders in your dressing room, all those unnecessary
restrictions about working hours. One man can take the scenery
to the stage door, another must take it in, and so forth—why,
the prop men often make more money than the actors with
small parts. All this makes for a certain commercial strictness

and confinement which, I think, destroys the fun of the theater and the comradeship we used to enjoy.

But one must not complain too much—the world goes on, and nothing is ever the same, particularly when one is not young anymore. One always looks back to one's early days with nostalgia and is convinced that nothing is quite as good as it used to be. My parents did the same when I was young, and I used to laugh at them. But without being bitter or spiteful or pessimistic, I think it's awfully hard to catch up with the modern trend. In America it's always been a matter of smash hit or failure— there hasn't been the medium tolerance we have in London for a play that isn't quite a success, and this tolerance does give a lot of plays a chance. But even in London, now, the chances are that you have to get a headline of a particular kind in the newspaper or you have to get television to advertise you. Then there's been all this fuss about ticket-scalping in America. All this jockeying for tickets seems, to me, very sad and wrong, and such abuses have smothered the intention of the theater. And, though every- one goes around talking of repertory theaters, the only one I can see here that's really carried out its intention is the APA Theatre, which does seem to have weathered three years with enormous success and has gotten a more or less permanent company, and is a great honor to have in New York. The danger is, now, that they are apt to build the theater before they get the company. The great contradiction to this is Olivier —I don't know if he knew it was coming, but certainly his Chichester venture two years ago, which I thought was rather a harum-scarum idea, justified itself abundantly from the very first year when he had one or two big successes there, and from it he built the foundation of a brilliant company which he was able to take to the National Theatre. (The National Theatre is not built yet; they're still playing at the Old Vic.) But by the time the National Theatre *is* built it will obviously have a ready-made company—not only a company, but a repertory of fifteen or twenty plays from which they can choose the best to open their new theater. This is awfully important. Men like Barrault and some of the continental companies have had these conditions for years. When Jean-Louis came to England, for a visit of two weeks, he produced eight different plays with a company of something like one hundred actors. I believe the French government paid for a great deal of it, but they recognized it as a wonderful example of what had been achieved over the years, and knew that there were very few companies in the world (certainly none in England or in America) that could take such an ambitious program to another country and be proud of it. I think it is always dangerous to export less than the best. In this day of the airplane we are fond of exporting things—God knows I've been lucky myself going all over the world with my recital, and also in doing Shakespearean tours in Europe and shows for the troops during the war—but the danger is that if we present something that isn't really good (and some of the British Council tours aren't good enough) the people in India or Israel or Argentina or America will judge us harshly. It's bad for prestige. The National Theatre will find it very hard to send tours in England, out of England, and keep a company in London as well. It really means that there will have to be three companies, and now, with the competition of television and films, it's very hard to assemble even *one* first-class company. In the two countries of England and America, I doubt if there are more than thirty-five first-class actors and actresses for classical work, and as much in demand as they are, it's impossible to get them all together in the same company. If you could it would be a miraculous thing. Yet the influence of these principals, if properly distributed, can create companies in many other places. There are always five or six really talented people in each company who could be inspired by one or two truly outstanding leading players.

In the 1930's, when I was directing and Olivier was acting with me, I thought of us rather as the "middle" of the company. There were the young people, who were not truly experienced—who were raw, on one side; and the older people of the company (in those days it was not hard to find actors and actresses because television and the movies hadn't siphoned them off) who were inflexible and rather hard to control because they were very set in their ways but fine experienced, skilled actors on the other. Between these three types of actors—provided we ourselves were a good center in our leading parts—we achieved some all-around good companies. Naturally, some of the actors broke away as they became more successful. I remember that at one time in my own company—in 1937—I had Anthony Quayle, Alec Guinness, Harry Andrews, Peggy Ashcroft, Angela Baddeley, Gwen Byam Shaw, all of whom have done wonderfully since. You can only hope to keep people together for a short while, but perhaps you can assemble them again for a certain production, and, if you've gotten on well together, you'll find that you fit wonderfully when you come together again. It's like a school reunion.

One of the happiest aspects of my stage career is that every few years I've had the pleasure of working again with the same leading ladies or the same men that I've worked with before in other plays. They know me and I know them; we begin on known and exciting ground on a project new to us all. This gives an enormous enthusiasm and rapport to a production, whether the play is new or old. Occasionally a totally unexpected venture can come off with this same flair—for example, when I worked with a new director, Peter Brook, on the old play *Venice Preserved* by Otway, which everybody thought was a relic of the past, resuscitated as a kind of joke, but it turned out to be a most brilliant and wonderful theatrical spectacle. When these things happen one is proud and excited to be in theater.

N.   How do you react to critics? Or to the art of criticism as it's practiced?

💐   GIELGUD: Of course I never like what the critics say. I don't think any actor does. They are either wrongly kind or too unkind. If they are unkind you think they're malicious, and if they're kind you think they haven't noticed the things you did *really* well. But looking back (which I haven't done very often) at scrapbooks and mementos, I don't find that they've often been unfair to the plays I have appeared in, on the whole.

I think we're all too raw and vulnerable directly after an opening. Of course the critics have an enormous influence on the box office, and it's terrible here in New York when plays come off in two or three nights (plays, that is, that should have lasted longer), yet in some ways it's preferable that a bad play die quickly. (In London a play that is not good can trail on for seven or eight or ten weeks to poor houses; you know you're not giving pleasure and that the audience is rather forced to come in.) But for the actor, of course, who needs the money badly, immediate failure is an appalling disaster, and the amount of money lost on big productions here is terrifying.

Now, I can't feel sorry about the failure of a musical like *Kelly* which obviously was no good. Everybody involved should have recognized that fact long before, and it's incredible, to me, that they can raise that much money for musicals. It's just like betting on horses, but people must think, I suppose, that any musical will automatically be a success as long as some good names are attached to it and they simply plunk the money down.

It's very hard to get money for a good play in this country, it seems, but perhaps this is because nobody has any great trust in any particular management. In the old days either the managers backed their own plays or very discreetly had their little syndicates (this was in England). I don't know whether or not Belasco, McClintic and those men had angels; I think they possibly had two or three backers who were personal friends and who trusted their judgment and discretion. They had their failures, too, of course, but somehow there was more dignity in the backing of plays, more dignity in the casting of plays, and more dignity in the decline and fall of plays, than there is today.

N.   You mentioned, before, that you have appeared in a few plays that flopped. What does it feel like?

❦   GIELGUD: Miserable. It's misery because one has worked quite as hard as one does in a play that is a success. You know, you tinker with a play after it has gone wrong. I have had two failures in England in the last year or two, modern plays which we never stopped rehearsing and changing and trying to mend on the road before we came to London. In each case I really didn't want to come into London, but I was persuaded to do so, and I went on the first night each time knowing the wretched thing would be a failure—and it was.

On the other hand, nobody knows the miracle that sometimes saves plays nobody believes in. *Nude with Violin* got terrible notices, but it ran for almost a year; the public wanted to see it. I didn't feel so happy about it all—I would rather the play had been praised—but we played it to full houses for many months, so I couldn't be altogether ungrateful. And it was a new kind of play, a new experience for me, so I got over the bad notices fairly quickly.

Many actors say they don't even read notices until two or three weeks afterward. This is probably the best plan; a bad notice can play unnecessary havoc with your performance as well as with your morale. Now, yesterday I happened to come across an old *Show* magazine in the apartment I'm taking, and in it they had an absolutely scathing notice for *The School for Scandal*. Naturally, it didn't affect me the way it would have two years ago, when I'd just started playing it. But dead notices, you know, fortunately are as dead as dead performances or dead critics or dead actors. One mustn't allow acting to be like stockbroking—you must not take it just as a means of earning a living, to go down every day to do a job of work, and to gauge success only by the present status. The big thing is to combine punctuality, efficiency, good nature, obedience, intelligence and concentration with an unawareness of what is going to happen next, thus keeping yourself available for excitement, the ability to absorb new impressions, new writers, new thoughts.

Audiences don't seem to me to have changed in any way since I was young. All that has changed is the way the plays are written and the style in which we have to play them. But the audiences remain the same; they sit and are either attentive or inattentive, they either wait for you at the stage door or they don't, and they listen while you talk and applaud at the curtains just the same.

If you worry too much about your inability to keep up with the times you become rather gloomy and old-fashioned—you are certainly aware of what is new, particularly your part or lack of part in it, but the "something new" often comes into your life quite automatically.

One of the reasons I did *Tiny Alice* is because I didn't altogether understand it, and I thought that I must be in a play which is difficult and which is in a new style to see if what I've learned over the years stands me in good stead or if I'm simply hopeless. I think that, as far as I can, I carry through this part as the author intended (and he more or less wrote the part with me in mind, in itself a great compliment that makes me feel I must make the effort to justify his gesture). It wasn't that I wanted the job so very badly, but I wanted desperately to be in a new modern play by a new modern author, and I wanted to play it in America, where I've never played anything that I hadn't played in England first. So I don't regret *Tiny Alice* in any way, although I don't think it has been the success we all hoped for. It does break new ground—it's an ambitious and exciting play. Albee writes with great imagination and power, and if it isn't quite the play I would like it to be, I must presume it's the play *he* wants it to be. Or maybe he's disappointed, too. Who knows?

It's so ephemeral, our business. A player, a performance, the way one acts—all are such short-lived things. It's only for the moment that you're doing it. One night it may be brilliant, one night it may be terrible, or it may be regular but dull, or brilliant but undisciplined. You're working with people who have so many different sides to them, so many bits of unexpectedness. To me these surprises—a little lack of certainty—are the breath of life.

People say to me, "You've never been hard up, you've never not known where the next meal is coming from, so you can afford to want surprises." Perhaps this is true. The fact remains that unless one hopes that tomorrow will be more exciting than today, and that next week will be more exciting still, it's rather futile to go on living after fifty, especially in this torn world. So as long as one can hold one's own with the new people who come into one's orbit, and have a few plays suggested to you, and manage to keep your head and have some kind of views about scripts and about the people you like to act with, and a sense of importance regarding the work you're trying to do, you can have quite a good time. Heaven knows I ought to be thankful for the extraordinarily varied and exciting career I've had. (One is assailed at times with a terrible gloom, of course, when one thinks everything is ghastly.) But we do get the reward while we're working before the public in a way that poets and musicians, sculptors and painters, often do not. They obtain some concrete satisfaction from completing their work, at least a measure of it, but it's rare that they make a fortune during their lifetime. Our work is born and dies at every performance. The only sad thing for us is getting older and feeling we're losing our memory or our looks or our hold on the public. But if we worry too much about that (and it can become a great obsession) we lose ourselves for no reason at all.

If one can move with some sort of philosophy into another decade, even with the world in the state it's in today, I don't think that one could find a more exciting or a more rewarding profession than the theater.

Films also fascinate me, and I'm hoping to do more films as I go on, perhaps because I've worked with one or two interesting directors in the last few years. I did a lot of stock films when I was young—they were not very interesting, and I took a great dislike to the work, but last year I was directed by Tony Richardson and then by Orson Welles on location—without makeup and without studio settings—and I found it marvelously refreshing and exciting to try to give a performance in another medium without stage connotations. In the Shakespeare films, *Richard III* and *Caesar*, I had in some way to adapt a stage performance to the screen. But to create a new part on the screen was in some way original; in *The Loved One* I had a completely fantastic part and in the Orson Welles film I play the old King Henry IV (Shakespeare's). I'd never played the part on the stage, so it was quite fresh. (I only hope I found the line I was talking about before, the one Brando never found in *Caesar*.) Playing Henry IV on the screen—especially under

Welles' direction—was an exciting experience, and I hope it may turn out to be effective.

The Loved One was also fascinating. Tony Richardson allowed me to improvise quite a bit. We added a lot to the scenes as we went along, and he seemed to me a most brilliant and relaxing man to work with. I don't know how the public is going to take the picture—it's so offbeat—it may turn out to be even more avant garde than *Tiny Alice*.

N.   The final question, and one involving an answer you've undoubtedly touched upon more or less before: What advice could you give aspiring young actors?

GIELGUD: It's very difficult—they all come to me and say, "I want to go to England and learn to speak English and to play Shakespeare." Now I have never seen a completely Shakespearean production in this country with an all-American cast, unfortunately, so I don't know what to say to them when they say, "We can't do Sheridan, we can't do Congreve, we can't do Shakespeare, because we don't know about the verse and we haven't got the feeling for the costumes and the style." I suppose it's true that we English learn how to wear clothes better because we looked at the right pictures when we were young, and we know the types portrayed in the English Classical plays. But there are a lot of pictures to look at in this country, too, and if young actors would really steep themselves in a period I would think that they'd eventually find a way to present it.

Some of our period plays are not much understood or appreciated in America. I did *Love for Love* here with an English company and the public didn't like it; they found the big wigs and the long speeches very artificial and strange. But aren't a number of good American playwrights producing a number of good plays in the American vernacular, so to speak? And aren't more theaters like the Guthrie Minneapolis Theatre and APA springing up to offer repertory? I think the young actor who really wants to act will find a way—there's no advice you can really offer except to keep at it and seize every opportunity that comes along. The universities and colleges are certainly trying in this country to encourage an interest and understanding of the more difficult European theater—the Greek and Restoration Comedy, the minor Elizabethans and so on. Racine, Molière too, quite apart from the enormous interest, study, and experiment in Shakespeare, which is quite as active as it is in Europe.

"I'm afraid many actors don't know what they have, but it may be valuable not to know what your special charm is . . ."

❦

GEORGE GRIZZARD

Watching a young American actor establish himself is
a rewarding experience. The flame of talent, backed
with guidelights of ambition, ingenuity, intelligence
and direction, does not flourish as often as we would
hope. Hollywood claims its share of promising performers, television siphons off others, and failures of
all sorts bedevil a majority.

George Grizzard is obviously fired with the will to
succeed. Talent, plus an iron determination, already
mark the distinguished path he is following all the way
to the top.

❦   GRIZZARD: I was born in Roanoke Rapids, North
Carolina, in 1928, but when I was six we moved to Washington,
D.C., and I grew up there. For college I went back to the
University of North Carolina, studied radio broadcasting and
specialized in advertising—I wanted to write and produce radio
shows. Television hadn't been invented, then—rather, it had
been invented but it hadn't come into its fruition—and after
college I worked for an ad agency in Washington for a year. I
hated it since there was no radio production. But during that
year I worked with amateur theater groups (I'd done quite a bit
of that in college). There was an amateur stock company

outside of Washington named Bailey's Crossroads, and we rehearsed at night and played at night, so you could only be in
every other play. I spent five summers here, before, during and
after college, and I suppose acting got seriously under my skin
because after a year of that damned advertising job I just quit.

I went down to the Arena Stage, which had just started—it
wasn't an equity theater, but it was a professional theater that
paid. I said I wanted an audition, and they gave me one because
they just happened to have a play coming up that had a part
that wasn't cast. So I auditioned and two days later I went to
work as an actor and I've been acting ever since. That was in
1950, and I was at the Arena for three months when I decided I
should go to New York to show my wares. So I came to New
York and starved all through 1951. The only important thing I
did was study with Sanford Meisner for about three months
before I went home for Christmas in 1951.

The Arena had now become an equity theater, and the man
who had started the theater and ran it said that if I could come in
for one play I could get my equity card, which might help me
in New York, so I stayed to do a part in *School for Scandal*. I
played Rowley, the old retainer. But one thing led to another,
and after I'd appeared in four plays they asked me to join the
resident company, so I stayed on for two more seasons, up to
May 1954.

At that point I'd done a play there titled *All Summer Long*
which I knew was coming to Broadway and I was offered a
chance to come along as an understudy. (I wasn't allowed to
play the part I'd played down there because I didn't have a
name.) I wanted experience on the proscenium stage again
because I had been "in the round" for almost three years, so I
left Arena, first going to Hyde Park (I was there for seven
weeks as a resident juvenile and did seven plays) before I came
on to New York to start rehearsals for *All Summer Long*. I was
assistant stage manager and understudy for John Kerr.

When that closed I auditioned for and got a part in *Desperate
Hours*, the first play in which I appeared on Broadway. It was a
big success and ran for a year. Then I went on the road with it
for three months. The next year I worked in television and

waited and waited because I wanted to do a comedy. Then *The Happiest Millionaire* came up, and there was a part I wanted, so I auditioned for it and got it and played for a year on Broadway, then a year on the road with a national tour after that.

After the national tour of *The Happiest Millionaire* I went to Europe for three months. Came back and started rehearsals with Jason Robards and Rosemary Harris in *The Disenchanted*, which ran about eight months. Rosemary talked to me a lot about the values of the classic theater because she had gotten her training and experience in England, and she was going up to Wellesley that summer to what used to be called "Group Twenty" but was now "The Theatre on the Green" to do *Much Ado About Nothing*. She thought it would be a good idea if I tried to get in, and I made it and went up to play Claudio in *Much Ado* with Rosemary. I left, but Rosemary stayed for the entire summer and did Eliza in *Pygmalion* and *Peter Pan*. At the end of the season she and Ellis Rabb were married, and after that they started APA, which is now in its fifth year and functioning very well.

Other parts—well, I was a founding member of APA, but only worked with them for two seasons. There was *Face of a Hero* with Jack Lemmon, which only lasted a month, and the same season I did *Big Fish, Little Fish* with Jason Robards and Hume Cronyn, Martin Gabel and Ruth White. Gielgud directed, and it was a marvelous production. They invented ensemble acting awards to give us that year. After *Big Fish* I went on tour with APA for the summer doing *Twelfth Night*, *School for Scandal* and *The Tavern*.

Then I did that film, *Advise and Consent*, then replaced Barry Nelson one night a week in *Mary, Mary* on the chance that I could go with it to London. Instead *Virginia Woolf* came up, so I did that instead.

In the meantime Dr. Guthrie had asked me to come to Minneapolis to play in his new theater, so I knew, when I went into *Virginia Woolf* that I could only stay with it for three and one-half months because I had to be in Minneapolis in February. While I was in New York I worked with Phillip Burton, just to have a place to do my soliloquies and be criticized (I knew I was going to do *Hamlet*) and I worked on Voice four days a week because I'd had no voice training at all, and Voice is Dr. Guthrie's big department. I left *Virginia Woolf* and went to Minneapolis and spent the season in *Hamlet*, *The Three Sisters* and *The Miser*.

Between that season and the next at the Guthrie I did nothing but television shows. Then back to Minneapolis for *Henry V*, *Volpone* and *St. Joan*. I left the season two weeks early to come back to New York to do *All Honorable Men*, a play about Alexander Hamilton that never came off. So I really haven't been on the stage since my last Guthrie season and the revival of *The Glass Menagerie* we're doing now.

N.   To focus on the Guthrie Theatre, how do you regard your experience with it, and what do you think of the place of classic repertory theater in America?

❦   GRIZZARD: They don't know much about repertory in the United States, and I don't think they knew much about it in Minneapolis. Nor did the actors who were brought out there to play know much about it. (We'd had it in Stratford, Connecticut, but even Lincoln Center isn't repertory because if a play doesn't work they pull it out.) But at the Guthrie we knew we were going to do four plays all summer whether they were popular or not. They became popular, and audiences came to see them, and the end of the season was better than the beginning. The audience had been built up.

It was nice, too, for an actor to know that he wouldn't have to do *Hamlet* twice a day. If we did *Hamlet* in the afternoon we did *The Miser* at night, or vice versa.

But I'm still not sure that if they'd said, "Leave this hit Broadway play and come out to Minneapolis," I'd have gone. I would like to think I'd have done it; I wanted to play Hamlet, and I wanted to work with Dr. Guthrie. There are very few theater masters left, and he's one of them, so I was anxious to work with him. He taught me a great deal, what with the emphasis mostly on voice and speech and rhetoric and poetry. It was like learning a new language, and it has helped me a lot. I'm sure that my performance in *The Glass Menagerie* (the narra-

tions are, in essence, soliloquy) is greatly improved because of
my two years out there. Those speeches have builds and peaks,
I know how much I'm going to do on one breath; the flow of the
poetry depends on the way the poet has written it, and you
can't mess it up by stopping to take a breath in the wrong place.
Dr. Guthrie called all these things to my attention and beat me
into some good habits.

I think the Guthrie is a great theater. I think it's the best
theater in the country. There are classes, there is great discipline (which I enjoy because I have so little of my own). I had
a speech class and a movement class each day, then a five-hour
rehearsal until the play opened, then no more classes because
our energy was needed for the audience.

It seems very exciting to me, now. Here I'm playing in one
play on Broadway and making a lot more money than I made
out there, but I'm not nearly as happy doing this one play as I
was out there working ten times as hard. I want to go back to the
Guthrie—but not to the kind of season I had last year because I
personally don't have the physical stamina to play three parts
as large as the ones I played last year. I got scared that I wasn't
going to make it through the summer.

N.   In your first season you played the uncut version
of *Hamlet*, didn't you? How did you feel about your success
in it?

❦   GRIZZARD: We cut a page and a half—the players
business, which was sort of a joke about the London theater of
the time, not very comprehensible to modern audiences, but
that's all we cut. We ran from eight o'clock to midnight, and it
was a well-paced show. I saw the same version in London and it
ran twenty-five minutes longer, but I think Dr. Guthrie was
responsible for the better pacing we had.

Actually, *Hamlet* was successful to me only because I did it.
I had never done Shakespeare before, with the exception of tiny
parts in comedies, and it was a great challenge. I was determined
not to hedge, not to get drunk the night before we opened or do
anything to keep me from being my best. Well, I did the best I
could, and what happened opening night—I think Walter Kerr

put his finger on it. (He's the most perceptive critic I know of; he seems to know what goes on inside actors.) But he said that I knew all the answers before I asked the questions, and he was right. I held onto the form that night. I was the hollow man, but the form was there, the movement, the speech, the phrasing, because that's what I had worked on. I didn't have the humanity. (I usually base my performance upon the humanity, but this time I concentrated so hard in holding onto the form of what Dr. Guthrie and I planned to do with Hamlet that I was hollow.)

Actually, my Hamlet improved a hundred percent in the six months, and that was the marvelous thing. Because it wasn't good that night we didn't take it off. We ran it for six months and I was allowed to grow in it, improve in it. It changed, and I think I got rather good, and now I have a place to start. I want very much to do *Hamlet* again some time during the next three years.

N.   Are you, as an actor, aware of any tangible sense of obligation? If so, to whom?

❧   GRIZZARD: Oh, yes, to the playwright . . . always the playwright. I think actors—as much as I hate to admit it—are interpretive artists; we're only there to interpret what the playwright has to say. We do it through our own experience and knowledge and emotions and what we know of humanity. Seven actors can play Hamlet and they'll all play it differently, yet each can be as right as the other. I think the audience—well, let me go back to something Dr. Guthrie talks about. (A pearl dropping, again; he doesn't teach, he just drops things, and one thing he dropped which I think is really important I suddenly remember.) He says that an actor must have the will to be understood, the will to communicate. Now, I've worked with some marvelous actors who do not have the will to communicate—they work for their own satisfaction, and they let the other actors onstage know what they're about, but they won't make the stage choices (a wave of the hand or an angle of the head, as examples) that will communicate something to the audience. I'm not very articulate about this, but—well, for an example, take *The Glass Menagerie.* There's a place at the end of the first act where the girl, played brilliantly by Piper Laurie, shows me a little animal from her menagerie, and it's a moment of the brother and sister coming together to share her little world, but what she chooses to do (because it's her little joke with me) is to show me tiny little things which amuse me and amuse her but fail to communicate to the audience what is going on. So I said, "Show me things big enough so the audience can see what you're doing, otherwise it looks as though we're playing a private little game up here. If you show me a big animal I can hold it up and watch the light come through it and people in the balcony can see what we're doing."

I think that an audience will get angry if it can't hear. And too many actors don't have the sense of responsibility to project, vocally, what's going on. If they can't hear they go away angry and I don't blame them. I get angry with light people who don't cut on enough lights. And you know, it's harder to hear when you can't see.

There are so many ways of communicating. The body, for example. Lots of actors have marvelous voices but can't move. Now, I can move but I don't have a vocal instrument. I have to keep working on that constantly, getting the voice so it will do what I want it to do. It's a long way from what it should be, still, but it's getting there.

There are so many ways to communicate, and the actor owes it to the playwright to develop each of them.

There's also this ESP thing. I don't know what it is, but there is an emotional thing that happens that makes audiences stay absolutely quiet, because something goes on inside of you that sends out—thought waves? I don't know. But it's a method of communication and should be used as often as possible in a play.

I have a streak of arrogance in me, I'm afraid. I'm not proud of it, but I feel that I have the ability to love people abstractly—1200 at a time—when I'm in a play. But my obligation to the playwright and to the audience ends when the curtain comes down. After the show—NO! I don't feel that I belong to them.

I can't understand people who collect autographs and I can't understand them grabbing at actors. I don't understand these large ladies' groups (usually consisting of large ladies) whose sole object is to get close to the actors; finally, when you talk to them about something, you find out that they want to do all the talking.

Nor have I patience with a noisy, inattentive house. I know that Olivier is not like this. When they don't love back, his next scene is driven by the thought, "How am I going to get them to love me this time?" I guess that's the way it should be, but I'm not sure it always is.

It's awfully hard to have love going just one way, and an audience-actor relationship is a give-and-take thing. The actor must always lead them, but the audience must follow and react. A lot of the time it's our fault if they react to what they see, and what they see is wrong enough to bring on the wrong reaction.

I like to be a leading performer because I like to have some small sense of the artistic control of what goes on. In the play I'm in now there are four leading performers and we take alphabetical star billing and we all love and respect each other but there are times when things go wrong and you can't just say, "Hey, don't do that!" In other productions a leading performer can.

There were times in Minneapolis when I would go to the stage manager to straighten something out, but most of the time, because I liked all the actors, I would say, "What happened? Why weren't you onstage for this scene?" because we were running a professional theater out there, and a lot of people, the extras especially (and we had about fifteen) had never worked in professional theater and would not wear makeup on nights they chose not to, and I thought this nonprofessional attitude was wrong and I tried to see that they learned the right and wrong way of doing things. They can do anything they want in amateur theater, but *not* in the professional world. Again, the obligation . . .

N.   Is your performance influenced by the reaction of the audience?

GRIZZARD : I'm getting much better about this. I'm getting so that I don't take it out on them, but rather upon myself. I now know that it's my fault if they don't react the way I want them to; I've learned to be a leading actor and I should be able to lead an audience. If they don't follow in the right way it's my fault; I led them wrong or I didn't lead them at all. Most of them don't know. An actor onstage says a funny line and the little lady in the audience says, "Oh, he's good!" Well, it's the playwright that's good, but the audience doesn't know the difference. The trouble is, we've got so much free theater on television that everybody is a critic, everybody's ready to say, "Oh, he's good!" or "Isn't he lousy?" when they don't know their ass from first base. Dr. Guthrie said a great thing—"Everybody who goes to the theater has a right to his own opinion, but he doesn't have a right to have it taken seriously."

Eventually you can even discount most of the critics. I know I'm going to go on acting for thirty years and they're going to go on writing about it. Sometimes I'm good and sometimes I'm not, and sometimes they're good and sometimes they're not. I just can't take what they say every time, and they can't expect me to be better every time, either.

N.   How do you feel about theater criticism? It's quality and its influence?

GRIZZARD : I hardly read them. I read Walter Kerr and I read *The New York Times*. I'll read notices on an important play that I'm in, or a review on something at the Guthrie, but otherwise I steer clear. The magazine critics—well, I have feuds with them. They don't know about it, but I have feuds with them. I think they did a wonderful thing in Minneapolis when we opened *Hamlet*. They printed fifteen reviews, side by side, from all over the world, and you could see the range of opinion. Some said it was marvelous, some thought it terrible; some thought Ophelia was just great, and some thought she was a little girl from some prep school. You could say, "All right, all of you go shut yourselves up in a room and fight it out because no matter what you say or think we're going to go right on doing *Hamlet*.

You don't need a critic to tell you when you're good and when you're bad. Sometimes the critic also reviews the horse shows and the garden club, and I sure as hell don't need anyone like that telling me about my performance. The actor depends upon the director, upon his own idea of what the playwright had in mind. The critic writes about it—the actor does it.

N.   How do you feel about the trend toward the light comedy with the small cast that's become so popular? And the big musicals?

❧   GRIZZARD : I think costs have as much to do with this as anything, and it's a factor the playwright has to keep in mind. If they write plays they want them performed, and if they want their plays to make money they have to be performed many times, and on Broadway; if they write a play that calls for eighteen people and five sets it isn't going to be done on Broadway, so they're better off writing a two- or three-character play with one set. Cruel, cruel economics—but it's what's making playwrights turn out plays for smaller casts, with fewer sets.

Musical comedies appeal to me—I love to go to them. I even like most of the bad ones, as long as they have singers and dancers and enough bright music. It's fun—like going to the circus. They're entertainment—and if this is what the theater is meant to be, musical comedies fill the bill. However, theater can and should be more than entertainment, but the commercial theater is so constituted that entertainment seems to be all it can offer. That's why we're beginning to have other kinds of theater springing up all over the country to provide the more serious plays and the classics. Apparently people aren't allergic to going to the theater to think.

N.   Do you think that American audiences are truly receptive to more serious theater?

❧   GRIZZARD : I don't know. We do a play and they come if they want—I don't think that I ought to have to go out and sell it to them. That's what the press department is for. You can't make people come to the theater, and if they don't want to come I don't think they should be made to come.

We had an audience the other afternoon—a couple of bus loads of high school students—that was whistling and making hissing sounds when the lights went on and I came out to do the first narration. They didn't stop, so I did part of the narration and said, "Kids, will you please be quiet? This is not a movie, it's a theater, and it's a play you're watching." The audience applauded.

But a lot of people don't know how to behave in a theater. They forget that it isn't a movie or television where the performers can't hear them. Those kids, for example, probably hadn't been to a play before, where things go both ways. In Minneapolis the audience would see us at parties and say, "We can't hear," and we'd say, "Yes, we know, we're working on that, the acoustics are too live and the actors with resonant voices are hard to understand. . . ." Well, we worked very hard, but we kept getting the complaint, and one night Douglas Campbell, the director, said, "You just haven't learned how to listen. We are not a television set you can turn up, you must damn well learn to concentrate when you come to the theater and do a little work, too. We can't do it all for you." I think there's something to that. People get spoiled by being able to turn up the set when they can't hear. I don't think we should make things deliberately difficult for them, but I do think they should learn how to listen.

N.   To turn to the matter of accepting or selecting a role to play. What do you look for in a characterization?

GRIZZARD: Humanity. Something I can understand, either in terms of experience or in comprehension. Then I can say, "Look, this is you, the way you are when you make a fool of yourself" or "the way you are when you cry" or "the way you are when you're in love." Or I can extend some part of human life to the stage so that they can understand and say, "Oh, yes," and they can identify and in some way be richer and know a little more about themselves, or be a bit more amused by the way things really are.

I think that humor is an essence I need in every part—there must be some kind of humor because it is so intensely human, even when we laugh at ourselves. I think there must be a nobility somewhere in a character, too—for example, even the weakly absurd Charles in *St. Joan* has a nobility, no matter how tiny it is, and it was important to find the nobility in this pitiful little king. I think it's important to show this, so that any man can find some bit of nobility in himself and respect himself more.

I don't know—but the big thing seems to be how men treat each other and why, and how they are influenced by their belief or disbelief in God. I think these are the basic premises of drama—man's relationship to man and his relationship to God. I think these must be in every play—otherwise I don't enjoy being in it, or I choose not to be in it. I find it hard to explain why I didn't want to be in several of the comedies that are on Broadway now—why I turned them down when they were offered. To me they were just amusement. Perhaps another actor could take them and shape them into things that would be more. I didn't see anything in the characters that interested me—laughs without substance, nothing more.

Yet if you're preaching you must also entertain, so I guess you have to be subtle about showing the pulpit.

N. How do you approach a role? What sort of preparation and homework is involved?

❧ GRIZZARD: The most thorough preparation I've ever gone through was with *Hamlet* because it was the most foreign to me—the language, the play, the style. It was "big" Shakespeare, so I went through the play by myself, line by line, until I knew what every word meant. There were always alternative choices of meaning, so I had to make a choice.

I did all of these things before I went to Minneapolis, and I went out there two weeks early to work alone with Dr. Guthrie before the rest of the cast came. He answered my six months of questions in one morning. We read the play together and he helped me with phrasing when meanings were obscure. He knew the play terribly well, I knew it rather well, most of the audience wouldn't know it at all, and I felt that it was up to me to communicate, as best I could, what the playwright was trying to say. I wanted to do the simplest Hamlet I was capable of doing (and believe me, I was capable of doing a simple one). I didn't want any of the nonsense about the homosexual attachment to Horatio, I didn't want any of the incest with the mother. The play is rich enough without any of that claptrap. (I think that stuff is 20th century Freudianism put on top of the play.) I wanted to present a very simple story of an idealist in a very imperfect world. Many people said they now knew what the play was about—but they knew what I thought it was about. They knew my interpretation of the play, and Dr. Guthrie said, "It's got to be your interpretation—I'm only there to help you; I've got to stage it and bring out anything you want to present." He was marvelous; he gave me complete freedom in the interpretation of the Prince.

For *Henry V* I went to the library and read about the wars so that I knew where Agincourt was; I looked at maps to learn the battlefields. I knew what Henry was up against.

When I do a contemporary play I do very little homework. It doesn't call for background, so I do most of the work in rehearsal. I don't think I have to go and work in a shoe factory to play Tom in *The Glass Menagerie*. (I once worked in an office where I ran a mimeograph machine or addressograph machine or something. A factory couldn't be much different.)

Homework on the big plays is largely technical work—speech, phrasing, knowing what the play is about, making decisions on the line that will keep the audience from being confused. You at least make some decision, and are consistent enough and definite enough about it so that someone can confront you and say, "No, that's wrong." Well, to *them* it's wrong, but at least I'm doing something definite, something I think is right. As for the pomposity of critics who say, "This is absolutely wrong"—well, screw them. They have no more right than I to say what is right and what is wrong. I have my idea, they have theirs, but infortunately they have the ninety thousand readers, so a lot of people will read a review and not come to see me. I do get mad at critics, don't I? And what is the recourse? Well, there are two I'm going to hit if I ever meet them. They reviewed *Hamlet*—and I accepted the reviews from the responsible critics—but these were two completely irresponsible critics of the play and they were inane. There's no way to get back at them the way they got at me—the hurt they gave me—but a solid punch will help. They shouldn't be allowed to get away with inaccurate, irresponsible, vindictive criticism— the kind that makes readers say, "Oh, so-and-so must be terrible in the play."

These men will be terribly hurt when they meet me.

N.   How vulnerable is the actor to criticism?

❀   GRIZZARD: You're always affected—there's a wonderful childlike quality in actors that lets them get hurt like children. I've seen some of the best actors in the country set back by the idiocy of someone's newspaper column. At this point I say, "Don't bring them around—I don't want to read them." Rosemary Harris tried to teach me that when I worked with her. She doesn't read reviews. She just asks, "Are they good?" and they'll say, "Yes," or "No," and she'll say, "Fine." But she won't read them, because if they say ". . . the way she moves her hand in that scene"—well, you'll never move your hand that way in that scene again.

I think it's best for actors not to read reviews. The audience, and the producers who depend on them for money in New York, have to read them, but I think actors should stop. When they're bad they hurt, when they're good they give us praise we don't need. The audience claps or it doesn't clap when the play is over. We know when we're bad—we don't have to be told. As Jason Robards says, "Actors don't need criticism, they need love."

N.   Could you state your own very personal objectives as an actor?

❀   GRIZZARD: It's as tenuous as saying, "I want to be an important actor in America." I have to work terribly hard because I don't have that much talent. I have to develop it constantly, and I have to grow and stretch because the idea of staying put, playing the same thing, bores me. I want to do as many different things as I can.

I think it's important to know your limitations. I know mine, some of them at least, and it stops me to a degree but it also makes me want to overcome them. Dr. Guthrie says I can never play Greek tragedy because I have no voice at all, so now I want terribly to play Oedipus.

I know I can do comedy because I have the sense of humor and the sense of comedy born in me, so to speak—it comes easiest to me. For instance, last year in Minneapolis the part that came hardest to me, the one I felt was least successful, was *Henry V*, but the part of the Dauphin in *St. Joan* was the easiest thing to do, and the most successful, and I could have played it blindfolded, with my hands behind me. Mosca was great fun— difficult because the language presented a great problem, also the physical energy every actor needs in great quantity, and I was tired by the time I got to that play and should have had more to offer than I did.

I want to work primarily on the stage because I'm not a handsome fellow, and the parts I want to play I can't play in Hollywood because they've got more than enough of the handsome fellows to go around. The movie audience tends to identify with beautiful people, and if I were there I'd play second or third parts. I'd rather stay away and play leads on Broadway or in the classic theater. It's more interesting for me to stretch, to take on a play in which language is a problem, or in which style or movement is a problem; you use yourself totally, not just one-tenth of yourself, which is all most plays on television and most modern contemporary things require.

I would also like to have a greater degree of emotional free-dom—I'm born in April, I'm an Aries, and I can't always do emotionally the things I know intellectually. This bothers me. It's why it's so much easier for me to do comedy, because you're not usually as emotionally involved in comedy as you are in serious plays.

But I want to do the great parts. And I want to have somebody write a play for me. I would like to play several of the Shakespearean parts. I love the poetry of the theater, and I'm learning the poetry because Dr. Guthrie has taught me the value of it and the necessity of learning it. These are challenging things to me because I don't have a classic background. I didn't even study Drama at the University.

The things I don't have are the things that fascinate me. I'm afraid many actors don't know what they do have, but it may be valuable not to know what your special charm is, what makes people keep looking at you—if they do. There is, according to Laurette Taylor, always a certain percentage of the audience born hating your personality, so you can never get them all on your side. This has stopped worrying me, but I want to fulfill my potential, whatever it may be, and stretch it if I can. I'm fascinated with the total combination of technical skill which includes movement and voice and emotional freedom. You don't see it very often, and I don't know that I've ever seen it in our theater. To me the best American actor is Jason Robards. I've learned a lot from him, and I wish he were more disciplined. The tendency is, however, when you have a greatness, an excitement, a fire, something which is alive and exciting, to be ashamed of it and destroy it whether you intend to or not. I've seen technical actors that have no heart, and heart actors that have no technique. I want to see one American actor have both. Most actors have a little of each, but to have a balance, and be free—

You know, I used to protect myself all day. I wouldn't do this or that, wouldn't go skiing on a weekend because I might break a leg, wouldn't play baseball because I'd end up going to the theater Thursday night bruised and tired—I came with my little talent held in my arms, protected safely, and dropped it on the stage. There wasn't even a clatter.

You can't protect yourself that much. You must be battered around a bit. I still haven't loosened up enough, but I've improved.

I'll probably be around for a while and I ask myself what I'm going to do with the time. I can certainly spend a few more years in Minneapolis. I can certainly spend a year doing films.

I don't know anything about films. I had almost convinced myself that I could spend two years doing a television series because I don't know much about film acting, but could learn. Yet I couldn't do a television series; it would bore me, and I don't want that identity. There's a great paradox of wanting to be rich and famous, yet not have everybody know who you are. It's complicated, but it seems to be my goal. So perhaps, if I stay on the stage, I can be rich and unknown (the only people who identify me on the street are those who saw "Password" on television, not those who've seen me in plays).

But I can't live the public life of the actor—I can't hump on an international level. I like and respect Richard Burton tremendously, but I can't drink with him because he intimidates me simply because he's such a celebrity. Now, Paul and Joan Newman are old friends—ten years ago my first play was his second play, and I was his little brother for a year and we went around together a lot. Now I think, "My big brother lives in Paris or London or Hollywood or somewhere"—I never think of him as being a movie star, probably because he's still the same nice guy, and to me he's still a big brother.

I'm not very good with successful people—international, notorious, wealthy people. I'm like a small-town farm boy when I'm around them, and the going gets sticky when they put on an act and pretend to be more international, notorious or wealthy than they are.

I should be a teacher. Eventually I think I will be, teaching and directing at a university. But not for another thirty years.

*"I want very badly to play Lady Macbeth . . . . I'd like to do
Peter Pan."*

❦

JULIE HARRIS

You do not forget Julie Harris. Her beauty is unique, for it combines a bit of the gamin with an ethereal incandescence, a touch of innocence with an imp whose naïveté has happily been erased. As if this weren't enough, she possesses a vivid dramatic talent, a presence both commanding and provocative, and a musical but husky voice that is the sexiest in the business. What man in his right mind *could* forget her?

❦　　　　HARRIS: I was born in Grosse Pointe, Michigan, just north of Detroit, and lived there and was educated there up until my junior year in high school when I was sent away to a school in Providence, Rhode Island. (My senior year was spent in another school in New York, Miss Hewitt's.)

My interest in the theater began in high school back in Grosse Pointe. I had a very young teacher, a graduate of Vassar College, Betty Spencer, and her first assignment brought her to our school to teach drama. She was full of ideas and put on wonderful plays; I tried out for them simply because it was fun. I had always loved the theater—I'd started going with my parents when I was about ten. (I'd seen children's plays before that and mother used to take me to the ballet, and I'd grown up with the movies, and they were a great influence.)

Perhaps because I was a very poor student in school—not really very interested in most subjects—the extra-curricular drama class seemed to make it all worthwhile. (To some extent I was always an actress; my brother and I would come home from movies and act them out. I notice, now, that children seem to have this instinctive tendency; my son does the same thing.) But I loved the drama classes, and on top of that people said I was funny, a good mimic, and complimented me, and this compensated for my denseness in mathematics and Latin. (Everything seemed to conspire to present insoluble problems for me. English —when they gave me a story to write—could be fun, but most of the time school was an agony.)

Acting was something I felt I could do, and when I was about fourteen I began to think of studying to become an actor. I heard of an acting camp in Colorado, Perry-Mansfield at Steamboat Springs, so I wrote to them and was accepted as one of their scholarship students. I studied with Charlotte Perry, who taught the acting courses, and I also studied dancing with Valerie Bettis and Merce Cunningham for three summers. Miss Perry was the first person who encouraged me to think of acting as something I could do as a career. This staggered me because I hadn't thought of myself as possessing the capacity for being a *real* actor. (I had seen Helen Hayes, Katharine Cornell, the Lunts, Maurice Evans, and Ethel Waters in shows that toured and came to Detroit, and I'd never begun to consider myself in league with them.) But Miss Perry encouraged me, so when I left high school I applied to the Yale Drama School. This was at the end of the war when they were accepting non-graduate students to fill their classes, so I attended it for one year. During that year I met Dione Lewis in the school; she knew someone who had written a play that was going to be produced in New York, and she suggested that I come to New York to audition for a part. I applied, and read, and several days after I'd gone back to Yale I heard from the producers; they wanted me to do the play.

This bowled me over. I went to Walter Prichard Eaton, then head of the School and said, "What should I do?" (The play meant that I would have to interrupt my studies.) He said, "You want to be an actress, don't you? When the opportunity comes to act you have to take it." So I took a leave of absence from school and came to New York and began working in the play.

I was so inexperienced that the director actually frightened me and I kept to myself. On the fifth day of rehearsal I was handed my notice—they were firing me. It came as a great shock, but when I think of it now I realize they should have done it sooner. I was intimidated, and I was a bit intimidating—I thought I knew it all; when I was given some direction I thought, to myself, "How dare they tell me how to do it? Don't they assume that I know how?"

And so, through ignorance, I lost the job. But the playwright was very fond of me. Curt Goetz was a wonderful man—he had written the play and carried the lead. He said, "I want you in the play, so don't get disheartened; I'll figure something out." Two days later they called me back again. I opened in the play and we ran for six weeks. *It's a Gift* had been a great success in Europe when Mr. Goetz had done it there, as a one-act play, and he had enlarged it. The play presented an amusing idea, but it didn't run very long. When it was over I went back to Yale and finished out the year. They do three or four major productions each year and I was in the last one. I didn't do anything until the following winter when I came back to New York and lived with Miss Hewitt—the headmistress of Hewitt's Classes. She was in love with the theater and she had seen, when I was in my last year of high school, how passionately fond of the theater I was. She had taken an interest in me and had taught me a great deal, including a wonderful background in Shakespeare and a love for Shakespeare. She introduced me to some people from the Amateur Comedy Club of New York, one of the oldest organizations of its kind in the city. They do three productions a year, at that time staging them at the theater at Hunter College. We did *The Devil's Disciple* and I played Essie.

Whatever an actress does is good; you not only learn, but you gain associations with your colleagues. You learn some new facet of characterization and the fine points of collaboration. So much of theater is collaboration—not like the painter who sits alone in his studio; what goes on the canvas is up to *him* only. A play is a collaboration of many people. Once it's been written the playwright must suffer a little in the collaboration because the actor cast for the part may not be totally able to give him what he conceived. (Eugene O'Neill said that only twice in his lifetime did he have an actor who lived up to his expectation of the part. Of course, the longer I'm in theater the more I believe that a playwright shouldn't set impossibly high standards because it's impossible for actors, who are human and individual, to adjust to them.) Back to *The Devil's Disciple*. While I was in that Richard Aldrich, one of the producers of Theatre Inc. (no longer in existence) came backstage and said, "We are very interested in finding new young people; would you come to the office and give us your address so we can keep in touch with you?" I did, and that spring the Old Vic Theatre Company was brought over by Theatre Inc. with Sir Ralph Richardson, Sir Laurence Olivier and Joyce Redman, Margaret Leighton—the magnificent company that completely changed my life the first night I saw them perform. I was unbelievably lucky; I was taken in as a walk-on with the company. Three American girls and six or seven American men were added to the company so that crowd scenes could be filled out. We were used in *Oedipus* and in *Henry IV* Part II, but we were allowed to watch any of the performances we wanted to see. I was there every night, and I have never seen such brilliant ensemble acting. In fact, I'd never believed it possible. What absolutely overcame me was the sense of precision, the constant illusion of reality. It didn't vary, like a musical performance. The notes were struck the same way, with the same intensity, yet it always seemed to live, of itself, for the first time, as though it had never happened before. It was scored, I should imagine, like a great symphony orchestra that can't allow for note-by-note variation. We say now, in modern theater, that you can't possibly do the same thing over and over again and have it meaningful; so the Old Vic was a contrary revelation. (I used to watch Sir Laurence when he played Mr. Puff in *The Critic*. To the identical syllable, in each performance, he would take off his hat, take out the hatpin and stab the hat with the hatpin. He didn't vary a hair's breadth from performance to performance, yet it was always funny and always astonishing.) It occurred to me that it is possible to be a well-trained instrument, to perform as a craftsman without ever becoming ordinary, and that if there is such a thing as perfection in acting it's worthwhile living for and striving for that perfection.

After my Old Vic walk-ons I got a job in a summer stock company in Maine—ten weeks of doing one side after another. My first play was Claudia, then I did a part in *The Little Foxes*. I was set to play the younger sister in *The Philadelphia Story* when the girl who was going to play Tracy (the Katharine Hepburn part) got a job in New York and left. They told me I'd have to play Tracy. It was a very long part, and I had to sit up all night for several nights to learn the lines.

Opening night of *The Philadelphia Story* was ghastly. I was panic-stricken, and on several occasions I had to turn my back to the audience and try to remember the lines. I was so nervous I couldn't hear the stage manager prompting. They hadn't had a summer company up there for years, and our opening night with *The Philadelphia Story* was our first sold-out opening, and it was agony to not be absolutely sure of everything. So we didn't want a disaster, and it wasn't. I suppose those moments when I thought, "What am I going to say now?" were more painful to me than they were to the audience.

That whole summer was quite an experience. It was exciting, but tiring, and I don't know that I'd want to do it every summer. In a company like that you were thrown entirely on your own resources, your own wits, and if you couldn't remember a line you had to make up something that made sense. It was improvisation in a way because you were never totally prepared. Yet there was a wonderful sense of power in throwing yourself into a part, and by virtue of your own concentration, your own belief in a situation, making it come alive for the audience. Then (heavens; I didn't know my life was this long) I came back to New York. I has a small part in a revival of *Playboy of the Western World*—a wonderful play. I was one of the village girls that bring Christy presents. (Someday I would like to play Peggie or the Widow Quinn.) I did another play with the Comedy Club, *The Idiot*, then a series of plays that had very brief runs—a week or a few weeks at most, hardly raging successes. Soon after I auditioned for The Actor's Studio, the first year they were in existence, and I was invited to study there. The first year I worked with Elia Kazan and at the end of that year we worked on a play titled *Sundown Beach* by the short-story writer Bessie Breuer. It was a beautiful play and we worked on it as a class project. Some people who saw it got quite excited and suggested that we do it in stock that summer, so we did, and we brought it on to New York in September but it only lasted a week. I had a wonderful part in it, and Harold Clurman saw me, and almost two years later he suggested me for *Member of the Wedding*. That play was really the beginning of everything big for me; it was the first time I got a really major part in a beautiful play that succeeded.

N.   This sounds corny, but do you believe in such a thing as a "break" or a catalytic event that actually creates success?

❦   HARRIS: Well, Charles Gilpen, who played *Emperor Jones* wasn't an actor. Someone saw him, and thought he'd be right for the part. I believe that every human has a part in him that can be brought to the theater if the director is good and understanding. If the circumstances of the play are right for that particular person they can play it even if they are untrained. Acting is essentially very close to human events; we all have imagination, we all act out things that happen, sometimes in our conversations, sometimes before a mirror, sometimes in the privacy of our minds.

If I hadn't been in *Sundown Beach* I wonder what would have happened to me. That led, in a direct line, to *Member of the Wedding*, and that play made Julie Harris a known and recognized commodity.

N.   I've always been impressed with your uncanny ability to subordinate your personality in a role. In other words I never think of Julie Harris, but of Joan, or Ophelia, or

Sally—whoever you happen to be playing. Do you consciously assume a new identity?

❧   HARRIS: I think that grows with time. When I did *The Lark* I read all the books I could possibly find relating to the life of Joan of Arc. I read the original trial records, and looked at hundreds of pictures of her, and I wondered how I could possibly convince anyone that I *am* Joan of Arc. She has to be such a symbol of all the strength and courage that can exist in a human being, and you could so easily strike the wrong note in playing her.

Well, when I read and pieced together all the facets of personality I uncovered I discovered an astonishing number of notes to strike. She was simple and true and sturdy, but she was also extremely witty. She was humble, yet she had a great ego, a terrific passion, a sense of herself. I think it was painful for her to fall in love with her position as a leader of men, to become enamored of the heroics of war and the destruction of the enemy.

It would have been hard for Joan to have survived. She would have had quite a problem of readjustment. She always said that once Charles was crowned and the English were on the way out that she would go back to the farm. Without the excitement of leading men, without her horse and her banner and her sense of destiny, I think she'd have been lost.

Shaw chose to dramatize this aspect, and honorably so.

At any rate Joan was a complex person, not a simple country girl. I think anybody who has visions must be a complex person. There are so many mysteries in life, and I suppose I have the ability to believe in mysteries.

Last September I did a play for television for Hallmark—*The Holy Terror*, based on a portion of Florence Nightingale's life. I read a lot about Florence Nightingale and came across this simple fact: she had a niece who had a child and she very subtly tried to persuade the niece to name the child Balaclava. Well, Balaclava was one of the great place-names in the Crimean War, and Florence said that it was the most beautiful name in the world. I thought of the feeling that went into that, when you think of the circumstances of her life, her being so sheltered and so carefully brought up, then suddenly going to the Crimea and for two years living under such dreadful conditions and making order out of such terrible chaos. It took a mighty will. Then, the way Mary Stanley was also sent to the Crimea by the War Office . . . and Florence got rid of her so fast. She had a phenomenal sense of destiny and she was not going to share the command.

There are always many sides to a characterization, and I've been fortunate enough to work with directors who helped bring out the best in me. Harold Clurman, with *Member of the Wedding*, gave me a wonderful sense of that girl. I was twenty-four, at that time, and Frankie Adams is supposed to be twelve and three quarters years old, so I was twice her age. He never said anything about acting childish or acting like a child. He said, "Your age doesn't matter. You could be fifty-two and still play that part. If you put yourself in the circumstances and properly feel her pain people are bound to think you're the right age." That was so sensible, because it's the actress who must convince the audience of a given set of circumstances. They say that when Ellen Terry was almost seventy she used to give recitals of Juliet and that when she ran on in the scenes with the nurse the audience would think she was fourteen, voice and everything. So this, to me, is the thrill of acting; of trying to tell a story in terms of acting.

N.   Recently *The Times* of London ran a rather negative article on Method Acting; the overall view was that it has become an excuse for too much introspection on the part of the actor. What are your feelings toward Method?

❦   HARRIS: Two of my favorite actresses—Geraldine Page and Kim Stanley—are Method actresses, and their work constantly seems to improve. I understand that they believe very strongly in the Stanislavsky Method, and have studied with Lee Strasberg. I know that other actors seem to have hurt the Method, but I think that involves misconception. Josh Logan, who just directed me in *Ready When You Are, C. B.* studied with Stanislavsky. As I see it, the Stanislavsky Method is closely akin to psychiatry, and if you are going to attempt it and really know yourself deeply, in that way, it undoubtedly takes a long time and requires all of your concentration. I think the misconception has come about because certain actors have given the impression that Method actors mumble, they don't have good speech, they can only play one type of role. Those accusations are made against Method actors, but Stanislavsky never meant beautiful acting to be mumbled or spoken with bad enunciation. There were things that intrigued him . . . when Duse did a scene from *Camille* there was a moment (I've read this) when, at the mention of a man with whom she had once had a love affair, she blushed. (She was very pale, but suddenly her face would flush.) Stanislavsky said, "How could that happen? Because it is an emotional experience; it is not just technique, she has involved her emotions." It's been said that during her last tour, before she died in Pittsburgh, that when she came off the stage after each performance she was a little less than when she went on. She spent herself.

Now, this is what I believe the Method strives for. It's like a bullfighter who goes into the ring, a really great fighter who engages the bull in his dance of death, and teaches the bull how he should do it. It's like the lover instructing the one he loves in the method of loving. The actor teaches you what you should feel in the play. This requires a certain kind of actor, and Sir Laurence Olivier (who has had a different sort of training—we haven't repertory theater nor all those great Shakespearean companies where the young actor spends years working up to leading roles, but plays all roles, small and medium-size, in getting there) is always truthful in his acting and his acting is actually the Method. He can't make the audience feel as he wants them to feel if he's not truthful. His technique, which is flawless, is only part of it. He must possess emotional intensity, belief . . .

Did you ever see Laurette Taylor in *Glass Menagerie?* Her performance shattered me. I felt as though I was on fire, or about to burst. It was so personal I couldn't believe I was seeing it. She was so funny and so sad. Julie Hayden idolized her. And it was said that in rehearsals Miss Taylor used to mumble her lines to herself and that the other actors were unsure of what she was saying. All this is sometimes a personal way of getting to the truth. Instead of racing into rehearsals and giving a superficially exciting reading in the beginning, then trying to live up to that, some actors go at the role very slowly and back away from the intensity of it for some time until they really understand the part; then they can plunge into it without thinking about it.

I think that criticism of the method from the English is quite unfair. We don't have the same opportunities that the English actor has. We could all migrate to England to share their opportunities and training, but that wouldn't be fair.

N.   I'll turn to *Ready When You Are, C. B.* Is that an enjoyable role?

❦   HARRIS : I like it very much. The characterization is interesting because the girl changes during the course of the play; she grows into something stronger. It's a very human sort of comedy. She has been an actress, and really wants to be, but after a series of disappointments she has rented her apartment out and makes a living as a landlady—an excuse, really, for not living anymore. That's the comic side.

There's a real side, however. I remember that when I used to make the rounds I expected people to act in a courteous way. Most of the time I was disappointed, but the competition was staggering, and when somebody said, "Oh, no, you're not the type," I thought it was the end of the world. So I can understand Annie saying, "Oh, well, I'll forget all about that and just be a landlord." She is going down a blind alley when the play opens. Then a series of adventures change her life and let her decide not to be afraid, anymore, of what life puts in her way.

N.   We haven't discussed *I Am a Camera.*

❦   HARRIS : That was an exciting part—it was so totally different and unexpected. I remember reading for Mr. van Druten one afternoon in September. I read the whole play, and I was in a fever when I left and terribly frightened. Sally Bowles was so flamboyant and outrageous and marvelous that once I got over the fear of saying, "Oh, I won't be able to convince anyone that I am this girl," it was nothing but pleasure.

I've liked all my parts, really, without exception. It was thrilling to know that Joan of Arc can be brought alive for people 500 years later, and that she's still meaningful. It's such a powerful story that no playwright can have the final word, nor can any actress have the ultimate characterization.

N.   As far as the future is concerned, what roles would you like to play?

❦   HARRIS: Well, I have some rather fierce longings. I've played Ophelia, now, and I've played Juliet in Canada and I want to play her. I want very badly to play Lady Macbeth. I have definite feelings about her, the woman she was (again, a complex person).

Then there's something special, very special, I'd like to do on my own—a program of Emily Dickenson's poems and letters, the way Hal Holbrook did the Evening with Mark Twain, and Emlyn Williams did Charles Dickens. I'd like to *be* Emily—to look and dress and perhaps even sound like her.

Another odd one—almost a standard desire, I suppose—but I'd like to do Peter Pan. I want to do it fiercely, not at all sentimental. It should be as Tyrone Guthrie said: you should cheer for Hook and shiver when Peter comes on because Peter is the villain and Hook is the hero. Goodness, it's a fierce play. Barrie says that children are gay, innocent and heartless, not a sentimental view. When Peter gnashes his teeth, his six-year teeth, he does it with all the fierceness of a boy who says, "I'll never grow up, no matter what you do to me!"

Barrie wrote a book that reveals so much of him, and of his mother, Margaret Ogilvy. It's a small book, but it's piercing. You can't say, after reading it, that Barrie was sentimental. He was fierce, though his capacity for love was boundless. He had sentiment but he was not sentimental, and the sugar-plum-fairy version of *Peter Pan* isn't correct.

N.   How do you feel about theatrical criticism as it's practiced today, particularly in New York?

❦   HARRIS: I guess I compare it, in my mind, to a prize fight. You have just that one match—that first night when the critics are there. Everything is staked on it, and you have to think of it that way. It's desperate, because if you fully realize that this one night is so important you might get so frightened that you won't act well. But that's the way the game is played, so you have to control yourself, to reach that peak of perfection, because that one night is the only one that's forever meaningful as far as the play is concerned.

I don't know if it's fair or not. Yet when you go to hear a symphony played you want it to be absolutely perfect, and you judge it on that performance—not what might have been or could be.

The public pays so much attention to the critics—they decide to go or not to go on the basis of what they read. I can't blame the public because an evening at the theater, from the time people leave home to the time they return, portal to portal so to speak, is an expensive proposition. Production costs, for example, are so unreasonable that I hope that someday an agreement will be reached between all the people collaborating in a theater that will allow the prices to come down. Otherwise we're going to have maybe five shows per year surviving.

N.   If you were to give advice to the talented youngster who wants to act, what would that advice be?

❦   HARRIS: I think the first thing I'd say is: "Go to wherever you can learn the most and have a classical training." I have a friend who's daughter is nineteen and has gone to England to study. I've suggested that to other young people because I don't know of the equivalent in this country—of a school or a way of obtaining repertory experience—that will teach you all aspects of theater art—music appreciation and painting, sewing and costume designing, singing and diction work, plus training in the classics. Some colleges have very good drama departments, but I don't think any of them have this classic all-theater background English and French schools have. The person comes away knowing the craft.

You can't minimize the importance of knowing how to dance

very well, and to sing; all these aspects should be explored so
that you can be as close to a perfect instrument as you can
possibly be. Your voice must be developed, your imagination,
your memory.

This isn't thought of, here—at least it's seldom talked about.
Not long ago I read a play with a group, a poetic play,
Calderon de La Barca's *Life Is a Dream*. Some of the speeches
were three pages long, and I had to memorize them. It's staggering, when you first begin something like that, but it's possible,
if you keep your memory trained. The beginning pianist has
to play scales; the actor has to train his memory.

N.   As an actress could you state any obligation you
might feel?

❦   HARRIS: I think the first obligation I feel is to fulfill
the direction that has been given me, the line of art in the play.
I must, as fully as I can, sustain the author's intentions all along
the way to give the audience a moving picture of what's happening, to let them follow the inner workings of the character as
well as hearing the lines.

I owe the audience the best performance that's in me at the
time, the best work I can possibly do. Sometimes you come on
and you don't feel absolutely right on top but you quickly
have to remind yourself that *they* don't care if you don't feel
wonderful; they're seeing you tonight and they've paid their
money to get in and they're going to go away with an
impression of you and the play based on that night's work. So
you forget that you don't feel so hot.

N.   A final question, quite personal. Your voice is one of
the most hauntingly lovely voices in theater. Have you always spoken like this, or is it a result of training?

❦   HARRIS: I think my voice is now stronger than it
was, but I always did have a low tone. On the stage I think I use
a higher pitch, but it never gets too high. I hope my voice
continues to get more flexible—I've been in theater twenty
years, and it's said that it takes twenty years to make an actor,
and the voice is such an important instrument I'd like to play it
better.

"_. . . theater has always been my real life . . ._"

HELEN HAYES

She is the First Lady of American Theater for many profound reasons. Three of them are *Mary of Scotland*, *Victoria Regina* and *Harriet*. Film triumphs include the unforgettable *A Farewell to Arms* and *The Sin of Madelon Claudet*. In personal life she has enjoyed stability and happiness and endured shattering tragedy. But at no point has she ceased being one of those preciously few stars whose talent, appeal and dedication can invariably dominate a stage—and fill the theater.

HAYES : I was born in Washington, D.C. My name has ten letters, I was born in 1900 in the tenth month on the tenth day. I think a numerologist would flip over this coincidence of events. I went to school in Washington at the Sacred Heart Academy—they very nicely honored me a few years back. I never managed to get through to the very end of high school because of the way my childhood and youth was split between school and theater. I made my debut in Washington with the Columbia Players—it came about because my mother had been stagestruck since her twenties, and had made the acquaintance of the man who ran the stock company. (Not that she had ever performed; they were merely good friends.) At any rate he asked her if she would let me appear in a piece at the Columbia Theatre when I was five or six years old.

I've been in theater ever since. The first years, of course, were limited to summer engagements with various stock companies, and these appearances were not steady—I was only called when they needed a child. But they'd always put on a production for me because it was discovered, at the very beginning, that I could manage myself on a stage without making terrible mistakes like falling down or blowing my lines. Besides, I was local talent. All my father's business associates and my mother's friends went to see me, so that helped out greatly at the box office.

It was probably only a bit, but I must have shown signs of talent, because all of the actors connected with that Columbia Stock Company conspired to push me on and get me jobs in New York. After three years of this encouragement they finally persuaded my mother to take me to New York to try our chances there. I must have been eight, quite young, but she did. She took me to see Lew Fields—he had expressed interest in me when he saw me in a little dancing school recital three years before. (I forgot to say that I went to Miss Minnie Hawkes' dancing classes before I ever went on the professional stage, and that every year she had what she called "The May Ball"—a demonstration by the youngsters of what they had learned over the year. I didn't learn any dancing, but my mother had me do some miming, and it was during my little act as a Gibson Girl that Lew Fields came into the theater to pick up his mail and stopped to watch. He was playing in Washington at the Belasco Theatre, and he saw the child up there miming and said to the theater manager, "If that child ever wants to be an actress you tell her mother to bring her to me.")

So three years later, persuaded by the director of the stock company and many other well-intentioned persons, we went off to New York, my mother taking me by the hand.

You asked me where my interest in theater started—well, like Topsy, it just growed. I didn't have any of that yearning most young people (stagestruck young people) have when they feel they're wasting their lives away in school and high school. So often they come to me looking wan and frustrated and say their parents won't let them go on the stage and they just know that they're losing all those valuable years and the experience . . . Well, I didn't lose any years and I didn't miss any experience because I was right in there being a pro at the age of five. The first time I was really on the stage (I must qualify the miming episode Lew Fields saw; I was five then, six when I appeared with the Columbia Players) rather fixed me to the theater because from then on I don't think I missed a year. This early career was limited to summers, of course, but I did three shows with Lew Fields—musicals that were a wonderful experience I treasure to this day. I remember every detail of them, the marvelous performers I played with.

N.   Did you sing and dance, too?

HAYES : Gracious, no. There was a society called the Gary Society which was a protective organization for children. It succeeded in putting through legislation which prohibited children from singing and dancing. It wasn't airtight legislation because children could do everything *except* sing and dance. You could stay up all night long, you could be in any cabaret whatever if they needed a child that wasn't called upon to sing or dance. I mimed—this seemed to be my particular forte, it was the thing Lew Fields had first seen me doing—so he always had a little act written into his shows specifically for me to mime. The first show in which I appeared with Mr. Fields was called *Oh, Dutch!* and it had a score by Victor Herbert, who directed the orchestra. I remember that very impressive head down there in the orchestra on the opening night. My sadness is that *Oh, Dutch!* was not one of his major scores, and I haven't heard any of it for decades. (It would have been nice to have been in *Babes in Toyland* or one of his other hits—things you hear on the radio all the time.)

I did two other shows with Mr. Fields and he always had a special little thing written in for me—but singing and dancing, no.

You see, at a very early age the theater became a normal way of life for me. Everything outside of the theater seemed extra, somehow; even when I would go home to go to school and

spend my winter with my family and my girl friends I felt
that I was just visiting. It wasn't until I got back with the
troupers in the theater that I felt at home. I don't know when
that subtle change occurred, but it seems as though theater has
always been my real life, and the other was like playing a
part.

N.   When did your first dramatic roles come along?

❧   HAYES : My first dramatic role came as the result of
the help of one of the stock company actors. I had played with
an English actress named Jessie Glendenning—a very charming
person—who'd been at the Columbia Theatre for the summer
season. I had been in one or two plays with her. Well, a wire
came rather abruptly from the Charles Froman office to absolutely startle my mother. (Froman was then the great shining
name in the theater, you know. It was magic.) It was all too
dazzling. I was then twelve, had played my three seasons with
Lew Fields, and there wasn't anything else coming up—I was
back home, attending school at Sacred Heart, and along came
this! It was at the very beginning of the school session so we
went to New York to look into it. We discovered that Jessie
Glendenning was in the play, and that they needed a child to
look about twelve. Jessie remembered this child who'd been at
the stock company in Washington and recommended me. (I
forgot to add that John Drew had the lead in this play, and that
they'd tried several little girls and he wouldn't have any of
them. They were a little artificial—the overcurled hair,
slightly tinted and everything.) So on I came, with long,
straight hair, and I was given the part.

That was the beginning, and it all followed in a sequence. We
never came to New York seeking a job except for that first time
when we came to see Mr. Fields. We always came up after the
receipt of a telegram, and those telegrams always came from
some actor who had played with me in the stock company and
remembered me. I must have been rather impressive in those
days because these calls would come a year, two years, three
years after they'd played with me, and they'd say to a
producer, "I know just the girl; she's down in Washington

. . ." and that's the way it followed. I always went home between engagements and went back to school and carried on a regular girl's life, but those stretches were never long.

N.   Did you study dramatics at all?

🌷   HAYES: I never studied dramatics until I was twenty-one, after I'd achieved stardom. (I was the youngest star I'd heard of—certainly in those days I really *was* the youngest. Since then, of course, we've had several who have achieved stardom earlier than I did; Susan Strasberg was seventeen or eighteen and became a star on the opening night of the play, *Diary of Anne Frank*.)

At any rate, I was a star at twenty-one, and my mother was wild with rage. But they had put my name up there, and they wouldn't take it down. She threatened to yank me away and not let me play the opening night in New York. It was all very dramatic, and her scene with the producer was played in high color. At any rate, she was wise. Maybe I paid too much attention to what she was saying; perhaps it would have happened anyway; but it was bad for me. She told this producer, "You're taking that name down; you're not giving Helen too much responsibility, a responsibility far too big for her, at this time of her development. It will put her under some kind of strain—the very knowledge that she's a star, and her name is up in those lights in front of the theater, isn't good for her and for her performance. She won't relax."

As I said, it may have been the power of suggestion, but I got very strained in that play, and that's when I did some studying.

N.   What was the play?

🌷   HAYES: It was called *Bab* by Mary Roberts Rinehart. And here, if you want to know the awful truth, was how I got starred in the first place. You see, the title of the play couldn't fill the tremendous sign in front of the theater. And the name "Mary Roberts Rinehart" was too long, but you couldn't say "by Rinehart" or "by Mary Rinehart"; you couldn't shorten it because it was her trade name. Well, since the pro-

ducer couldn't put his name up, mine was the only short-
enough name they could use.

I suppose, in a way, I wasn't altogether starred because it read
"BAB with Helen Hayes." But the sign was big, and the letters
were bright, and my mother felt it placed too much of a load on
my very young shoulders. She was right, too, because (from
the first night we opened in New York) I got strained, shrill, lost
control of my voice, and tightened up inside. So two great
friends who'd played in Washington (my mother was great for
making the right friends), Ruth Chatterton and Ina Claire, took
counsel and sent me to Ina's teacher—Frances Robinson Duff. So
at twenty-one, as a star on Broadway, I started taking drama
lessons and voice and body movement and I never stopped until
fifteen years ago when I got lazy.

(Perhaps I always had the feeling that perhaps each year
would be my last, and that I should take lessons of some kind, to
improve in some way. It got to be a nervous habit.)

N.   What about the preparation involved for some of
your great roles? How did you approach *Victoria Regina*, for
example?

❧   HAYES: The first thing that comes to mind is the
way I vigorously avoided reading any biographies of Victoria.
I've held to this with all my biographical plays, and I've done
quite a few. The reason for this is the fact that I don't want my
approach to a role to get cluttered with too many facts and too
much knowledge that isn't shared with the audience. I try to
approach the role purely as the author of the play conceived
it—just as I would play a fictional character conceived by a
playwright. (What I am playing, after all, is *his* Victoria or
Mary Stewart or Harriet Beecher Stowe, not one found in
reference books or histories.) So with Victoria, as far as her
characterization was concerned, I took my cue entirely from
Lawrence Houseman. I did do one thing, however, that might be
called research. I went to England to look at her dresses at the
Victoria and Albert Museum because I had an urge to do so.
Then I had an appointment made with the Marchioness of
Milfordhaven who was then tucked away in Kensington Palace.

(She told me that was where they put their indigent or aging royalty; she explained to me how she and her sisters and all her family had invested their money in Russia because her cousin was the Czarina, and you can imagine where *that* money went.) Anyway, the Marchioness was the daughter of Princess Alice, the daughter of Queen Victoria, and the Princess Alice had died when this Marchioness of Milfordhaven was a little girl and had been raised more or less under the care of her grandmother. So I reasoned that she and Victoria must have been close.

Now, the reason I wanted to meet her and talk to her about her grandmother was this: one thing troubled me about playing Victoria, my American accent. I was afraid to assume a British accent for an American audience because they don't want to take this from an American actress—they won't accept it. (I'm very good at accents, and always have been; I have good ears, you know, and mimic, but however well it was done I sensed they would say, "Oh, come now, Miss Hayes, don't try to be British on us." So what was I to do?)

Somewhere I'd heard that Queen Victoria had a German accent. She was a German princess, after all, and hadn't been in England until she was brought to Kensington Palace, so the chances that Victoria had a German accent seemed quite strong. That was why I wanted to see the Marchioness. In the course of our visit, when she sat with her hands fluttering like little birds with her tea, I asked her if her grandmother, her majesty Queen Victoria, had any discernible German accent, and she said, "Ach, no, she hadt no more accent than you or me." So I played Victoria with a German accent.

I have another favorite role—Barrie's *What Every Woman Knows*. I loved that play—I'm a great admirer of Barrie, anyway, and I'm afraid I will just go on crying aloud in the wilderness that it is unsophisticated and stupid to call him an overly sentimental, marshmallow writer. This seems to be the general opinion of Barrie. Now, I realize that there are too many ribbons and bows on his prose, but he wrote during the Edwardian period, a period of rather curlicued writing and cute little phrases. Perhaps the writing was a bit saccharine at times, but the ideas Barrie had, and the things he had to say, are so incredibly deep and profound—far more meaningful, and often more startling, than the work of some of these sophomoric writers who are shocking New York today. *What Every Woman Knows* is full of insights; in fact, every play of Barrie's startles me with the painful clarity with which he saw us all.

Even *Peter Pan* is far removed from whimsy. A psychologist today would be very interested in a child who is afraid to grow up because such a child would be an extreme case of normalcy. Every human born on this earth is born with a tragedy, and it isn't original sin. He's born with the tragedy that he has to grow up. That he has to leave the nest, the security, and go out to do battle. He has to lose everything that is lovely and fight for a new loveliness of his own making, and it's a tragedy. A lot of people don't have the courage to do it. I know a dozen Peter Pans who are twenty-five or thirty-five or forty-five years old, don't you? (I'm not trying to be startling; I think all this is really there, if you look for it.)

I loved *What Every Woman Knows* because I felt that it has great wisdom, immense charm. I took liberties with the Barrie phraseology and took out some of the sweet little phrases— they're the only things wrong with Barrie. (You know, theater people learn Shakespeare the way other people learn their prayers. I've often thought of how pleasant it would be if we could slip in a word here and there that is known to our generation instead of using those that are obsolete or vague. "It confounds thy fame as whirlwinds shake their buds . . ." [Kate's speech to women] simply means "It destroys your charm." "Confounds thy fame" is obscure, unnecessarily puzzling, and Shakespeare is full of such things.) At any rate I took liberties with Barrie, removed the sweety-sweet little words, and had one of my greatest successes.

I loved *Harriet*, the story of Harriet Beecher Stowe. Just the other day I read that last speech again; it's so apropos of Selma and all that's going on right now. In the play she says, "Our hope is that there will always be men who will stand as our President has done and accept scorn and vilification for the truth." (I'm paraphrasing.) It should be our hope that we, as a people, have learned that in a nation in which some people are happy and others are miserable, that nation cannot endure. And when she said, "Our danger is that when the war is over—when the conflict is done and the war-weariness sets in—we may be tempted to forget and to slide back into the old ways. Then, and only then, will our sons have died in vain and the war will have to be fought over and over again." This was Harriet Beecher Stowe speaking, way back then.

I played *Harriet* twenty years ago—the authors had written these lines in then, and here we are now, in full circle. Fighting it over again. A hundred years have passed since Lincoln freed the slaves, and we haven't made much progress.

N.   Did you enjoy your movie roles?

&   HAYES: Yes. Of course, I have a particular senti- mental attachment to the role my husband created for me, the role for which I got the Oscar, *The Sin of Madelon Claudet*. He wrote it to order; it was custom-made, and he used everything in it that he loved about me, allowing it to be shared with the world—a gesture here and a mood there. I don't know how he managed to fit everything he admired into that one role, but he did.

A Farewell to Arms was a great thrill. I enjoyed playing with Gary Cooper. He was a wonderful actor, a very sensitive man. And I loved *Arrowsmith*—you know, I was very lucky out in Hollywood. I didn't stay long, but in that short time I had some peachy roles. Irving Thalberg was so kind . . . I asked him to let me do *What Every Woman Knows* and he did. But I suppose, objectively speaking, *A Farewell to Arms* was my favorite.

I rather went downhill out there after the first five startlingly marvelous pictures I made. I played the Anastasia role under protest—I didn't want to do that at all. It was the last thing I did on the screen, and I've not been tempted to go back to do another, but I regret the Anastasia. I'd refused it, and they'd accepted my refusal, but they came back after Charlie died and said, "Come on, why don't you do it now?" And all my friends . . . you know, after you've led an active life, and had a blow, they all get nervous and want you to plunge into something, do something . . . "Don't just stand there, do something!" . . . and they helped push me into it. I think I really knew, in my heart of hearts, that what I really needed to do was to sit for a while and mend, but I went off and "did something" to satisfy them and get out of their way. (It's hard on them to have you around.) So I went out and did the Anastasia, but I didn't like me in it, yet it can't spoil the memory of the really wonderful pictures I did.

N.   To return to the theater—what obligation do you, as an actress, feel toward any given entity—say, the playwright, or the audience, or—

❦   HAYES: I'm glad you mentioned "playwright" because when you started the question I knew exactly how I was going to answer it. My first duty is to the playwright, and despite the fact that I took some of the sugar coating off Barrie's language I did it out of respect for him because I knew that he wouldn't write that way today for today's audiences. But this was the only time I was ever disrespectful to an author, or have taken liberties. I detest such liberties (perhaps I should keep my Barrie tamperings a secret—I don't want to encourage any actor to do this), because it's my belief that none of us know more about the play and about the part than the man who wrote it. If we could write better than the author then we should stop acting and take up writing.

Then, too, it takes some of the fun (and certainly much of the challenge) out of the actor's job if he adjusts lines to suit him, instead of adjusting himself to the lines. This is a part of the great challenge of acting—"That line is hard for me; I don't know how to say it. I find it almost impossible. It is completely opposed to my expression, yet I must say it because that is the way the author imagined that character thinking and speaking" —and it is really part of the joy of acting, the losing of oneself.

This is why I'm a little startled and confused about going inside, within yourself, this method association . . . calling upon oneself to react. To me it has nothing to do with your performance. What you're doing on that stage is projecting yourself into someone else entirely, into the mind of the author, into the being of the character. You are trying to settle down to be comfortable in that character and speak the author's words. You are merely an instrument for what he is saying.

Running parallel—not first, not last—is my duty to the audience. They are to hear the words of the author; I cannot indulge in any private performances for my own amazement. I do not indulge myself on the stage. Sometimes it seems to be more convincing and artistically pure if you don't try to project too much, don't try too hard to convey to the last row; it might be more in keeping to just mumble (if mumbling is indicated in the character's emotion) but you mustn't do that. You must share everything with the audience.

Then there's the terrible task of keeping yourself well. This is your responsibility to the company, to the cast. Their livelihood depends on your well-being. And now, of course, theater is more than ever dominated by your investors. It's become a big-money affair, and you have to think, "Oh, I'm this little bit of quivering flesh, but I'm worth hundreds of thousands of dollars in a production, so if I don't keep myself well I'm robbing people of money."

So you live your life—as I did in my more active days, in my heyday—you live your life like a prizefighter in training. I was always dieting, exercising, denying myself anything that was fun.

N. What major changes did you find in theater during your career?

❦ HAYES: Not any major changes . . . not permanent changes, at any rate. You know, we go by cycles. One little cycle finishes and you enter another, then another, but one thing remains steady and constant: the difference between good and bad acting. Whatever the style, whatever the mode of the time, it all comes down to good acting and bad acting.

Types of plays come and go in cycles, too, but there are plays that have a certain sturdiness and durability and those plays live. Many of the flashy popular successes please their season and die.

The same thing goes for actors—the flash successes, the enduring performers. I'm sixty-four, now, and since I was twenty-one I have watched a legion of Duses and Bernhardts come and go. Almost yearly there's been a new genius, a new Barrymore or Duse, and they come and go, come and go, and out of them only a tiny handful endure. It's comforting, in a way, because you know that the sudden and unworthy success, either in acting or in writing, the flashy and spectacular things, don't always make for enduring fame.

N.   In looking at theater right now what do you find most admirable or most deplorable?

❧   HAYES: I don't know. I thought, for a while, that we were getting a little too morose. I don't mean that I want all plays to be funny and purely entertaining, but it seemed that everybody thought it quite sophisticated to ape that Hammerstein lyric—"They say the human race is falling on its face and it hasn't very far to go" . . . well, I'm a cockeyed optimist who refuses to believe that the inherent dignity of man is withering or has withered. I'm proud to be a member of the race.

I didn't like it when institutions like Motherhood were so blatantly condemned. I don't think we should stand back in awe of motherhood, but they overdid it a bit and slapped mother down a little too often. It was terrifying. If you were a mother you were a monster. Then the wives became instruments of destruction—deadly creatures, and this got tiresome. I'm awfully sick of the "heart of gold" prostitute right now. In fact, it has seemed that anyone living quietly and gracefully and decently had no real good within him . . . that unspeakable evil lurked in the girl or boy next door.

I think that sophistication got lost in the theater. It takes a lot of sophistication to be corny, and when that word "corny" was invented we got into a lot of trouble. Everyone was so afraid to be corny that they got sophomoric about it, particularly our writers, and I deplored that trend. But when a play like *A Man For All Seasons*, about a man like Saint Thomas More can open and capture the American public I feel good again. I know we're all right when playwrights will dare to write plays of affirmation about man.

The theater of the absurd is a phase, and it will pass, and the existentialism of the theater is a phase, and it will pass, too. They simply don't contain truth, so they can't live.

N. How do you feel about the influence of the critics upon American theater?

HAYES: It's easy to glibly blame them for the diminishing of theater, and in one respect they must be held accountable. I've been watching this for a long time—and it's been distressing me frightfully—and this is the fact that the New York theater-going public has a vastly different taste than I find in the rest of America. (Here, of course, the public must be guided by the critics because it's too expensive to gamble. You have to be sure something is recommended before you go to spend all that money.) But so many plays that are successful in New York are sent out on tour and they simply haven't been received.

They're not the things the rest of America identifies with at all. The only things that New York seems to have in common with the rest of America are the musicals; consequently, musicals are more and more dominant in the American theater.

Yet there are always a few non-musicals that are so good they're loved in New York and Chicago and Timbuctoo. They break through the barriers. But it's depressing to find New York's taste so different from the rest of the country's preferences.

N. If you were to offer advice to the aspiring actor or actress . . .

HAYES: I hope I don't discourage any young person who wants to go into theater. I remember that in my day it was sort of fashionable to say, "Oh, keep away, the theater is on its way out." Certainly that is more true now than it was in my early years when I got that advice from older actors or actresses.

Anyone who is determined to act will do so, in drama groups, in high school, in college, and even if they don't pursue acting as a career, and give it up, they will be enriched as people.

For example, they will at least learn to speak better. I always feel that if a young woman had a bit of drama training she might have less trouble with her marriage; I'm sure a lot of marriages are shaky because the poor man has to listen to some horrible nasal twang over his breakfast coffee and he's put off for the rest of the day. If she'd just learn to speak a little better he might not be so irritated by her.

Let them go into the theater · if they want. I'm sure that many thousands don't get beyond the drama department of the college, but it' isn't wasted time. Then, if they do get beyond the department, and go into theater, the chaff is winnowed from the wheat very quickly. Only a true actor with a deep-seated compulsion is going to stick out the struggle that goes with being in the theater. It's brutal, it's worse than a Marine boot camp, and they drop out by the thousands. But they have also been enriched by the experience they've had.

I don't really believe that many of the dropouts go home embittered for life, and are miserable and lost with the boy from high school they marry and the children they have. I don't think those little tragedies happen very often, but perhaps I'm a fatalist. From the practical standpoint the winnowing is a good thing—the theater doesn't offer much continuity of opportunity to the youngster for the development of talent and the learning of craft.

However early, however intensely, that youngster is dedicated to the theater, I think he should finish high school and probably college. A major in drama is very good, but to leave school to go into the theater is to limit one's opportunities. Instead of getting a head start it leads to a delaying action.

In my day I didn't have a choice; I suppose that if I had I would have said, "Oh, I want to get on with my career"— though maybe not. (I was happy in school, and perhaps I would have preferred staying there, gleaning everything I could. I've been studying ever since, trying to make up for the things I didn't get during those normal study years.)

There's an awful lot of crying out for help by young people, and I don't blame them for it because it's such a desperate problem to get recognized nowadays. But they must realize that one can only be given a start—the merest push—and that the rest of it is up to them and perhaps the state of theater as it limits them.

N. A final question, and a personal one. Is the almost legendary story of your meeting with Charles MacArthur true?

HAYES: I think it happened the way you read it. I was taken up to this salon that Neysa McMein held every afternoon at her apartment. She was a great favorite in New York; she was a commercial artist who used to do covers for *Colliers*, and she owned a studio in which there were two pianos. About five o'clock every afternoon you'd find Irving Berlin and George Gershwin pecking away at those pianos and the place full of all kinds of great and exciting people—it really was a salon. Well, one afternoon I met Marc Connelly on Fifth Avenue and he scooped me up (I was about to do a play he and George Kaufman wrote called *To the Ladies*) and took me to Neysa's for my first visit—and I was shaking with terror because here were all these sharp wits—Dorothy Parker, Alex Woollcott, Bob Benchley, Frank Adams—and I was scared to death to be in there with them. I didn't know how I'd be slapped down, so I ran off into a corner and sat there in terror and misery, cursing Marc for bringing me and leaving me flat.

Then came this beautiful young man with the little bag of Planter's Peanuts and he offered it to me and said, "I wish they were emeralds." He said it rather lazily, but I was so grateful to anyone who would speak to me that I was overwhelmed.

But it wasn't just gratitude. I sensed his sensitivity and his compassion (he had, after all, spotted this character huddled in a corner, lost and out of it and come to her rescue). But from then on I was a goner. I didn't come back into my orbit for ages—or what seemed ages to me—because I just couldn't think of anyone else or see anyone else but that young man. He was very beautiful, inside and out.

"You see, I don't play 'background music.' I play 'foreground music' . . ."

CALVIN JACKSON

I had read a rave notice in *Time*, caught a few of his Canadian telecasts, yet was totally unprepared for the power, feeling and taste pianist Calvin Jackson revealed the first night I heard him at the Beverly Hilton. From his magnificent interpretations of standards like "My Funny Valentine" to a Chopin étude, from the best of Gershwin to the most thundering Rachmaninoff—this cat, to put it in the shortest possible way, *has it*.

JACKSON: I was born at the Lying-In Hospital at Race and Cherry streets in Philadelphia on May 26, 1919. I attended Philadelphia public schools through high school.

My interest in music became apparent when I was three years old, and by the time I was three and one-half I could pick out a few tunes on the piano. We had an old Storey & Clark player piano which fascinated me; I could see the keys going up and down with no one touching them, and I learned what was up and what was down, and about the different intervals. (I didn't know about them as such, then, of course.)

One night at a church recital in Wayne, Pennsylvania, I heard a cousin, Corinne Hill, play a song titled "Melody of Love." It was the first time I'd heard the song and after the recital I was brought home and put to bed, but about four o'clock in the morning I got up, went down to the piano, and started playing the tune—using both hands. Heads started peering around the door, and the family decided that my fourth birthday present would be my first piano and theory lesson. At that point we were living in Haverford, Pennsylvania, and I'll never forget my grandmother taking me into Philadelphia, to 53rd and Thompson Street, to Carl Diton (who had studied with Karl von Sternberg, and who taught in the very strict European style; he felt that if you started the child with Theory at the same time he began playing he'd be helped, later on, with Composition). It must have been a funny sight to see my grandmother, a very tiny woman, under five feet tall, and me with my satchel dragging on the ground, going for my lessons. As a matter of fact I met Billy Kyle on my very first day; he now plays with Louis Armstrong, at one time played with the John Kirby Sextet. He was ten or twelve at the time, and he was playing very well. We used to visit one another, back and forth between Haverford and Philadelphia. I took the music course in school, all through Junior and Senior High, and then took an entrance examination for a fellowship at the Juilliard Graduate School of Music in New York and passed it. This was in 1937. I took extra credits at New York University to round out my education in a formal sense, but actually, I've never stopped studying.

You never stop studying music. As a matter of fact, it's unfortunate that life is so short that you can only glean one iota of what you would like to learn from an intelligence standpoint about any subject, let alone music, which gives rise to the hope that there's some sort of plane of existence where you can continue.

While I was in school I wrote for different bands like Jimmy Lunceford, Al and Lee Reiser—two piano team and orchestra, Benny Carter, Colman Hawkins and Andre Kostelanetz. (Earlier on, in high school, I belonged to a band, a regular jazz band, where I learned quite a bit about orchestrating for a jazz orchestra. Dizzy Gillespie was in this particular band, along with Charlie Shavers, who later joined the same John Kirby band that Billy Kyle had been with.) After I finished school I became very friendly with Teddy Wilson. I played at the Cafe Society Downtown a few times, and he told me that Paul Draper, the ballet tap dancer, was looking for an accompanist. I applied for the job and got it and soon found myself in Rio de Janeiro. We came back and I did a concert tour with Larry Adler; and for about a year and a half I was with Paul and Larry. Then I formed a two-piano team, came to California and opened in Los Angeles at the Swanee Inn. After that we opened the Swing Club, owned by Billie Byrd. This was in the latter part of 1942. Benny Carter's band was the big feature and we played intermissions.

We had a few dates on "Hollywood Showcase," a radio show MC'd by Ken Niles and Mary Astor, then we went to Riverside, California, to the Somerset House. (While I was there a young fellow, all of eighteen, who'd just gotten out of the Air Force—a tall, lanky, Lincolnesque sort of guy—approached me and told me that he played piano and wondered whether studying composition would help his playing. I say, "Of course," and encouraged formal study. I met him years later, when I was living in Canada. A slightly older Lincolnesque character I didn't recognize came up to me and said, "Do you remember a young fellow walking up to you in California and asking you about whether composition helped playing the piano?" It was Dave Brubeck.)

Our piano team went back to Los Angeles where we broke up. I had gotten an offer to write arrangements for the Harry James band. We were at the Lux Theatre doing Chesterfield radio shows and I stayed with the band for about nine months. Then back to New York, playing at the Astor Hotel, then to Chicago to the College Inn. Then back to California, where I had a wonderful time at MGM writing for a picture titled *Bathing Beauty* and another, *Two Girls and a Sailor*. So I left the band and joined the staff at MGM as arranger and composer. I did fourteen musicals there—*Anchors Aweigh, Her Highness and the Bellboy, No Leave, No Love, Holiday in Mexico, Two Girls From Boston, On an Island with You, Kissing Bandit*, etc. I left California and MGM in September, 1947, and returned to New

York. I stayed for two years. I appeared at the Roxy Theater, did the "Rhapsody in Blue" when the Danny Kaye show was there—we used the orchestra and the choral group, and it was very interesting. They had one of the biggest crowds they'd had in the history of the theater during those three weeks. That was because of Danny Kaye, of course. They also had an excellent picture showing, but I forget what it was. I played Cafe Society in 1948, also Baker's Lounge in Detroit, a lot of short engagements thrown in.

In 1950 I went to Canada and took up residence for six years. I appeared with the Toronto Symphony Orchestra in 1955. I had a television show for two and a half years, did a great deal of radio, and played at the Park Plaza Hotel for four and a half years. I took a quartet on the road, played in New York, Philadelphia, Cleveland, Chicago and Detroit and appeared on Steve Allen's "Tonight" show and also "Music '55" that Kenton had for a summer.

I came out here at the end of 1956. Since then I've been playing clubs, and recently finished part of the adaptation score for *The Unsinkable Molly Brown*. I did one television series that was short-lived, "The Asphalt Jungle" at MGM. I'm at the Beverly Hilton now, of course, and hope to be for some time, but I've played different clubs like the Villa Frascati and the Frascati Grill and the Frascati Rotisserie (I've just about done in the Frascati's, though they have three more restaurants I haven't hit). I appeared with the Hollywood Symphony when Ernst Gebert was at the helm—he died a short time ago. We did the Gershwin Piano Concerto. After his death I conducted the memorial concert—Beethoven's "Egmont Overture," the "Siegfried Idyll" by Wagner, the Rachmaninoff "Vocalise," and Brahms' Fourth Symphony. On Sept. 11, 1965, we're going to perform a benefit (symphonic) concert here at the Hilton, in the International Ballroom, for the Kennedy Memorial Library. (I met Jack Kennedy in 1941 in Rio de Janeiro, Brazil, at the Copacabana Hotel. We discussed a number of sociological issues and I liked him, so in 1963, on his birthday, May 29, I decided that he *had* done something to rectify some of our problems in the U.S. and I started to compose a symphonic composition for piano and orchestra to be dedicated to him. He was assassinated six months later, and never will hear it, but the hotel heard about this piano concerto and decided that we should present it as a benefit. We hope it comes off very well.)

N.　　　　This is undoubtedly a naïve question, but how is the musical scoring for motion pictures done?

JACKSON: In the first place the picture is generally shot before any scoring is done. If it's a musical there are pre-recorded numbers. They have to be shot to fit, so you do your recording beforehand, then get on the set with a playback machine and the director shoots the action to fit the sound. All other parts are scored after seeing the finished product and the music is fitted to the action. It can get very intricate at times, working down to split seconds. You find, for instance, that you have to stop at 22⅓ seconds—not ⅙ or ⅔, but 22⅓. The scoring has to fit the action, that's all there is to it.

Motion picture music has come a long way. I think Dimitri Tiomkin was the first composer to really score a movie. *Lost Horizon* was the big breakthrough. There hadn't been a great deal of scoring used throughout a picture earlier than that. Even the musicals had just the production numbers scored.

N.　　　　Which of the movies you've scored did you find most satisfying?

JACKSON: I enjoyed *Anchors Aweigh*. We did a full ninety-minute score plus all the pre-recorded material with Sinatra, Gene Kelly, Kathryn Grayson and Jose Iturbi. *The Unsinkable Molly Brown* was also challenging, and I think we did a good job.

The television series, "The Asphalt Jungle," which I scored on my own, was a great experience. And there were a few other movies that stand up . . . *The Kissing Bandit*, for example. Vincente Gomez and I wrote a flamenco number for that, a whip dance for Sono Osato. *Music for Millions* was a pleasant departure because there was so much symphonic music in it.

And I did about twenty-five minutes of the score for *Meet Me in St. Louis*. It was a charming movie, beautifully thought out. For a musical it had a lot going for it in the way of a script. (A lot of times the scripts are very bare. If you had seen a goshawful trifle like *Thrill of a Romance* without any music put to it you'd wonder how in the world that picture could have made eight million dollars when it was first released. But Joe Pasternak seemed to have a touch that made money, whether the story was good or terrible. It was during the war years and I don't suppose those things would pass today. Movies, probably because of the competition from television, have gotten better from almost every standpoint. Maybe television would get a lot better if it had competition, like subscription television. As it is, the TV set has replaced going to see a B movie.)

N.   How do you enjoy club appearances—for example, your six-night-per-week stand here at the Beverly Hilton?

❧   JACKSON: I enjoy playing, no matter how many people are out there, as long as they're quiet. Sometimes we start playing the first number and the din is horrendous—the crowd isn't composed of aficionados but of those who come in to play their own neuroses, people who are pent up most of the week in offices and have to come out to be noticed. But if the first number doesn't calm them down, a remark like "Thank you very much, ladies and gentlemen; good evening and welcome to the European theater of World War II" will help, and if it's a particular table that's causing the disturbance you say, "Thank you very much, ladies and gentlemen and members of the debating society," and *that* helps. Sometimes there is absolute silence, and you wait for these times as far as night club performance is concerned because then you can hear yourself think, and you can give the same sort of performance you would give on a concert stage.

Now, I realize that proprietors have to sell drinks, and that there are people who come in not to listen to entertainment but to talk and have a jolly good time with their friends, but I don't think they should perform at the expense of someone sitting next to them who wants to listen. You see, I don't play "background music." I play "foreground music" and I mix up the more popular stuff with classics such as Chopin's G Minor

Prelude or Debussy's "Maid with the Flaxen Hair." Or I'll give a classical treatise on, say, "My Funny Valentine," which I start out as a fugue.

But it's interesting to see the number of aficionados that you do get during the course of an evening. They hit the door like D Day, and they sit and they listen and they make intelligent requests. They're your reward.

That's about all I can say on night clubs. It is exposure, it is exercise, and it is good for a person. But to keep your stomach and psyche in shape you have to take three orange juices against one drink, because you wouldn't be able to play at all if you had a drink with everyone who wants to buy you one.

N. I'd like to go to an even more commercial area—the work you do writing (or scoring) television commercials.

❦ JACKSON: It's interesting work, and we've done things for Foremost Milk, Bank of America, Purex Soap Company, Skippy Peanut Butter, Dodge, Flying A Gasoline, Allstate Insurance, Folgers Coffee— and many more. The commercials only play a minute, but you'd be surprised at the exhausting amount of work that goes into them. You begin with the agency man's ideas, and your ideas (from the musical standpoint) and the ideas that come from whoever's doing the photography or cartooning. You've got to be careful not to tread on the toes of any other product or person, you've got to have individuality and quality without going over the heads of your audience, and—frankly, I don't see how the advertising agency man can avoid ulcers. He's everybody's in-between man—he's between the talent and his peer at the agency, between agency and sponsor, between talent and sponsor. It's tough enough just being on the musical side of it, and I've seen some very good men fold up under just that amount of pressure.

But it's a lucrative business. As a matter of fact it pays far better than writing scores for motion pictures or writing arrangements for recordings. But the work you do is intense and has to be right. Not every musician can do it because it takes a certain sixth sense to be able to supply something that is meaningful and is, at the same time, an undercurrent. The ulcers come subliminally. So when a certain Folger's Coffee commercial comes on and I want to say, "Listen, they're playing our song!" it's not just because of the money coming in but also because I know how much hard work went into it.

N. To return to your personal appearances, club and otherwise, do you, as a pianist, feel any obligation to the pieces you play?

❧ JACKSON: Well, I have an obligation to the composer to play his melody first, in an A-B-A form, sonata form. Then I do it as *I* would do it, then I reiterate his melody once again. In other words, "This is what I'm playing; this is how I like to play it, how I envision it; and *that* is what I played."

N. Can you pick out any single events or sustained experiences that stand out—because of either significance or pleasure—from your career?

❧ JACKSON: I would say that both appearances with the Hollywood Symphony, the one appearance with the Toronto Symphony, the performance back in 1948 when I conducted the Carnegie Pops Orchestra and we did a treatise on Fats Waller's "London Suite" (I used a piano team in one of the sections of the suite, Ferrante and Teitcher). I enjoyed my work at MGM consistently.

Actually, I enjoy all music, whether I'm hearing it, playing it, composing it or studying it. It's safe to say that my entire life has been spent in and around music. (I did a bit of sports when I was in junior high and at the university, but it didn't amount to much. They used to say "Hey, Calvin, they went that-away.")

The big highlight, however, will probably come when I premiere my own piano concerto.

N. *Anchors Aweigh* got an Academy Award for musical direction, didn't it?

❧ JACKSON: I didn't get any part of it, because in those days they didn't give Oscars for adaptation. The Society has rectified this, now, and if the picture were released today I'd share in the Award. I lost out because of the terminology. In fact I was nominated for adaptation of *The Unsinkable Molly Brown* this year.

N.　　　　What did you do, precisely, during your six years in Canada?

JACKSON: Primarily I worked for the CBC when there was no commercial television whatever in Canada. They presented my show on a sustaining basis. This was very interesting because it must have cost them a bundle—we had a 21-piece orchestra and I was with them for two and a half years.

I remember when Stewart Griffith, the program director (now program director for commercial television in Canada) came to me and said, "How would you like to do a jazz program?" I said, "What type of program?" and he said, "Of your own choosing." I asked him how much of an orchestra I could have and he told me I could have as much as I wanted. So I said, "Now, before I wake up, what kind of say-so would I have regarding the production?" and he said, "Everything. You work with the producer," and I said, "What kind of supervision will the company have?" He said, "None, until the end of the season; they won't touch you." I said, "Thanks a lot and goodbye," and that was it—for two and a half years the program was a success. When we first went on we had a 68 per cent viewing average (and Canadians could pick up NBC and CBS from Buffalo; but then, we found out that a lot of people in Buffalo were listening to CBC. For that matter, people in Seattle get CBC from Vancouver, and in Detroit they pick it up from Windsor. There *is* an audience for culture). I found out that I could talk to an audience in a thoroughly adult and knowledgeable way, and that there was an audience to respond. I guess that's about it.

N.　　　　What is your opinion of the music we hear today— new music in either pop or concert format?

JACKSON: I feel that through our mode of living we've lost a lot of romanticism and we've lost it in our works of art, too. There seems to be a striving to be different just for the sake of being different—of having lost a love for tapestry. It's all plywood and tinsel and sounding brass.

Now, I like effects as a splash, as emphasis, as dramatization, but I don't like effects just to be effects. There must be a reason, some sort of sanity whereby there is cohesion.

For instance, in my piano concerto I dared to write the second movement in the romantic tradition, and in the third movement I went a little modern as far as the ⅝ rhythms are concerned, some of the chord combinations and the linear aspect. But I had a reason, and the reason will be explained in the program.

I've always felt—in listening to Prokofiev and Stravinsky and even Schönberg and Hindemith—that though they are great composers in a modern and often startling way, they never lack cohesion. Bartok is a great example of innovation with purpose. Leonard Bernstein's "Jeremiah Symphony," for instance, has a complete seven-eight movement—a sort of dance that is absolutely remarkable. Prokofiev has used different rhythms, Shostakovich is startlingly experimental modern at some times and Scarlatti-ish at others. So is Gian-Carlo Menotti. Khachaturian—I love the Moorish sort of music he writes, the Armenian feeling in his music. It enters into a specific area and state of feeling.

William Walton, Ralph Vaughan Williams, Benjamin Britten, all have too much to offer; they explore, musically, to relate specifics.

I won't go into the caterwauling stuff being palmed off as popular music. After all, if civilization has survived the bubonic plague and a couple of world wars it can get through the Beatles.

N.   In the course of getting to you I've met with your personal manager, Albert Saparoff. What role does he play in your career?

❧   JACKSON: Well, he's a most unusual man—he's actually my partner, manager, overseer, and an all-time Dutch uncle. He's the concert master of the Hollywood Symphony, was in the violin section of the 1943 Harry James band when I first met him, and has played with the motion picture orchestra at MGM. He's had as wide and varied a course of experience as

I've had. As a child he was a prodigy, and went around giving concerts at motion picture houses and vaudeville theaters.

He became my manager one day when he decided that I wasn't getting the right sort of promotion; this was five years ago, and when he gets an idea he stays with it. He's invaluable to me—whenever I do a TV score or a TV or radio commercial or conduct or play he's always at my shoulder, straightening things out. He sees to it that arrangements are copied, that the orchestra is called, that there is the proper union break in between the hours we are recording, that the sound engineer is on his toes and that I'm on my toes. He lines up concerts at schools, and when anyone calls me I tell them they have to talk to him first. He's also a very stubborn man. When he gets an idea he follows through, and if it succeeds, great, and if it fails he goes down with it. This sort of determination is wonderful in any man, but it's absolutely great in a personal manager.

And to top it off he's given up most aspects of his own promising and successful career to put me over.

N.   Getting even more personal: Has the fact that you are a Negro inhibited your career?

❦   JACKSON: At times it has. And in some ways, oddly enough, the disadvantage of being a Negro has been (accidentally) an advantage. For example, when my teacher in Philadelphia tried to get me into a conservatory there, they had a color bar, and that's why I went to New York to take the examination at Julliard. It's a good thing I went to Julliard because I was exposed to a much larger city, the heart of the entertainment world, actually, and it removed me from what had been the limited environs of my life up until that time.

Later on I found that the racial aspects were much the same as they'd be in any other business or profession. If I'd aimed at a Wall Street or an oil company career I'd have run into the same obstacles. The way might not have been paved for me, as a Negro, or for the members of the many other minorities who make up the majority.

I decided long ago not to let the racial thing be the cause of my existence or non-existence. I've gone along and done the things I can do to the best of my ability, and I've always sought to move in the circles I wanted to move in.

I must say that many Negroes—Marion Anderson, Roland Hayes, Paul Robeson, Leontyne Price—have been able to enter the inner sanctum in varying degrees. Yet even a few years ago there wasn't a chance for a Negro musician to get into a symphony orchestra, so what was the sense of studying French horn or violin or viola or cello? You studied the instruments that could get you into a jazz orchestra. (There are entertainers like Sammy Davis, Jr. or the late King Cole who are strictly entertainers; what I'm speaking about is the strictly classical field.)

In the last twenty years a lot of inroads have been made and they're continuing to be made. The last four years have really brought progress, and the next ten may see the problem dispelled to a point where a man's talent and conscientiousness and his intrinsic worth as a human being will be the things which move him ahead—without reference to race or religion. The moment we face that great moment of truth we'll be the society we inherently would like to be.

I feel that my son will have it much easier than I had it, and I had it a lot easier than my father had it, and so on back (even though there was that long waiting period). But as we, as an ethnic group, become more educated to the different skills of the world and of the country, more of these doors will open. I have a positive feeling about the future, and I think this is the feeling that not only insures survival but growth as well.

N.   A final question: If you were to look back at Calvin Jackson from, say, a century away, how would you like to have him appraised in terms of accomplishment?

❧   JACKSON: I want to leave some sort of musical legacy from a compositional standpoint. I feel that conducting, playing, arranging, etc., are of the moment and for the moment and fade very quickly. We know there was a Bach, but there may have been many contemporary musicians of his time who were better musicians but who just played, and we don't know anything whatever about them. The composers, the writers of the world, leave legacies. An architect like Frank Lloyd Wright leaves designs, a way of living, a way of being. An actor can be remembered for fine performances, but not recalled as securely as a playwright. Shakespeare will outlast Olivier and Rachmaninoff will outlast Rubenstein. And I'm fairly sure that well within our lifetime a Beatle will be something you step on, quick. (I hate to dwell on them, but they're not at all like the Sinatra thing, where girls swooned all over the place. Those girls have grown up and they don't swoon anymore but they still like Sinatra because Sinatra has talent and taste. Once a kid grows up the Beatles will be remembered as something that happened at the same time she had braces on her teeth.)

It's very interesting—life itself. The short sojourn we have here, the things we surround ourselves with in a materialistic sense. What is it all about and where do we go from here? What is being?

There's a favorite expression I have when I've met someone who is of a fine nature, whom I admire and have respect for. I say, "Thank you for being," and this about sums up my whole attitude toward living.

"*I can never tell when a flight of fancy is coming on.*"

❦

DANNY KAYE

He sings, he dances, he acts—and he is one of the truly great comedians of our time. Those who crowd to see him, in London or in New York or in a television studio, do not comprise an audience; they are captives. The magic of Danny Kaye originates with the consistently brightest, freshest material to be had. But it is brought to life by the engaging, mercurial charm of the most versatile man in show business.

❦ KAYE: I was born in Brooklyn and educated for the most part right there. I quit school, however, just a half year before I was supposed to graduate, and spent most of my university time abroad.

I once said—when I was being given a doctorate at an American college in New Haven, and a lot of talk was going on about education—that I didn't believe in education. This was kind of facetious on my part, but in an odd way I think there is some measure of truth in that statement, even though it startled that group.

In a funny way there's some measure of truth in what I said. If I had wanted to become a doctor (which, indeed, I did) or a mathematician, or a lawyer, it wouldn't have occurred to me not to go to school and be educated. But what education you can give a performer is an open question, and when I should have been in college I was working in China at my profession. I learned far more in the practical experience of playing in a foreign country, and even in my early professional work here, than I could ever have learned by going to school. I knew at a very early age that I wasn't going to make my living as a mathematician. I certainly wasn't going to be a lawyer. I did feel, somewhere along the line, that I might have gone into medicine, but long before I left high school I knew I had been cast for this profession. How that came about, I don't know.

N.   Were there any incidents that jogged you along in that direction?

   ❦   KAYE : I don't know how I managed to get into show business. I don't think there was any one event that catapulted me into the theatrical profession. I think, rather, that there was a series of events that telescoped themselves into making it virtually impossible for me to do anything else.

N.   Can you isolate any of those?

   ❦   KAYE : They're vague—not so much vague as unimportant. No big or dramatic or climactic moment. It isn't like I met somebody who said, "Come with me, they're trying out a bunch of fellows for a show," and I said, "No, I don't want to do it," and he said, "Oh, come along, it'll be fun," and I went and kind of half-auditioned and the fellow said, "Yeah, that's the fellow we want!"

It didn't happen that way at all. I couldn't get a job for years, and I couldn't get a job for a very strange reason : I did too many things. I was never able to say, "I am a singer" or "I am a dancer" or "I am an actor" or "I play sketches." Somebody would say, "Do you sing?" and I'd say, "Well, kinda," and they'd say, "Do you dance?" and I'd say, "Well, I'm really not a dancer but I suppose I could dance." They'd say, "Are you an actor?" and I'd say, "Not really, but if there's a part . . ."

I never had any positive statement to make about what I could do and in a peculiar way it was a drawback, in the beginning, and later became an enormous virtue.

The reason I'm in this profession, now, is that it's the greatest means for self-expression that I have. That's a rather general statement, but my whole attitude toward what I do, toward my profession as a whole, is general.

To begin with, I perform mostly by instinct rather than analytical dissection. I think I know what I'm about because I've spent many years at my profession, having a fairly good set of eyes and a rather acute ear and being receptive, generally. Things have rubbed off on me, sometimes willy-nilly, whether I realized they were rubbing off on me or not, whether I wanted them to or not. (For example, witness the fact that I now enjoy cooking Chinese food enormously. I was exposed to Chinese food thirty years ago, but it wasn't until recently that the desire to cook and eat Chinese food began to insist itself.)

This is true of what happens to me in my profession. It is best exemplified by the way this television show works out. We do a run-through on Saturday, then we do a dress rehearsal, then we do the show. It is likely that those three performances will vary enormously, depending upon the need for a particular kind of expression at the time, depending upon the need for a particular excellence for myself and for my fellow-performers.

Sometimes, too, the variations will be instinctive on the basis of a protest. Sometimes the need to make a protest in what I'm doing will color the way I am performing. Basically all this is instinctive, not something I've consciously learned.

There are times, though, when I can't work that way. Last night I worked with a quintet and we did a musical jazz thing. Now, when you're singing five-part harmony you can't suddenly decide to take off somewhere because there are these other people singing very closely related notes. This requires discipline of another kind.

I always think of my work as undisciplined discipline. I know exactly where I am all the time but should I ever try to channel it, to be exactly the same every time, my work would lose its vitality, its imaginative quality, and it would hamper me in my flights of fancy (and these sometimes occur in the middle of a performance).

I can never tell you when a flight of fancy is coming on. It might be some catalyst resulting from a reaction to my material, something someone says, or a mood. I don't know. Somebody once said to me in London, when I was having a big success over there, and we had a group of psychiatrists and physicians in the audience, "What is this magic you have with an audience?" and I said, "I don't know what the hell you're talking about."

Well, they had lots of theories, but I said, "Don't read things into something or we'll end up making this a kind of mystic cult." There's no mystery. I go out on the stage and try to entertain as well as I know how, and when I do that I am sparked by the audience or the audience is sparked by me. There is a kind of communication I can't begin to explain because it doesn't always happen. You become technically proficient enough to make it look as though it's always happening. Like I can go and play in Vegas or in a theater in New York or a theater in San Francisco and you can see the show seven nights running and feel certain it's the same show each night. This is because one becomes technically proficient enough to make it look the same Yet you would know, if you were inside me, that there were some nights when there was *real* communication, some nights that were a joy and others that were not.

N.   Does the audience—the receptiveness of the audience—make a great deal of difference?

❧   KAYE: An inestimable difference. Audiences don't come into a theater knowing how they feel. Basically an audience is going to a theater to have a good time. Now, the fact that they might not react the same way last night's audience did doesn't make them an inferior audience. They don't know how loudly the audience laughed last night. *You're* the only one who knows, and if you want to judge the quality of your performance simply by the quantity of your reaction, this is something you have to deal with yourself. I have many nights when—

You know, this can't possibly become objective because I am now trying to explain to you about my private personal reaction to what happens to me on the stage. I don't want, for one single instant, to confuse it with any dictums I could lay down for show business or for young people. I am not making rules. There are no rules in this profession because the very thing that works for me might not work for someone else, and the thing that works for someone else might be hopeless for me. If this were the kind of thing you could stamp out like bottle tops you wouldn't have the incredible variety of personalities in my profession. A doctor can't make one diagnosis and give one particular medicine for each and every illness. If doctors weren't allowed full play of their skills and their intuitions and instincts everybody could be a doctor.

But I didn't answer your question—I'm being political. Yes, the audience does affect the show; it affects your relationship them. It's one thing to do a dance and it's one thing to sing a song when you make a record or even when you're on the stage. It's another thing to work from a comedy reaction. You know that if there is nobody in the theater you can still sing the song, possibly as well. It might not be as exciting, but you could conceivably sing the song with the same kind of fervor. But if you go out on the stage to do a comedy sketch or a comedy number and there is no reaction whatever (and indeed there have been many such times in my life) there's no possible way to function. But you do it because you know it's either a matter of doing it or ending up in the river.

N.   Earlier you said there were several years when you couldn't get jobs. This goes 'way back, but what were your first professional engagements? What material were you using?

          KAYE: One of the first real engagements I had was with two friends. We had an act. They were dancers and I used to sing while they danced and then the three of us would dance. There wasn't much talking. I'd do a sort of comedy dance, too, while they changed for ballroom numbers. One day—in Utica, New York—I came prancing out on the stage and fell flat on

my can. Dave Harvey said something I'll never forget as long
as I live. He just looked down at me and said, "Wait for the
laugh." That turned out to be the beginning of a crazy idea of
what might amuse people. (On the contrary there are the
inhibitory factors that make a performer perform the way he
does, but I don't know how to explain these. I don't *really* know
what makes me perform the way I do or what makes Red
Skelton perform the way he does or what makes Jack Benny
perform the way he does. It has to be a sum total of what you
are, really.)

But I did things before that. When I was in school I belonged
to a fraternity, and I used to sing with another guy; we called
ourselves Red and Blackie. We did some radio, we'd entertain at
fraternity meetings and parties, but we were beginning to get
paid. Later we joined an outfit called the A.B. Marcus Show. It
was a highlight in my life because we were playing in Detroit,
our act, when Marcus came to look us over. "Those two people I
want. That tall redheaded fellow I don't need." Marcus didn't
care about whether or not we had an act. He didn't need me, but
my friends wouldn't break up the act so Marcus decided to pay
the three of us what he was originally going to offer the other
two. We wound up going to Japan, China and the Philippines,
and it was as broad and fruitful an education as anybody could
have, especially somebody in show business. In the first place I
was dealing with audiences that didn't understand English : it's
one thing to communicate with an audience that knows what
you're saying, can respond when you ask them a question. It's
another to try to make them understand what you're trying to
do when the only way you can communicate is through pantomime and sign language. But it certainly does develop your
ingenuity—many facets of ability that are otherwise hidden.
And in a funny way—although I had dealt with kids before—I
think that's where I began to learn, through playing these adult
audiences, how I could best communicate with kids. Remember
—I said before that I had soaked up this affinity for Chinese
food and cooking that didn't manifest itself for many years?
Well, it occurs to me now that those years I spent in the Orient
dealing with audiences that didn't understand me probably

manifested themselves later in dealing with children who didn't understand me. I once said, "Adults make the best children," and that's sort of true, because the very same things I would be doing for that adult audience I found myself—twenty-five years later—doing for children.

At any rate I enjoyed this tour of the Orient, but there came a time when I figured I had to come back home. It was a tough decision to make because I was very comfortable—I was with a show that had eighty or ninety people in it, I knew everybody, and we were one very big happy family. Remember, it took us seventeen days just to *get* there so we not only worked, but we'd lived, in close proximity. I was safe here, I had a job as long as the Marcus Show lasted.

There was a group with that show called "Behe and Rubiat" —I think the fellows were from Lebanon or Syria and they used to philosophize with me a great deal. Behe (I don't know whether he's still alive or not) and I struck up a fairly strong friendship, and when I talked to him once about the advisability of leaving the show and striking out on my own he said, "Danny, it's very safe to stay here," and then he uttered a proverb that's become old hat, as all proverbs have, but was fresh and apt 'way back then. "He who travels fastest travels alone." So with a great wrench I left the show and didn't do anything for the next nine months while the show traveled all over the United States and went to Australia and back.

They were playing in Newark, New Jersey, one time, and I went to visit them. I saw all my old friends, and it was the same kind of warmth and gaiety and I wondered, "What the hell have I done? Why did I leave all this to come sit at home to see agents and bookers and not accomplish anything?" I went down to see them off a few nights later and they wanted me to come with them—I could buy clothes in the next town and be safe and secure again.

That may have been a turning point in my life. I was sorely tempted to go along, but some other instinct prevailed and I very sadly said, "No, I'd better go home."

N.   But then you did start working?

❦ KAYE: I got odd jobs here and there. I worked with a fellow named Nick Long, Jr., a little later and I played the Casa Manana and some theaters and then we got booked into the Dorchester Hotel in London with the Chester Hale girls, Bobby May, and Norton Wayne, who was one of the greatest MC's I've ever seen. And, the night we opened in London at the Dorchester was the night Hitler marched into Czechoslovakia. (I still remember one incident; Henry Sherek, whom I still see occasionally, said, "I got a call from the American Embassy— they're advising all Americans to go home." I said, "Why?" and he said, "Oh, the bloody Kraut is making some sort of a mess. No need to worry—just go out there and keep your pecker up." That's the first I'd heard the phrase in *that* context.)

Well, I was the most resounding failure that the London café set had ever seen. It was hopeless, and I struggled along for six or seven weeks and they finally told me to take a walk. Nick Long stayed on for a while, and it was nine long years later that I got back to London to play at the Paladium.

N. And now they won't let you go.

❦ KAYE: In between, remember, a couple of things had happened. I'd done a few movies and some stage parts. The great story is opening night at the Paladium. They'd never had a band right on the Paladium stage, and they asked me how long I was going to be on. I said, "Jeez, I don't know, how long do you want me to stay on? Twenty, thirty, forty minutes? Maybe I should stay on as long as things go well." And I was standing in the wings when a fellow named Ted Ray said, "Ladies and gentlemen, Danny Kaye." I knew he was introducing me, and knew I was supposed to go on, but I didn't. I wasn't paralyzed or anything like that; it just seemed totally unreal. Again he said, "Ladies and gentlemen, Danny Kaye," and I still stood staring at him until Charlie Henry sort of pushed me and I stumbled onto the stage.

N. To retrace a few steps—what happened in that nine-year stretch between your English appearances?

❦ KAYE: The year after I was in London I met Sylvia, and we did a show called *The Barbizon Review* and a

few others, then *The Straw Hat Review* with Imogene Coca.
From then I went into *Lady in the Dark* with Gertrude
Lawrence and after that a show titled *Let's Face It*.

While *Lady in the Dark* was running Abe Glasgow, then
my representative, told Sam Goldwyn there was a fellow in
New York he ought to see. I played an effeminate role in the
play and Goldwyn came, saw and said, "Why the hell did
you bring me all the way to New York to see some fag?" He
was ready to go back to California when Abe said, "No, this
isn't what I want you to see—I want you to catch him at the
Martinique." I must have been a good actor because Goldwyn
really believed I was a fag.

After *Let's Face It* I came out to California to make my first
picture. I couldn't wait to get back to New York because California was supposed to be for the birds. I went back and forth
three or four times and finally decided that if I was going to live
anywhere I'd just as soon live in California. I was born and
raised in New York City and I'm crazy about it—we've just put
together an apartment in New York, as a matter of fact, a
beauty—but it's more logical for me to live here. When they
first started talking to me about doing a television show they
said, "You ought to do it from New York because New York is
the hub of show business." That's a lot of nonsense, really,
because you can get the same kind of excitement here that you
can in New York. I couldn't get working conditions like I have
here anywhere else in the world—this bungalow, the rehearsal
hall right around the corner, nothing but the best facilities and
arrangements.

N.   I remember—and I'll start with your first movie, *Up
In Arms*—how great your special material was—how funny
and intelligent. Is there any way of describing how it was
written, staged, put together?

❦   KAYE: It was all very intelligent and well-written
because an intelligent and talented girl wrote it. Sylvia is one of
the most gifted lyricists and composers I've ever met, and she's
spent most of her show-business life working for me. In an odd
way she didn't give her talent a chance to develop, and it wasn't

until I decided to do this television show every week that we came to the conclusion that she should finally do something on her own. Writing for a weekly television show is rough. Some people can't do it, just can't orient themselves to it. Frankly, I didn't know if I was going to be able to do it or not—I find now that it goes quite smoothly, it isn't really too great a physical drain. The worst thing about it is the fact that it's confining. For a fellow who's usually as free as a bird it's taken something of a toll. We do five shows, then get a week off. The last time I had a week off I decided to take a little trip to get the hell away and I went to Hong Kong.

N. How long will you keep your television show?

❧ KAYE: This is only my second year, and in all probability I won't stay beyond a third year. If I do I may take a year off in between. I like it, I enjoy it enormously, but I've got to watch how things go.

N. Do you have any plans for motion pictures?

❧ KAYE: No. The demands of a weekly television show are such that I couldn't possibly plan a movie. The only time I could do it would be during the vacation in summer, and that isn't even three months—it's only ten or eleven weeks— and I need that time to revitalize myself for the following season. When that vacation comes up I just bloody well don't want to do anything.

I've got a lot of other interests, you know, and I want to use the time off to go where I want to go and do precisely what I want to do. My life used to revolve only about my career, but a fellow can't work that way, live that way, all his life. When you get to a position of some eminence in your profession you should be able to satisfy some of your other interests. I'm interested in flying, in cooking, in sports, in traveling.

N. Are you conscious of any obligation as a performer? To yourself or your audience?

❧ KAYE: I feel a sense of obligation to me. If I function as a human being with any sense of obligation *to* function as a human being the rest falls into place.

Now, that answer may not be all I want it to be, just like some of my other answers may look a bit odd to me when I read them back. As you develop, concepts, ideas and attitudes change enormously. You think you've arrived at a point where—well, where this is it. And suddenly something happens (it doesn't have to be an overt thing) something consciously or unconsciously happens and you change. And you're not even aware of the change.

N.   I'd like to go back to your Paladium appearance, now, in London—your smash success nine years after your bomb.

❦   KAYE: I don't really know what happened. I can only explain it in terms of what was told to me by the English people themselves.

Actually, I think it had something to do with the times. The war was just over, Britain had resumed a policy of variety entertainment again, but the first few people who appeared weren't terribly successful.

When I came on they might have identified with my lack of inhibition. (I had such strange notions. I believed, like most Americans still do, that the English were cold and reserved and unemotional and had no sense of humor. Nothing could be farther from the truth after witnessing their behavior in a theater. The English are so quick, so theater-oriented, so show-wise, they are totally uninhibited and were some of the best audiences I've ever played. On the other hand the French are supposed to be volatile and passionate and outgoing but their behavior in a theater is the reverse. But no matter.)

Now, the British were used to their comedians (or so I was told) coming out wearing a long jacket or a short jacket or a red nose—something that said "comedian"—and I came out wearing sports clothes, looking as though I was going on to a country club luncheon. In fact, one day I said I'd like a cup of tea, so someone brought me a cup of tea and I sat down on the stage and drank it.

I did anything that came into my head when I was onstage at the Paladium—I behaved in a totally uninhibited fashion—

because there was all this terrible tension that had existed throughout the war years. The fact that I gave them a chance for explosive release from these tensions might have accounted for the success I enjoyed.

I don't know. I suppose people could make up very fanciful stories and big psychological dissertations on what the subconscious prevailing mood meant—the insecurity and horror of war gone and peace prevailing—or just the advent of spring—and write an endless thesis.

I've got a cup here—I use it for pencils and pens—that carries an inscription from a piece that ran in a London newspaper when I left England in 1949. It's titled "Our Danny's Gone Away" and it reads: "He capers, he dances, he has eyes of youth/ He writes verses/ He speaks Holiday/ He smells April and May."

That probably sums the whole thing up as well as it can be explained. All I know is, it was great fun.

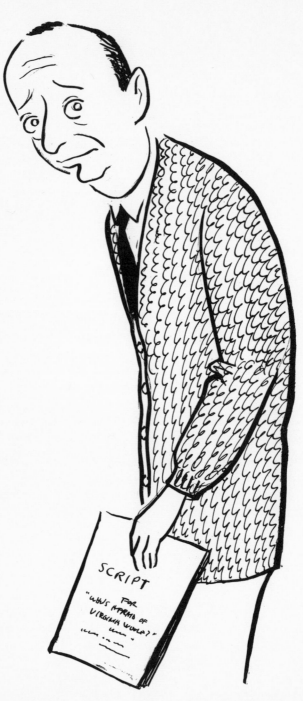

"Little do audiences know what we go through so that they can enjoy themselves in a darkened theater."

ERNEST LEHMAN

The credits that precede a motion picture go by all too quickly. Yet for years I've watched them closely, primarily to catch the names of the writers involved.

In recent years some of the best-written films made —many of them, in fact—have listed Ernest Lehman as screenwriter. *Executive Suite*, *West Side Story* and *The Sound of Music* are only three of his finest products. As writer-producer of *Who's Afraid of Virginia Woolf?* Mr. Lehman is now one of the most talked-about men in the industry.

He's an amazing man. Unassuming, a bit shy, strung on nerves that are not made of iron.

❦   LEHMAN : I was born in New York—on 92nd Street in Manhattan, to be exact—forty-odd years ago. The fact that I say "odd" indicates that I'm not happy about its being that long ago.

When I was five we moved to Woodmere, a suburb on the south shore of Long Island, where I spend fourteen years in a large, pleasant house, with ivy crawling up the red brick walls and squirrels in the attic. I attended Woodmere Academy, a private school, then switched to the public school system and graduated ninth in a class of 300 from Lawrence High School.

Came the depression, and the family manse became a New York City apartment. I entered the College of the City of New York and spent five years getting a B.S. degree in English literature. (I had thought I might become a chemical engineer, and began by majoring in science; but halfway through college I decided to become a writer, switched to literature, and graduated with the hybrid Bachelor of Science in English.)

The first writing attempts I recall are those I did in college— they made me aware of a definite flair for writing. I studied the technique of the short story in a class conducted by a rather famous professor, Theodore Goodman. Quite a few prominent writers passed through his class in narrative writing at CCNY. He gave me a B-plus but cautioned me on "slickness." He was right. My first job was in Wall Street. I became a copy editor of a financial magazine, and at the same time I started a novel. It was a road-company Jerome Weidman titled "Someone Should Have Told Me," and had a Wall Street background. But twenty-five pages was all I did. Ten years later I took out those yellowing sheets of paper and decided they could become the basis of a short story. (It was later published in *Redbook* magazine.)

The financial magazine suspended publication during a temporary recession, and I drifted into free-lance article writing. When I was twenty-one I had my first article published in *Collier's* magazine, a theatrical profile of Ted Lewis, the bandleader, written in collaboration with a very close friend, David Brown. It was titled "Is Everybody Happy?" and the sight of my byline was so exciting there was simply no doubt that from then on I'd write professionally. For about a year I wrote articles for national magazines—a tough way to make a living, but I was too young to know better. Then I lost heart and decided to take a steady job. I became connected with a publicity agency in New York that specialized in theatrical and motion picture accounts. There I worked, largely behind the scenes, as a writer, turning out material which eventually found its way into the newspapers under the bylines of all the famous Broadway columnists. In fact, there were times when I wrote entire columns for them. (As you know, press agents gain the good will of newspapermen by doing favors, such as writing their material; in return, the newspapermen print plugs and other material to please the clients of the press agents.)

This was my introduction to show business, really, and I was truly struck by the glamor and the behind-the-scenes skulduggery that goes on in the world of Broadway pressagentry, Broadway column-writing, night club life, Hollywood personalities on safari in New York, etc. I must have been quite impressionable at the time because I was moved to make this world my world of fiction, and I went on to write many short stories and novelettes about the denizens of Broadway. I even went to Provincetown and started writing a novel about this world, but (again) I lost courage and quit after turning out the first four chapters. However, being a guy who never wastes material, I took those four chapters and reworked them. The first three chapters became short stories which were published in *Collier's* and *Cosmopolitan*, and the fourth became the basis of my first novelette, published in *Cosmopolitan* and later as a book. It appeared under the title, "Tell Me About It Tomorrow," because Herbert Mayes, then editor of *Cosmopolitan*, felt that my title was not quite "right" for the magazine. I had called it "The Sweet Smell of Success," which became, of course, a very famous title when I later sold the novelette to a motion picture company here in Hollywood and wrote the screenplay with Clifford Odets. The title, as you know, has apparently passed into the language in a rather permanent way, and very few people know that those four words, "Sweet Smell of Success," were first juxtaposed one Saturday afternoon in the spring of 1949, in a small furnished room on the Upper West Side of New York City, rented for this particular writing effort. It seems incredible to me today that nobody had ever put those four words together before.

After that success I continued to write many short stories and articles for the national magazines before I wrote another novelette, "The Comedian," which created quite a stir in New York and Hollywood when it appeared in *Cosmopolitan* and in book form. Within a week of its publication I received a call from my agent informing me that Paramount Pictures was interested in bringing me, my wife Jacqueline, and my son Roger, out here. (Since then we have added Alan, now ten.) Paramount wondered if I had any interest in a Hollywood career, and frankly I was quite excited because I had always felt that I was destined to become a Hollywood writer. I had felt that I would fit in out here, that I would be rather good at writing motion pictures. I had always been extremely interested in films. (I'd constantly cut classes at CCNY to go to movies, and I think that if I hadn't come to Hollywood by way of magazine writing I would have stayed in New York a little longer, become a television dramatist, and eventually found my way out here via that route.)

One of my best short stories, "The Unguarded Moment," in *Cosmopolitan*, was dramatized on television and I received an award for the show. The young ad agency man I'd dealt with during my TV appearance to receive the award, Jud Kinberg, had preceded me out to California to become an associate producer with John Houseman at MGM. I spent a rather uncertain first year at Paramount, and when Houseman was looking for a writer to do the screenplay of *Executive Suite* Jud Kinberg remembered me, the work I'd done in New York as a magazine writer, the novelette "The Comedian," and he had a vague recollection that I'd once worked in Wall Street, so he thought I'd be suited for that picture. He called me to see if I might be interested in coming over to MGM if they could borrow me from Paramount. I had great admiration for John Houseman (he had just produced *Julius Caesar* with Marlon Brando, and *The Bad and the Beautiful*, which was to win several Oscars) and I was thrilled about going over to MGM to work with him. I read the novel several times and accepted the *Executive Suite* assignment with delight.

It became my first picture. Looking back now, I realize that I was extremely lucky. MGM could have hired any one of hundreds of writers who had actually written films—instead they hired (or borrowed) a completely unknown writer who was under contract to another studio. I started working on *Executive Suite*, the work went well, and it turned out to be one of MGM's most important all-star pictures. Even as I was finishing the screen play, word got out that it was good. And before it was even on film Billy Wilder, who had met me at Paramount, brought me back there to work on *Sabrina*, Audrey Hepburn's second picture. (But while I was working on *Executive Suite* at MGM, Paramount had let their option on my services lapse, so Paramount had to pay much more for my services in bringing me back than they'd have paid by continuing my original contract.)

Sabrina starred Humphrey Bogart, Audrey Hepburn and William Holden, and it was an altogether unforgettable experience. I received my first Academy nomination, and my first Writer's Guild Award, as well as the opportunity to explain Major League Baseball to Audrey. (The World Series was played while we were on location.)

After *Sabrina* I went to 20th Century Fox to do the screen play of *The King and I*. I had never done a musical, and when you stop to think of it, I was (again) an odd guy to hire. Why pick somebody who had written tough, hard-bitten, Broadway-underworld magazine fiction, and a highly dramatic film about big business, and a very modern romantic comedy? Why not hire someone who had written screen plays for musicals? But I am still grateful for the illogic of it all. Darryl Zanuck approved of me; so did Richard Rodgers and Oscar Hammerstein; and so did Charles Brackett, the producer, who had selected me—perhaps after checking with his former collaborator, Billy Wilder.

While I was working on that, MGM (which had had the chance to sign me to a rather modest contract while I was working on *Executive Suite*, but had obviously decided not to take the chance) decided to sign me to what was now a far less modest contract. And so after *The King and I* I returned to MGM and did the screen play for *Somebody Up There Likes Me*, based on Rocky Graziano's autobiography. It was, I think, one of my best film-writing experiences. Again, MGM might have inquired as to what I knew about the subject. I had never seen a professional fight, knew nothing about boxing. But I was eager to do the picture—it brought me back to my native New York, to cloudy skies and crowded sidewalks—all very personal territory. Next—the independent motion picture company,

Hecht-Hill-Lancaster, had always wanted to buy "The Sweet Smell of Success." I had always resisted selling it until I felt it would be in the proper hands. While I was working on *Some-body*, I sold H-H-L the novelette. The decision was made after I saw their *Marty* (which was to win the Academy Award). So I moved over to this independent company and started to work, for the first time, on a screenplay based on my own material. Halfway through the writing of the screenplay we all decided that I had the desire, and probably the ability, to direct as well as write the film, and so the deal and the announcement were made. I went to New York to start scouting locations, and came back to Hollywood only to be told that United Artists (they were financing the picture) had decided they were afraid of taking a chance on a new director, but that if I cared to I could produce the picture as well as write it. After a few unnecessarily emotional scenes I decided to accept the compromise—I couldn't bear to leave what I regarded as my baby.

Well, for reasons I won't go into, the whole situation eventually became untenable for me. A week before shooting was to begin in New York, I was told that I would have to do some rewriting behind the camera on location (Alexander McKendrick directed the film, directed it marvelously, and wanted to have me there). However, I felt the pressure would be too great, and my doctor was making noises. I had developed a very large pain in my intestinal tract—due, no doubt, to all the conflicts attending this film—so I wound up not in New York City, but for the first time in my life in a hospital. The doctor determined that the very large pain was due to extreme tension, and that I should not go back to work on that picture or any other until the pain went away, I went to Tahiti. And one day, lying on the beach completely free of care, I suddenly sat up and said "Good Lord, 'Sweet Smell of Success' is being filmed in New York and I don't even know who's in the cast other than Burt Lancaster and Tony Curtis." That's how wonderfully detached I had become. The film was not a financial success. It went too far over budget. But it was an artistic success in many quarters—*Time* magazine selected it as one of the best American pictures of the year, for example—it was one of the New Yorker's "current and choice" in boldface—and it still plays in art houses and at universities— but to me it was never quite as good a film as it should have been. Whose fault? Who knows? Perhaps mine. Nevertheless, with the passage of wound-healing time, I'm proud to have been associated with it as co-author. (The great Clifford Odets did some work on my screenplay after I'd taken off for Tahiti.)

So—back from Tahiti. On the boat from Papeete to Panama City I started writing another novel (I'm an expert at starting them) titled "The Riddle of the Sphincter," about my five days in the hospital. I finished only one chapter, and I'm surprised that I haven't yet found some way of turning it into a short story. I returned to MGM (I'd been on a leave-of-absence to do "The Sweet Smell of Success"), and there I wrote my first original screenplay, *North by Northwest*, for Alfred Hitch-cock.

There's one hell of a story associated with that picture. Hitchcock was committed to MGM to do a motion-picture ver-sion of a novel titled *The Wreck of the Mary Deare*. Originally I had turned it down—along with fourteen other projects— during and after the Tahiti stint, because I simply couldn't see it as a motion picture. So a luncheon was arranged for Hitchcock and myself. We liked each other, and convinced each other and ourselves that *Mary Deare* could be done. And soon, we offi-cially started on it. But after three weeks of story conferences, I slipped back into my original state; this was not a movie. It would be too static, deadly, dull. So with great reluctance and trepidation, I arrived at Hitch's house one morning and said, "I hate to say this, but you'll have to find another writer. I just don't know how to do this one." Hitch didn't bat an eyelash. (A great original expression I'll have to use sometime.) He said, "Don't be silly. I don't want another writer. We get along so well, we'll simply find something else to do." I said, "But what about *Mary Deare?* What about MGM?" and he said. "We won't tell them about it until we find something else to do." So for the next month, Hitch and I met every day and talked about various possibilities for a motion picture we could do together, and whenever I went to the studio, I'd walk down the halls, looking guiltily over my shoulder. Certain passing executives would salute me and say, "How's everything going, Captain?" (thinking I was working on *The Wreck of the Mary Deare*). Finally I told Hitch that I really felt like doing a Hitchcock picture to end all Hitchcock pictures—one that would combine everything he was noted for—suspense, wit, great changes of locale and an oblique sort of glamor. (But how can *I* define what Hitchcock is noted for?) At any rate, he liked the basic idea very much, and I went ahead with what was to become *North by Northwest*. Soon came the day when we realized that we had to let MGM know we were not going to do *The Wreck of the Mary Deare*. Hitch felt that it was up to me to tell them, but I said, "No—I can't bear to face them and give them this news." He said, "They'll be delighted—they've not only got *The Wreck of the Mary Deare*, which they own, but they'll have a completely new film they never counted on." Then, with a twinkle in his eye (I've got to use *that* fresh phrase someday too!) he said, "All right, I'll do *your* job *for* you. *I'll* tell them." So he set up a meeting with a half-dozen executives at MGM. Now, at that time, I really didn't know what more than 50 percent of the story would be. I knew we were heading for Mount Rushmore at the end, and that there would be a chase across the faces of the presidents, but much of the picture was utterly unknown to us.

Hitch called the meeting and told the executives that *The Wreck of the Mary Deare* was too difficult, that it would take too long to resolve, and that he felt it would be better if we did this film, and he would not tell them what it would be about. He thereupon spun the yarn in his inimitable manner up to the very point where he knew nothing else to say, and then he rose, said, "That's all, gentlemen, I have to leave now," and left them as if this were number eight of a cliff-hanging serial. They were thrilled. (What else could they afford to be?)

Hitch was at Paramount shooting *Vertigo* while I was at MGM writing *North by Northwest*, and when he finished his film he took off for a vacation in Jamaica. To this day I don't think Hitch knows how many times I called my agent and said, "I'm sorry, I have to give up. I can't write another page. I haven't the faintest notion where this thing goes next." There were days when I couldn't even face going to the studio. Somehow or other, I managed to get the first seventy-four pages written, mailed them to Hitch, and his enthusiastic letters and phone calls kept me going. Sets started building; locations were being worked out; Cary Grant started on salary at some astronomical sum per *day*. And yet I could not get the screenplay past page 136. I literally did not know where to go next, and the weeks went by, and there I was, stalled well-short of "The End."

Finally I broke the news to Hitch; "I give up. I don't know what happens next. I've painted myself into a corner and the room has no doors." We sat in his office, staring at each other very gloomily. Finally, he said, "Maybe we should call in—" and he named a certain novelist known for her suspense thrillers. "Maybe we should call her in and have the studio hire her just to sit with us and throw ideas at us." I said, "No, it would be much too embarassing," and we continued with our despair, and Hitch kept talking about calling this woman in and I sort of stopped listening and suddenly I looked up at him and said, "What would happen if she shoots Cary Grant?" He said "What are you talking about?" I said, "In the cafeteria at Mount Rushmore, our girl takes a gun out of her purse and kills Cary." His eyes widened as only Hitch's eyes can widen when he senses something cinematic. "But he's our leading man." I said, "They're not real bullets." A big smile came over his face. He hadn't the faintest idea nor did I, why she was shooting Cary Grant with blank cartridges, but he saw the scene and so did I. Despair vanished; I rushed to my office and began to figure out why our girl would do that to Cary Grant, and that was the end of a certain novelist known for her suspense thrillers. The rest of it was relatively easy, and before long I had managed to finish the screenplay. The picture was on all the Ten Best lists, I received an Academy nomination for best original screenplay, and all turned out very well at the box office.

I could write a book about *each* of these films—I haven't worked on *one* movie that hasn't had a full quota of complications. Little do the audiences know what we go through so that they enjoy themselves in a darkened theater. It's true that we're well-compensated in terms of money and recognition and sometimes glory, but there is something truly ridiculous about the agonies of creating pleasure for the world.

After *North by Northwest* came *From the Terrace* at 20th Century Fox, produced and directed by Mark Robson, based on John O'Hara's gargantuan novel—very difficult to adapt to the screen. I wish I had done better, but I believe it was commercially successful.

Then *West Side Story*, of course. In terms of Academy Awards, artistic acclaim and tremendous grosses, I suppose I would have to call it *the* outstanding picture I've done.

West Side Story was created for the stage in highly dramatic terms and therefore lent itself to the motion picture medium from the outset (something that is not true of all musical plays). As a screen writer, I feel that one of my functions is to see that we don't lose the intrinsic worth of the original material in turning it into a movie. So I didn't tamper with this one too much. (Frankly, there are times when the screen writer or adapter feels compelled to prove himself by throwing away that which he is working on and trying to do something completely different with it. He is caught between that desire and the knowledge that what he is working on is awfully good and ought not be tampered with.) Yet I think I did many things in making *West Side Story* into a motion picture that were valid and important but which might not have been visible to the naked eyes of people who hadn't worked with me on the movie. I think I had sense enough to leave the good things alone in writing this picture, but I mustn't be a shrinking violet entirely here because I do think the changes and innovations I made added up to a better movie.

After *West Side Story*, I wrote the screenplay of Irving Wallace's best-selling novel, *The Prize*. The picture starred Paul Newman, introduced Elke Sommer, and did quite well at the box office. It was difficult for me to write simply because—wisely or unwisely—I decided to make a fun-and-games, *North by Northwest* type of entertainment out of it. I felt that that was what the public wanted at the time. (And this was *before* the

James Bond films.) I would say that Wallace's novel was far more sensibly serious than my capricious approach, and though the picture got many very good reviews it also got some indifferent ones. I blame that on myself; if people failed to notice the tongue in my cheek, it was my fault as a writer, not theirs for dim vision. I'm not used to bad reviews, and the adverse ones really stung.

After *The Prize*—*The Sound of Music*. I feel that I have never taken a play and opened it up quite as much and made as much of a true motion picture out of it as I did with *The Sound of Music*. I went to Salzburg, in Austria, and spent several weeks just soaking up atmosphere, looking for locations and becoming thoroughly familiar with the locale of the Trapp Family story. I came back to California and did the screenplay, but I'm sure I wouldn't have written it as I did without this research. For example, the treatment of "Do-Re-Mi"—on stage, it was done in the living room, and it would have been terribly static done that way on the screen, but because I knew the physical background, I was inspired to break it up into many exterior locales so that the entire number takes place over a period of days rather than in one ten-minute period. Yet, musically, it continues unbroken, exactly as it was done on the stage.

N. Now you're at work writing—and producing, too— the film version of Edward Albee's *Who's Afraid of Virginia Woolf? That* must be a challenge.

LEHMAN: May I say that you have used the word advisedly? I had always heard about the *glare* of the spotlight, but I never knew that it could *speak*, too, and that all it said was, "Show me. I dare you." Forgive me if I seem disinclined to talk too much about the whole thing right now. Actual shooting of the film is several months away, and I have this fear that today's thoughts could come back on the printed page to haunt me tomorrow. All I can tell you with any degree of certainty is that Elizabeth Taylor and Richard Burton will play Martha and George; Sandy Dennis and George Segal will play Honey and Nick; and Mike Nichols will direct the picture.

N.   Perhaps you can speculate on your reasons for *accepting* the challenge.

❦   LEHMAN : The play was a shattering experience for me. I had read it, and was only horrified. Then, I went to see it, and was taken completely by surprise. I found myself laughing till it hurt, and then midway through the second act, I found myself weeping bitter tears, and that *really* hurt. There is no greater tribute that I, personally, can pay to a play than to be almost destroyed by it. *Virginia Woolf* is terribly funny and terribly sad, and terribly wise, too, and I know all the reasons why "You can't make a movie out of it," because I've heard nothing else wherever I turn, and maybe they're right, but I'm not interested, because all I know is that the attempt must be made somehow to get the genius of Edward Albee up on the screen. *Who's Afraid of Virginia Woolf?* is one of the great plays of our time, and if, through our combined talents and plain dumb luck, we can manage to deliver its emotional impact to the world's motion picture audiences, we will have done something worth doing. If we fail, we will have attempted something worth attempting. I hope we don't fail, because Edward Albee and his play deserve better than that.

N.   Why have you sought to produce as well as write?

❦   LEHMAN : I knew you'd ask that question and I wish I had a clear answer. I could say that I thought I would have more control over the ultimate fate of the screen play and the picture itself by producing it, and to a certain extent that may turn out to be true. It is possible that the cast might have been different and not to my liking, if I were not the producer, and that another director would be doing it, and that the script I finish might not have been acceptable if I were not the producer. One of my motivations might be rationalized as a desire for more control over the ultimate destiny of the work. However, I'm not foolish enough to believe that's the only reason. (It certainly isn't money, because, without going into the whole economic structure of the motion picture business, let me just say that it is a financial sacrifice to me to be the producer of the picture as well as the writer.)

I sense, however, that I also felt an emotional need to move into an area of possibly greater power on the Hollywood scene. Somehow, when you're the producer as well as the writer, you acquire a slightly greater status, and though that slightly enhanced status is for the birds (and I don't mean Hitchcock's) it leads into new experiences in motion picture making, some quite aggravating and frustrating. (I take back many of the harsh thoughts I've had, at times, about producers. I can understand, now, what they went through in getting my screenplays onto celluloid as successfully as they did.) So many decisions have to be made. One has to struggle with agents, with the demands of movie stars, and oh well—I think I'll be able to talk about this better once I've gone through the total experience.

N.   A great deal is bandied about pertaining to the committee-making of films. Is this a problem?

❦   LEHMAN: At times the "committee" as it's called has presented me with some problems. At other times it has been helpful. Each picture has been unique in that regard. It's easy to generalize and say that Hollywood writers have a terrible time because they work in committee, but that isn't always entirely true. Then too, the playwright working on Broadway has the same problems—he has to work with a director, with a cast, with a producer. A playwright, through his dramatists guild, may be protected so that nothing can be changed without his authorization, but he has to be professional enough to know that if a scene doesn't play, or an actress can't feel it, changes have to be made, and so there he is, working in committee.

Good pictures happen when the people involved are fortunate enough to know which battles to win and which to lose. There's a lot of give-and-take, and I know I'm stubborn enough to fight to the bitter end for something I believe is right, but I also know enough (I think) to give in when a pet idea doesn't seem to convince my opponents. But isn't the novelist often called upon to revise by his editor, and don't magazine editors ask for revisions and title changes, and doesn't the journalist have to conform to space and style—?

Any way you look at it, the writer is more vulnerable to

committee operation than any other creative or interpretive artist. There isn't *anybody* who doesn't have the right or the presumed ability to suggest to a writer that there is something wrong with what he has done. A writer has to expect that the director, the producer and the actors will feel they have a right to suggest changes in his work without in any way stepping on his toes or upsetting him. Yet what writer feels he has the right to suggest to a producer that he isn't producing the picture properly, or to a director that he isn't catching the writer's intent, or to an actor that he is not portraying the role as well as he might? This is my main objection to the writer's lot. Everyone feels privileged—if not obliged—to tell him what the hell to do differently. But the writer doesn't seem to have the reciprocal privilege. A producer can say, "What does a writer know about producing?" and an actor can say, "What does a writer know about acting?" without being seriously challenged. Yet the writer apparently cannot say, "What does a producer, or a director, or an actor, know about writing?"

But I must conclude my grumble by saying that whenever you find any writer in any medium complaining about the conditions that prevail, you can be certain that, deep down inside him, his true complaint is that he wishes he were a better writer.

N.   Are you sensitive about the reviews of your movies?

❧   LEHMAN: Oh, Lord. You are talking to the seismograph of screen writers. I can record a bad review in Bombay. I am unduly sensitive to reviews. It's all rather strange, though, because I seem to remember the few bad reviews much better than I remember the many good ones. Something has got to be wrong with a person who regards himself as a personal failure if his picture doesn't make Bosley's Ten-Best-of-the-Year list. At the same time I should qualify this confession by saying that I have made the list many times, but I'm disappointed when I don't. I could tell you some little anecdotes that would really make me seem ridiculous regarding reviews. I once burned a copy of *Time* magazine in the fireplace without reading the review it contained merely because someone phoned me and said, "It's really not so bad."

N. In talking to writers who live in California I continually run into the fact that they feel as though they're penalized by the critics for living out here. Have you noticed any prejudice of this nature?

LEHMAN: I certainly have. I think it's a very complex psychological problem, and I can offer only an opinion —I can't say, "This is specifically what it is"—but there *is* an anti-Southern California syndrome. Not just Hollywood, but Southern California as a whole.

I used to study this. I noticed the fantastically ingenious ways in which Eastern or Midwestern journalists used to manage to work in a slap at the Los Angeles area while writing something which had absolutely nothing to do with it. There is a great deal of non-specific contempt, hostility, perhaps even disguised envy, in non-Southern Californians toward this area. I don't know how it all started, and it may not be entirely groundless—things like that don't just happen without any basis in fact.

Obviously there was a phase of life in Southern California, perhaps back in the 1920's, that was legitimately open to ridicule. I wasn't here then, so I don't know all the details. Perhaps the Hollywood that Nathaniel West wrote about deserved ridicule—the Los Angeles of Aimee Semple McPherson and the various cults. Then, of course, Hollywood has always been the symbol of outrageous living, corruption, too much money, divorce, sex—everything that people would (consciously or unconsciously) like to have. Also, it has always been chic for journalists and critics to condemn Hollywood for its bad pictures, while conveniently forgetting all the great ones. (Maybe this attitude is taught in school starting with kindergarten.) When non-Hollywood writers settle out here to write their prose and poetry they seem to be dismissed as serious writers. Now, there's no doubt that, compared to New York, Boston, London, Paris, or Rome, Los Angeles has been a little late in getting with it culturally speaking. Yet I don't know of many people who are hostile toward *Pittsburgh*. I don't know of many critics who sneer at a writer for living in Milwaukee or Seattle. I think the snide hostility of the press toward artists who live in Southern California would be worthy of a very interesting Ph.D. thesis. You could write a book, in fact, on the anti-Hollywood, anti-Los Angeles, anti-Southern California phenomenon of the 1940's, 50's and 60's.

N.   Now if you were to give advice to the youngster— and we'll assume he's talented—what would that advice be?

☙   LEHMAN : I think that writers are to a great extent influenced by the company they keep. If a writer happens to grow up in a local culture (family and friends and colleagues) which values the so-called glamor or the so-called status of "Hollywood writer," or if he happens to grow up in a culture that values big money, I think he unconsciously acquires goals as a writer which would lead him in a totally different direction from a writer growing up in, say, a university town among people who placed great value on literature, the arts, as opposed to commercial culture (with a capital K). *In other words, a writer's destiny is apt to be shaped by the values of those people he is exposed to in his formative years.* In these early stages, I think he is fortunate if he happens to have friends who praise him for the right things instead of for the wrong things. Now, if he is talented and sensitive and wants to write literature, but lives and works among people who have only totally commercial values, it behooves him to find a new environment. Similarly, if he's longing for "glamor," and preoccupied with material success, he's doing himself an injustice to remain in an arty or academic atmosphere.

All the rest of the advice—the "read, read, read" and "write, write, write"—he'll get from every English and journalism teacher along the line. And you can't minimize the importance of reading and of practice. But if he places himself in the proper environment (proper for *him*), where he gets maximum encouragement and the right kind of assurance, he'll progress faster and—most important—he'll be happier. That is, assuming that a writer can ever be happy.

"If I don't play the piano every now and then I get a little stir-crazy."

JACK LEMMON

At least a dozen people in Hollywood had told me that
Jack Lemmon is the nicest and the brightest guy in the
business. At the time I saw him he was faintly tinged
with yellow, a victim of Infectious Hepatitis, and he
was still a bit weak in the pins. But as he talked, mating
in words his sensitivity, virility, perception and ambition, I found precisely what at least a dozen more
knowledgeable people had discovered before.

LEMMON: I'm a Bostonian, I guess. I was born in
Newton Center, one of Boston's multitudinous suburbs, and
when I was four we moved toward Newton proper, near Water-
town, still closer to Boston, and when I was thirteen we moved
into Boston proper. Because I was an only child we were no
longer in need of a house after I went away to school at Philips
Academy (Andover, as it's called).

The desire to act came when I was very young; I think I was
always determined to be an actor. I did *Gold in Them Thar
Hills*—an old melodrama—when I was four or five. I had a
small walk-on, and the show ran for a couple of weekends with a
professional director and an amateur cast. I think we were
raising money for a hospital.

My first key performance was as a replacement, a last-minute replacement at a school named River's Country Day in Brookline. I was about ten and I played the part with a very large black hat with a wide brim, Texas style, but worn like the old Barrymore bit with one side up and the other side down. I had a black cape, too, and this might have been important because I can still remember the relish of getting audience reaction and laughter by doing something I hadn't planned on doing. I didn't have time to learn the lines—there were two pages of dialogue I couldn't assimilate that quickly—so we had a teacher in the wings as prompter. The only way I could perform was to say a line while I walked across the stage, then pretend to think and ponder while I walked back to the wings to get the next line. This set up a peculiar pattern of oddball pauses that fractured the audience and I loved it. From then on I did carnivals and spiels at school, continued with shows at Andover when I got there. As a matter of fact I was class of '43 and for some reason they voted me Class Poet. Why in hell they did this, I'll never know—I never wrote any poems. By then I'd also become interested in music, in writing it, something I still do for my own amazement. But at Andover, for the first time in that school's history (a long and sometimes illustrious one), a bunch of us wrote and performed a musical comedy for Class Day instead of doing the regular exercises. I wrote some of the music and a lot of the skits and it was quite successful. We were then eligible for V-12, ROTC, and so on, and we were going off to war or college or whatever, so there was one absolutely God-awful song I wrote that went "I'm in the U.S. Army/ and if Hitler ever sar me/ he would never dare to harm me." (I am NOT responsible for the lyric.)

At any rate, after Andover I didn't know whether I wanted to go to Yale or Harvard. I got accepted by both by the skin of my teeth, but the Navy sent me to Harvard because I was eligible for the V-12 program. They had lowered the requirements until they got to my level. I was never a good student; I spent too much time on music and dramatics, so I was really very lucky to get to Harvard at all. At Harvard I continued with dramatics as much as I could and wrote one of the Hasty Pudding Shows—wrote the music and acted in the skits. We couldn't go on the road as they usually do because it was wartime and they didn't want us tootling off, but the run, local as it was, was successful.

All these things further whetted my appetite, and by the time I was commissioned (with, I was informed by a Captain, the lowest grades of any member of the entire program that had gone through Harvard) the war was over. After three or four months of active duty I had enough points to get out. I needed one more credit from Harvard, went back for that, and then went booming off to save the American theater. This was in 1946.

Roughly, the career went as follows. For about two years nothing much happened. I did the "starving actor" bit—you don't really starve, you just don't eat much—and I didn't make enough money to pay taxes. Then things happened, and life was good.

Off and on I worked at a joint called The Old Knick—short for Knickerbocker Music Hall. (It's now the El Morocco, a funny bit because when I went to the opening of the New El Morocco as a Hollywood actor in my damned tuxedo, with all the cameras going, I stepped out of the car and said, "My God, it's the Old Knick where I first worked!") This was my first real job, outside of a bit of summer stock in New Hampshire and with the Marblehead Players and in New Hampshire.

My salary at the Old Knick went from $0 or $5 a week all the way up to $75 a week, depending upon how the club went. It was great experience. As George Burns says, "There's no place left for a kid to be lousy anymore," meaning that the days of vaudeville are gone. That club offered the same thing vaudeville did in previous years. We did everything from old-time melodramas to waiting on tables to community sings to M.C. bits to oleo bits (meaning anything in one). I was also the orchestra (a piano I played by ear, but we'd rehearse enough so I'd know what the singers were doing and I'd accompany them). Sometimes I'd play Master of Ceremonies, sometimes headwaiter. We did anywhere from sixteen to twenty shows per night and didn't repeat. A show went on every ten minutes, and if there were ten customers six of them may have been there for the last show, so it meant an awful lot of thinking on your feet, doing things that weren't always safe, revising old burlesque routines. It was great experience, not necessarily from the standpoint of acting but definitely in performing in front of people and feeling an audience, of knowing when you have them and when you don't. Often I'd go fifteen to twenty minutes, make an exit to no applause, hearing a big zero. A lot of very good people went through the Old Knick. I remember one show—and our salaries may have been $25 or $35 per week—a melodrama that featured Maureen Stapleton, Jack Albertson, Bob Simon, Dean Barry, myself, a few others. Summer stock seems secondary to this. Maybe I didn't do enough of it. (How much can the youngster do now? A young actor then could get great experience and training in live TV, winter repertory, summer stock. All of those are practically extinct in comparison to the way they existed then. Everything is stars, now, and big business. In television even small parts are played by established actors.)

When I broke into television there were no such things as stars. Lucy and Milton hadn't even come on the horizon, and they were the first two stars to come on the scene. I can remember in the early days of Studio One that I got a good part for $50—in fact both Chuck Heston and I got $50 doing a show titled *Channel of Substance*. I got my part because Worthington Minor, the producer, was in the expanding CBS building and they didn't have a door on his office yet. I walked in, and there he was, so I started spouting in an Irish brogue and I ended up getting the part, but that's an example of how free and easy and accessible things were then.

That's not about to happen today. That comparatively small part of the priest would be played by a well-known actor, tens of thousands of dollars would be spent on the production; then an hour of production cost four of five thousand. At one point I had a series on ABC. We had a thirteen-piece live orchestra, the first big boom camera, the biggest studio, and we turned out a half-hour comedy show for something like $12,500 a week. Today that show would cost $85,000 or $90,000 to produce.

Anyway, I did an awful lot of live TV—comedy and drama —over 400 shows in four or five years. So maybe this was my repertory period, and again I consider myself lucky. (I think the biggest problem kids face now, certainly as far as network TV and films are concerned, is just being able to put in an apprenticeship. They have one hell of a time.) All the while I was working in television and doing bits of summer stock I was interested in the stage. I looked down on the movies—a typical New York attitude, I guess. I wanted to be in Theater. Finally I got a part, and a good one, in *Room Service* and we opened at the 48th Street Playhouse. It was a bomb—a depression play. It was no longer funny in 1950 A.D. to show five guys trying to raise $5,000 and starving to death and looking longingly at the pigeons on the windowsill and being unable to check out of the hotel because they couldn't pay their bill. However, I got good reviews out of it, and the reviews must have meant something.

At that time Max Arnow—head of casting at Columbia pictures—had seen me in a *Robert Montgomery Presents* and he thought I'd be just right for a part opposite Judy Holliday in a film. My agent called me up from William Morris and said, "I've got a thing about a movie here," and I said, "Oh, hell, I'm not interested in movies, I'm looking for another play or more live TV." Then he explained that the film would star Judy, whom I loved as an actress, and be directed by George Cukor, who was one of the few directors I was aware of (I loved the way he handled actors) and it was written by Garson Kanin. All these things made it more than a bit appealing, so I read the script, fell in love with it, and they asked me to test for the picture. Columbia told me I'd have to sign with them if I got the part and I said that I would as long as it wasn't an exclusive contract. It was a standard seven-year contract but I did get things nobody had gotten before. I had the right to do four Broadway plays, taking a year off from the seven years, and could do an outside film each year providing I'd done two that year for them. In other words it was a two-a-year non-exclusive contract.

After the first few weeks of confusion and ignorance I loved film-making and I still do. I think film is the greatest medium, as a matter of fact, and in some ways I like it more than I ever could like theater. *This* monologue will show you the danger of asking me a question.

N.   It's what I wanted—you're up to your film career. Now I'd like to jump, a bit, to *Some Like It Hot*. You were great, in drag. In the movie.

❧   LEMMON: I'm glad you said, "In the movie." Actually—and I think I've said this before—I've been a very lucky guy, a very fortunate guy, when the chips are down. I don't care whether talent is there or not, and I don't believe in astrology, but I'm positive that a little angel up there has given me some great breaks as far as timing is concerned. (I'm digressing, but only because I think it's important.) Now, a lot of people can walk around for twenty years with my quotient of talent and not be found—they may never be found.

At any rate, Billy Wilder happened to see a picture Dick Klein directed titled *Operation Madball*. He liked it and he liked me in it. In the back of his mind he had the idea for a film he was going to do, *Some Like It Hot*—kicked off from an old German film he'd bought the rights to, where (in a four or five minute sequence) two guys who were trying to run away threw mops over their heads and played in an all-girl orchestra. That kicked off Billy's project so he enlarged on that sequence, transplanted it to the U.S., and—

I was sitting in a favorite restaurant—Dominic's—when Billy came over one night and introduced himself and asked if he could join me for a moment. "I have an idea for a film about two guys that dress up in drag to escape some gangsters. They join an all-girl orchestra and you'll stay in drag for about 85 percent of the picture. Are you interested?"

I looked at him as though he was nuts, but I figured he was still sober, so I said, "Yes." He said, "Good, because I won't write it until I have my actors, so you don't see any script until you're committed."

Along came the script, the first sixty pages of it, and I literally fell off the couch—I was still in my little bachelor haven—when I got to page five. It is still by far the best farce script I have ever read, and I firmly believe that it should be sent around to colleges to be read by kids who are studying writing—especially scriptwriting—as a model of construction and of dialogue stemming from character. (Not just one-line nifties, but jokes that stem from character, behavior, the legitimate funny lines.)

If I can digress again: As far as the finding of a character is concerned there are two ways you can approach acting—at least as far as I can tell. One is the normal way, the Method or whatever you call it—it's like laying bricks. You start at the bottom and work up; actually I guess you start in the middle and work to the outside. You sweat and think and read until you get the various attributes of that character, the sum total of which makes you understand why that person behaves the way he does, why he says what he says and does what he does. Once you have this understanding and knowledge of the character you put the outside on, the mannerisms, the way he dresses and moves and looks. In other words, your makeup and your wardrobe stem from what the person *is*.

The other way to build a character is what would normally be called the wrong way—that is, to create a shell and crawl into it. To get the externals down first. The way the person dresses, looks, talks, behaves, comes first—then you make the character a person who lives up to externals.

This is what I did. I purposely went the wrong way with *Some Like It Hot* for a very good reason: this was a comedy, and the bizarre character masquerading as a girl was going to be at least 50 percent of the visual comedy. So we experimented for days with wigs and makeup, and when I got what I thought was the right face, the right vacant idiot look with the eyes, and the beestung lips, and Billy agreed—only then did I make the character the kind of person that would behave openly in that manner. I found a shell and crawled into it, like one of those goddam crabs.

I did the last thing on a new picture, *The Great Race*. It's a two-parter—I play two roles, like I did in *Irma*, only I play two totally different people who happen to look alike. One is a fop prince, a Wildean character, not quite faggy but with a sort of shrewd weakness he affects on purpose. He's a lace hankie character, but the externals were important, so important I made him behave in ways that lived up to those externals.

In other words, the things you first learn as an actor can be disproved. I went for result—saw what I wanted and made the character perform that way. But an actor has to have a great deal of experience to know how to do this. One of the plagues of actors in the old days of radio and television and movies (and it still happens today) is the bad directors—the result directors. Your direction can be stupid, and I'll exaggerate to make my point: "Be happy" comes on page eighteen. You can't play "Be happy"—it's not a specific, it's a result. It's a state of being, and you can't really play a state of being. You can play "to love," "to hate," "to anger" or "to provoke"—they're something definite.

In other words, acting doesn't have anything to do with listening to the words. (As you're first told in high school plays—"Listen, don't just wait for your cue, listen to what the other person is saying.") We never really listen, in general conversation, to what another person is saying. We listen to what they mean. And what they mean is often quite apart from the words. When you see a scene between two actors that really comes off you can be damned sure they're not listening to each other—they're feeling what the other person is trying to get at. Know what I mean?

Sorry—I get carried away with all this. Back to *Some Like It Hot*—you asked me about that hours ago. But it was one of those things I went at backward. (I hated directors, years ago, when I first began to learn this. There was a great fellow, a director out here now named David Alexander, who had a group class years ago. All of us were professional actors, working actors, and around twelve or fourteen of us would meet with him every week or two, and we'd do scenes—it was a scene study class with criticism on our craft level only. I learned a great deal from that class, and there again we were made so aware of result, of the traps of the superficiality of just playing for result rather than getting to something concrete.)

Now I want result direction. All I want to know is what result the director wants—I'll do the homework. I'll get the result. The interesting thing is that once I know *what* he wants I know there are possibly twenty ways to get the result, and the fun and delicious hell is trying to decide which way to do it. And the simplest way is the best—you don't need an hour of pseudo-intellectual imbibing and yapping about Method or any supposed deep-dish level of acting. Nothing is duller than somebody crying. And nothing is better than trying not to cry when the audience is crying.

Out of that class I also began to develop the approaches I now use as much as possible: counterpoint and obstacles. Dull scenes can certainly be made more interesting if you take them beyond routine. For example, a love scene staged out-of-doors: make it rain. You're trying to do a very tender love scene and you're sopping wet—at least it's more interesting.

I love obstacles because on the simplest level you have to achieve those certain things as an actor because they're there, they're written in. But now you try to put everything in the way of achieving what you must achieve and you frustrate the character. The frustration does two things. It creates a higher level of energy and dramatic conflict within the scene which therefore makes it more interesting and earns empathy. It gets empathy from the audience because they have frustrations and they tend to identify and so to understand and to care because of self-identification. I began to notice, in my reviews of recent years, that critics would say, "Lemmon again playing the put-upon guy who muddles through." This was totally unintentional on my part, but I realized that although I hopefully don't ever play characters the same there *is* one common characteristic: often the characters are frustrated.

A good example of this, from the directorial point of view, came in the introductory scene in *The Apartment*. Billy had to show that he had all these different people using the apartment, and he had them on the phone trying to juggle time. It was a long scene, about five pages of calling to change appointments. Hopefully, it would be amusing, but more than that it was necessary background to give the audience the plot. But Billy did a beautiful thing. He gave the guy a cold, and the scene worked because the poor son of a bitch had a temperature and a cold and was perfectly miserable and the audience knew how goddam lousy he felt and they loved the scene.

Another piece of Wilder's direction that I rebelled at, at first, but which made the scene, came in *Some Like It Hot*. (Honestly, I'll get back to it.) This is when Tony comes home and I've been out dancing with Joe E. Brown and I announce that I'm engaged and he says, "What the hell are you talking about?" and I say, "We're going to be married at Niagara Falls," and he says, "Why does a fellow want to marry a fellow for security, etc." Well, it's a great scene, but it was written straight, and when we came in to shoot it Billy handed me a pair of moochachas and said, "In between each line play them." I thought he was nuts—that he'd really blown his lid—that I'd be ruining the scene. Well, without the moochachas the audience would never have heard anything beyond "I'm engaged" and the whole thing would have lasted twenty seconds. This way the scene took about a minute and a half, and it did a second thing, perfectly legitimate. I was so happy and ebullient about the whole thing that I got up and started dancing around with the moochachas. The scene was great. Billy Wilder was great again. And that's *Some Like It Hot*.

N. Have any other roles involved similar bits of business, or an external-to-internal characterization?

LEMMON: Billy and I had a time with the old man in *Irma La Douce*. Remember, Billy writes his script after he has the cast, a great way to work if you can get away with it, and he has a good idea of what his actors can and cannot do. Still, there are things to work out.

Take the old man's accent—once, unconsciously, I lifted my upper lip and Billy liked that touch of phony exaggeration so I got some false teeth I could slip over my own and played the part that way. Then there was his posture—I worried over it and Billy said, "I think I see him as exaggeratedly straight, if anything tilted backward," and that did it. I stood back like that—like I had breasts and was showing them—and the outward behavior of the man took shape. Same with the cane and gloves.

I can't explain how and why these little things, silly little things, can set a character, but they do—whether you're doing *Hamlet* or a comedy role. But I am firmly of the belief that it is not only legitimate, but a matter of duty, for an actor *not* to try to be honest about how a character should basically be played because I don't think honesty has anything to do with the theater. (I thought so, when I was very young.) An actor is there for only one purpose : to perform in front of people that must be amused on the highest possible level. And by amusement I mean *Some Like It Hot* or *Hamlet* or *Othello*. That audience is there to be amused. If you can legitimately bend a character, if you can make him behave in a certain way, as long as it's logical that he *could* behave that way, and if that way is dramatically or comically more exciting than a standard behavior pattern, than I say bend that character. It's the actor's duty to find out the most exciting way a role should be played, then to play that role to the hilt. This could mean bits of business, like those we've discussed, it could be underplaying, it could be climbing up and down the walls, it could be chewing up the scenery, but if he doesn't give it hell, make his characterization as complete and compelling as possible, he isn't fulfilling his function as an actor.

N.   I don't want to head into the area of gossip, but since you did play with Marilyn Monroe in her greatest movie, what impressions of her did you come away with?

❧   LEMMON : It's very hard to answer. I know, during and after the film, that we got along very well—we were friends. Yet I never knew anything about her. I couldn't get close to her, yet I knew she was fond of me and I was fond of her. I think Marilyn probably mistrusted a lot of people. She had every reason to, as we know from the record of her life. I saw her several times after we finished the film—if I went to New York she and Arthur would meet me for dinner. (She almost never went out, so this was something.) But I still didn't know a damned thing about her. I could never really get close to her. She was ill during a lot of the filming, so as a result, during those interminable lengths of time when you're setting up or between shots, when the actors will sit around and bullshit, Marilyn would be alone or lying down. She felt lousy—she lost a baby during one part of the filming; she didn't know she was pregnant, then found out she was and lost the child. I think it was the second or third time it happened to her, unfortunately. She was also ill with——God knows what all.

Marilyn could be very ebullient and open when she was feeling well. She could be funny, a very funny girl, and she had a sense of humor. Her talent wasn't just a natural talent she didn't control. She wasn't just a personality who happened to have a marvelous odd-ball quality nobody else had. She knew damned well what she was doing.

Instinctively, I liked her. It was fascinating to work with her, and I had no preconceived idea of what she'd be like. I'd heard the rumors of how difficult it was to work with her—her habit of being late and all the retakes. Well, she was late very, very often, but it never really bugged me. And when we'd work, even though there were times when we did take after take, it didn't bug me because I was fascinated by it. She didn't do it out of temperament, playing the great female star, or calling attention to herself. I think she had an alarm clock inside, and if something wasn't going right for her it was the hell with whether the result would work or not, in someone else's opinion, she wouldn't finish it if it didn't feel right to her. She'd blow the take. I'm not saying she was correct all the time—it's very difficult to know when the result is right purely by how you happen to feel.

(Let me digress again. So often a director will say, "Cut, print!" and I know I do—all actors do—I'll say, "My God, Billy, you're not going to print that! I felt horrible, I wasn't really in it, I was aware of what I was saying." As far as I'm concerned if I'm aware of the dialogue I'm not in the scene—as I've said before, you don't pick all your words. Anyway, he'll say, "All right, do another one and we'll print them both." So you do another one that feels great and you'll print them both and chances are it'll come out that he was right—the first one was better.

In other words, it's difficult to know how well you've done

until you see the print, and it's difficult again if you're looking at yourself. It's a very difficult thing to be objective enough to be able to stand back at the same time you're performing and say, "This is good" or "This isn't good." You may feel you're not in a scene and the scene will be marvelous. Another time you'll feel great and the scene will be like masturbation—consumptive, total ego.)

Marilyn felt very strongly the opposite. If it didn't feel right for her it just wasn't going to be good, and I think she was one of those rare people who was right most of the time.

In general, Marilyn did some wonderful stuff. When her performances didn't work the whole picture wasn't too hot. She was cohesive and consistent, but if a scene didn't start out right for her—forget it. You'd stay there until it did feel right for her. This was one of the few indulgences she had, but it wasn't a purposeful indulgence (as we normally use the word) so much as something she felt deeply about.

N. Another world-in-a-nutshell question: Can you state your objectives as an actor?

LEMMON: For a long time I don't think I had a specific objective in mind—I'd wonder what the hell I was trying to accomplish but I could never state any objective beyond the fact that I wanted to act. I never thought beyond wanting to be a successful actor, a working actor. I never thought of being a star because I never thought of film. I guess I dreamed, like a kid dreaming of being a fireman or a policeman, of being one of the best stage actors in the world.

The only objective I have is to be the best actor I can possibly be, which means I'd like to be better than I am, now. I have great trepidations about it at times, and worry about it a great deal for reasons that never occurred to me when I was younger, but Christ! I can't let those get to me. There's a good deal of the child in most actors, I think. (This part will probably have no pertinence at all to the interview, but sometime it would be interesting to go into this with an actor who would really be honest about what is an actor, what makes an actor; I'm convinced that a great part of it all involves childishness and egotism we don't want to admit.) Basically, the more I grow up, I think that the childlike qualities inherent in many actors is just great. It's a shame that more people don't have it—that they can't daydream. They can't enjoy the real thing; they tell the boss off in front of the bathroom mirror or when they're on the freeway and it's all rather futile. But an actor can let it out, he can be somebody else and forget all his own frustrations. He can be a totally new character, and instead of that being a neurotic or unhealthy business it's beginning to dawn on me that it's healthy as hell, it's a great escape. I might very well be one of the people who happen to be an actor who is fortunate indeed to be working successfully at the trade. I haven't been analyzed, so I don't know a hell of a lot about myself, but I might very well be a neurotic mess if I was something else.

Yet acting isn't enough. If I don't play the piano every now and then I get a little stir-crazy. When I was a kid I used to bite my nails all the time, and the piano may be a more adult release of nerves and tension.

Sorry. I got sidetracked again.

Secretly, I would love to be called "the best actor." Who wouldn't? I think that desire is healthy—you should strive to be the best. One of the inherent problems of so-called success, however, is the definition, the ambiguity of terms. A man with five million dollars blows his brains out and they say, "Successful man kills himself." He wasn't a success—the poor bastard was a failure. The success was somebody else's opinion. The bloody fool was miserable.

At any rate, I want to be better than I am. I want to be called "a fine actor" as often as possible. I want to realize as much as I can of the potential I've got—which I think is big. If I don't walk away from things, if I keep getting good parts, and if I stretch to reach those parts, I'll continue to grow.

I said "stretch." If I look at a script, and I know precisely how to play a part, the hell with it. Why do it? If I don't know how to play the part, but respect the role and am intrigued by it, chances are it's a role I should do. A few minutes ago I mentioned the fact that success breeds problems. The worst one is this: The more successful you become the less you can do. I never realized this before. I just turned forty and I'm doing two pictures a year. Not too long ago, in a fairly short stretch, I did over 400 TV shows. I was growing by leaps and bounds and learning. Now, in England an actor is blessed by a setup which combines our star system with good common sense and great respect for acting, directing, and theater in general. You can play all kinds of parts without causing a hullabaloo. Here you can't. If I find a little gem, for example, that I'd love to do, but my role isn't the big one, I can't do it. Olivier can. Our public is as attuned as the industry is, and the minute I showed up in a character part they'd wonder what the hell happened to Lemmon, he must be slipping. It just isn't worth it.

The point I'm making is that by virtue of good fortune and hard work I'm a star, but I have to be more and more choosy. I was fortunate enough to get marvelous parts in pictures like *Some Like It Hot, The Apartment* and *Wine and Roses* to mention three in a row that were superb.

Naturally, you want to uphold that level and you start looking around for comparable parts and you don't find them, so you do a couple of other pictures in a row that aren't as good and people again wonder what the hell happened? What is Lemmon doing junk like that for?

Well, if you hadn't had those three great parts in a row they wouldn't call that "junk." They're just average pictures. You can't hope, really, to get two great parts a year, or even two in ten years, but you've got a problem that ties right up to the question of how good an actor you can become.

Basically an actor is more interpretive than he is creative. You have to work with the tools that are given you—the improvisations I talked about before are important, but the role has to be a good one to begin with. You are dependent upon the basic tools of the trade, the writing and the direction. Seldom will you see a memorable performance in a bad picture that's badly directed.

The trouble is, you can't get an *Apartment* or *Some Like It Hot* by calling your agent on the phone and ordering one or the other. So the problem with success is that you can't do just anything—and it's frustrating to have commitments to make pictures without having the right scripts for the kind of movies you really want to make. Right now, in two weeks of solid reading, I haven't found a damned thing that even remotely interests me. The kind of callouses I'm growing now have no relationship to my growth as an actor, and that's disturbing. Because you've got to grow, but in order to grow you've got to have the right parts.

N.   What is your idea of the right part? We've talked about some of your films, but what do you look for in a role?

❦   LEMMON : The answer has to be general.

To begin with, let me clear up one thing. I read everything and anything that comes along because I'm not looking for a comedy at one given time or a drama at another. Right now I'd like to find a drama because I've done four or five comedies in a row—I'd love to find the sort of thing that broke the routine when *Wine and Roses* came along. It was a great change of pace (a selfish way to look at it). If I said that I respect the writing, and the people involved in the project, and if I'm reading the script and am held by the story and by the character, and do not know how to play it, then I'm pretty well convinced that it is a good part.

When I say "don't know how to play it" that is 100 percent right. I don't think that any actor knows how to play a really good part. If he says he can read a script and grab the phone and say, "That's the part for me! I know this fellow, I can play him!" I say—baloney. He may want to play him, but if the part is really well-written he doesn't know how to play him. Oddly enough, the better a part is written the less clear it is. You might think that a very good writer would not include generalities and vagueness in his writing, that it would be explicit and clear and the character totally apparent, but that isn't true. It adds up to this : None of us are interested in people who are dull, routine, obvious and apparent. I've never met anybody interesting who was apparent. If you speak to someone for two minutes and know what kind of person he is, he's the dullest—he'll bore the bejesus out of you. He's a prototype. Now, this same thing applies to acting. Ninety percent of the acting we see isn't very interesting because a character-chewer is being created, not a character. The actor has the shell but he hasn't crawled into it. If there's depth and body to the character it's another story—and it's worth staying around for.

You know, a good psychoanalyst can take four years, perhaps, to get to the root of a problem in a patient he could be seeing three or four times a week. In many respects acting and analysis are similar. Both are the study of behavior in one human being at a time. Both are getting to the "why" of a character's actions and motivations. And once you know why, as an actor, you let the audience know what you've found out. Acting is the last step; 80 percent is analysis.

In other words, when you look at a good script you see an acre between each line. When you read it, if you're aware of that acre, there's something good—and you can't just pick the first thing that comes into your mind. You don't really know the character but you've got to get to know him. And it's a challenge, a big one.

Frankly, when I read *Wine and Roses* I was afraid of it. It's easy to protect yourself at times, to back away saying, "No, it isn't my cup of tea," when you're afraid, when you know you might fail in it. But you should do it, not back away, because only by doing it can you become a better actor. I was afraid of *Some Like It Hot* in some respects, too, but that was part of the reason why I said, "Yes, I'll do it." If I was afraid of it, and passed up the challenge, I'd be a complete fake, a charlatan, a living lie to everything I've said in this interview. I might fail, but screw it—I'd also learn a hell of a lot.

All these things add up to what makes me want to do a part. I don't mean that I'm afraid of every part I play (I've felt perfectly safe with lots of them) but if I *am* afraid of it there's an extra temptation to play it. But mainly if I'm excited and titillated by the part itself, and don't know how to play it, if it isn't routine, one of five thousand slight variations, then I'm for it.

Look at the parts I've had, though, and you see how very lucky I've been and how hard it is to play can-you-top-this when most actors don't collect a *Mr. Roberts, Some Like It Hot, Days of Wine and Roses, Irma La Douce, How to Murder Your*

Wife and *The Great Race* in a lifetime. Take just *The Great Race*—if that isn't a great part it's nobody's fault but mine; it's beautifully written. I come out of six or seven months of work with three parts. As Professor Fate I'm the arch-villain of all time, the "corner-you-in-the-roundhouse-Nellie" takeoff. Then I'm the fop Prince from Europe confronting and playing scenes with the professor. Then I'm the first guy realizing the look-alike and imitating the Prince. This has got to be an actor's field day.

So now I sit and start to read scripts and nothing interests me, so I'll probably have to cool it for a couple of months and stop looking for great parts. My luck has been so fantastically great I probably deserve to sit it out for a bit.

N. The final question—more toward the theoretical realm. What advice could you give to the assumedly talented young person seeking an acting career?

❧ LEMMON : I always feel lousy when I get letters, or bump into kids, asking for advice. Now and then someone will even say, "Oh, won't you help me get a job?" which is the most embarrassing thing in the world.

Unfortunately all young people—and we'll assume that we're talking about the talented ones—assume that you're supposed to give them a break, give them a job; that they don't have to learn a craft. This is ignorance, of course, and the only sound advice starts off, "Learn . . . get experience. . . ."

As we touched on earlier it was much easier when I was younger to learn, to get experience. The opportunities which were afforded me are now available to nobody except working stars and good supporting players. Summer stock is big business with names. It didn't used to be. Television is all names or all series where they're trying to build a name. The young actor has a hell of a time finding ways to get experience, paid experience or even semi-professional experience, and the best he can get is in schools and colleges. Or he might get into a group or a class, then try like hell to get small parts in some kind of professional company.

At any rate he's got to get the experience somewhere, but

there is one thing I feel is terribly important—that has helped me—and that is an education, preferably college. If there is any indecision in any would-be actor's mind about whether he should or should not get a college education, under the mis-guided belief that a college education would be a waste of time and that he'd be better off getting experience in the profession, I think he should get rid of the indecision and go to school.

College is bound to broaden his scope of knowledge, and his horizons, pique his curiosity, make him better-equipped to live in society, and certainly know more about people by being exposed to a variety of intellectual levels. The more he knows about people the better an actor he'll make. The more he knows generally, the more he's aware of, the more he's able to think and analyze, the better an actor he'll make. He's going to get a lot more out of college than from walking around looking for a job. College can't help but contribute, but with things as they are now, for actors, the walking may only give him sore feet.

End of sermon.

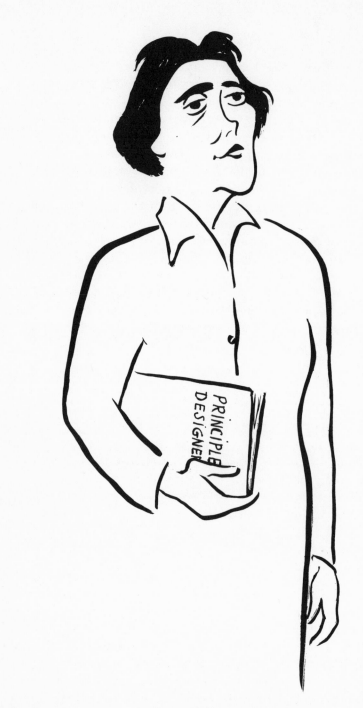

"I'm happy to see everything I design on the stage—that means it isn't taking up storage space."

TANYA MOISEIWITSCH

In addition to the inspired interpretation and the skilled performances that have distinguished each production by the Tyrone Guthrie Theatre in Minneapolis, one is consistently struck by the physical perfection of settings and costumes. This is theater in the grand style—dazzling, vivid, a spectacle for the eye as well as a feast for intellect and emotion. The artistic direction of Sir Tyrone Guthrie, Douglas Campbell, and Edward Payson Call, guide these achievements in some measure. Yet major credit for the visual impact unfolded play by play, scene by scene, character by character, must be given Tanya Moiseiwitsch, Principal Designer of the Guthrie Theatre.

MOISEIWITSCH: I was born and reared in London, and went to various schools. I didn't work very hard at the subjects I didn't like and worked terribly hard at the ones I did like—all of which seem now to have been connected, in various ways, with the theater. History and literature, drawing and painting, poetry—all the jolly subjects. I didn't work hard at mathematics, and now I'm sorry. I just thought I couldn't understand the mystery of numbers. I still don't, and it's a great loss. I had no idea of how it connected up with this job, and when it comes to measuring things I have no end of trouble.

Languages I didn't try, and I'm sorry about that, too. I'm half Russian, and apparently all Russians can speak at least five languages but I can't speak two and one half. I don't know Russian at all—this means I can't read Chekhov in the original, and we're working, now, with a new translation of *The Cherry Orchard* which I'm sure is great, but I'd rather like to prove one or two things for myself and I can't. I think I could learn Italian much easier than any other language. I lived there for at least six weeks, and I was beginning to laugh at jokes. Then I left and I've forgotten every word. Perhaps I lack a flair for languages.

Math and music are supposed to go together, but contrary to my neglect of math I studied music quite hard. I don't know much about theory, but I listen a lot, and it comes in useful in my work. Yet I don't think one should study only what is going to be useful, and I tell others this when they ask for advice. But no one should have *my* gaps in education.

Well, various schools taught me what they could, and I left at sixteen to go to art school for a three-year course. I completed only two. But I don't regret what happened that third year, for it was spent at the Old Vic Theatre as a student. It seemed to me that if I didn't grasp the chance of going at a time when there was a vacancy I would never get there. This may not have been true, but I'm glad I went because that was the year Tyrone Guthrie took over the Old Vic, so I saw him work at the start of that part of his career and at the absolute beginning of mine.

I was not trusted then, of course, to do anything but stir paint and carry buckets about and get under everyone else's feet. But I saw a lot that went on in the way of the development of the Old Vic, which at that time was a threefold operation—drama, opera and ballet. The paint shop was kept busy working for all three, so it was a very full year.

After this I got a job as an apprentice. This means that you are told precisely what to do by a designer who has far too much to do. In short, you paint the scenery. I was fairly well trained for this but was rather startled to learn that my first job would be to make shoes. It was terrible. It was like mathematics.

I knew nothing about making shoes, but I soon found out, because if the actors came in a rush to try them on and they weren't ready your face was very red. This was at the Westminster Theater in London, then a repertory that included classical and modern, comedies and thrillers, every kind of play you could imagine, all in a very short space of time. Then I was whisked off to the Abbey Theatre in Dublin as a designer—quite a shock. Hugh Hunt, the director, wanted a designer he felt he could instruct. He really wanted to do the designing himself, but he wanted someone to carry out his work for him. This was ideal for me because I was so inexperienced I would *have* to be told what to do. After three years I was doing a great deal on my own, but never totally on my own because I very strongly believe that a designer works with the director, and that he tells you far more than you ever tell him. He has to direct you as well as the actors. There's give and take, of course, because everyone has an idea to throw in, but to this day I feel I work for the director.

I slogged along for the next ten years, very pleasantly in weekly repertory, a play a week, designing and painting. Fortunately I had help—the actual painting is such a stint that you get so tired you can't think, and the director does want you to think a bit. As this was during the war there wasn't a great deal we could do with costumes—there was little money to spend, and curtain materials were all we could get without coupons, so within these limitations I learned the invaluable discipline of economy.

Then Guthrie invited me to go to Liverpool as a designer. They already had one, but she was becoming quite exhausted from the load of work, so with two of us it turned out that we only had to design one play every six weeks. This was my idea of heaven after doing one a week. Then Guthrie pointed out that next I'd want six months, and he was absolutely right. Six weeks was never enough. Eventually I got six months to prepare a show, a musical for C. B. Cochran in London, and six months wasn't too much. However, it was a marvelous experience. He took an active interest in every single detail. Even the knives and forks that were going to be used in the restaurant scene and to be exactly right—France, 1870, neither more nor less. And there seemed no end of new material for costumes. This hadn't happened to me before; working at the Old Vic one realized that the first part of a designing job was to go into the wardrobe and see how many of the existing costumes you could use as they were or how they could be "revised," so to speak, with the skirt taken off and put around the top, or the sleeves taken out and put into another costume. But everything with that musical was brand, spanking new, and it went to my head. It was a lovely show, too; it ran for a year and gave a lot of happiness.

It's the Old Vic I remember most. Lilian Baylis was wonderfully kind to me; she was a friend I thought I could turn to if I was in trouble. We were told that there was no money for a heater in the paint shop; quite often the paint froze before we could use it, and someone said to me, "I think you'd better ask Miss Baylis for a heater." I suppose they had all tried, and because I was new I might as well take a whack at it, so the first opportunity I had I brightly said, "It's very cold in the paint shop, Miss Baylis," and she said, "Well, you'd better jump up and down to keep warm."

I was never asked to ask for anything again.

Years went by. I worked in London most of the time; it was home. But then I heard from Guthrie about a new idea that was springing up and he was going to do it and would I like to go, too. It was a new theater—still just a hole in the ground, and I would design the stage for it, and the costumes for the productions, and it would be in Stratford, Canada. I said, "Yes"—and though this is all quite recent I can't seem to remember a time when I wasn't there. This was in 1953, and when we got there the theater was half-built, and I felt alarmed at what I'd agreed to. I have never been particularly timorous about tackling anything, but *that* was a challenge. But it seemed to go very well; in fact it developed beautifully and I'm more than pleased to have had something to do with it that very first year, when it was all touch and go.

Then, again with Guthrie, I helped get up a play in Israel, also rather speedily. He had been there before, but I never had, so I found it a glorious adventure. Everything took twice as long because it had to be translated as you went along. I'd like to have stayed there much longer. Another traveling job I adored was with the Teatro Piccolo in Milan, and with my colossal language deficiency this was another translating job. It was Chekhov, and I think they thought I knew Russian and had been with the Moscow Arts Theatre. I felt like a terrible fraud, but I did tell them I hadn't. I had to work in centimeters which isn't easy (especially for me) and a lot of translating went on and I worked like a savage and loved every minute of it. They're an incredibly good company, and wonderful crafts-men.

And now I'm here in Minneapolis.

I knew, when I was asked to come in as a consultant on the stage design, and as the designer of the costumes, that there would be more scenic elements here than we had in Stratford. We thought it would be desirable to have more individuality for each production rather than a basic stage—in Canada there's a set which is upstairs and downstairs and that's it, because it was planned only for Shakespeare plays and was made permanent. (In Stratford they are trying to get away from a total Shake-speare diet, and this year they're doing *The Cherry Orchard*. I'm not designing it, but their director said to me, "Now, where am I to put the bookcase?" a very important scenic element. When the theater was built the permanent set was never dreamt of as being a hazard, and I could only say, "I don't know, I have my own problems." But I'll find out, when I go to Strat-ford next week, where they put that bloody bookcase.)

Here there was more flexibility at the start because this theater was planned as a repertory for a variety of classical plays, not just the Shakespearean.

N.   Did you design this stage?

        MOISEIWITSCH : It was, as I said, a consultancy, which meant that the theater was already rather thoroughly planned—it was down on paper, and there was space left on the paper for the stage. It was actually a collaboration with Guthrie, and emerged from his experiences in Edinburgh and Strat-ford. Lack of space is always our worst enemy.

N. You seem to have a great deal of space here.

🌺 MOISEIWITSCH: Oh, you think so? That's fine. That's what you're supposed to think. You're not supposed to know that we're all standing on each other's heads at the back. Yet I suppose if you had limitless space, if you worked from here to St. Paul, you'd still complain about not having enough space. I think we're greedy.

There are limits put on the amount we can build, and that's just as well, because no one will ever be able to get grandiose Cecil B. DeMille ideas here. Storage space is a great problem, and after three years we're very pinched for storage.

N. What is the breakdown of your responsibilities as Principal Designer?

🌺 MOISEIWITSCH: I really don't know what the title "Principal Designer" means. Perhaps, because I'm older than anyone else, and I've been here longer, I ought to keep a motherly eye on the younger persons coming in, the students. (We don't have apprentices.)

Actually, the job is completely collaborative and cooperative, and I don't think the word "principal" means that much. There's a feeling of responsibility, certainly—and I am responsible for the way the stage is shaped, the mechanics of it. If that had to be altered for another production I would be consulted, but I don't really feel that I'm in a position to say, "No, I don't think that can be done." I think everything can be done, can be experimented with, as long as there is money and time. As far as costumes—I design them for the plays I'm assigned to do. So far they've all been plays I've wanted terribly to do, and for the most part they're plays I haven't done before, so I've been proud and pleased to accept each assignment. The risk of working on something you've done before is great. It should be easier, because you've done the prep, but it doesn't work out that way. You usually feel that you mustn't repeat what you've done before, and you wander far afield to find something new just for its being new. On the other hand it may have been a good idea you had before, and you'll rack your brain to put this good idea in again. That can be exhausting.

Now, I've done *The Cherry Orchard* twice before, but never with Guthrie, so it's like doing it a first time. But you have all that feeling of background from studying that particular play and that particular period, and you know some of the answers but you don't know them all.

N.   Is it possible to define your objectives? Or your principles?

MOISEIWITSCH: Not without sounding a bit pompous. You see, one's pleasure is in serving, in being of service, of being useful and contributing. In the course of this you get something in return—the pleasure, if all goes well, of having participated in a general effort toward something which is worth doing.

It is this participation, this collaboration, this working with others, from the director through the actors, the seamstresses and cutters, everyone, to produce something with energy, vitality, new life.

N.   How do the workshops at the Guthrie Theatre function?

MOISEIWITSCH: The word "workshop" sounds terribly mundane. It isn't like that at all. I don't think you could point to anyone here and say, "That man is not a craftsman in his field." Each person brings something specific, some training or experience of value. Even the youngest ones, who are learning, soon find that they have a special talent for something, even if it's the making of buttonholes.

To speak less generally. In real life, if you wanted a bookcase made, you would go to a cabinetmaker. Here we'll find a carpenter who has the taste and the relish for the wood, the workmanship, the craftsmanship, and he'll work from your specifications but he'll add something of his own that you didn't dream of. And when it comes alive it's beautiful and interesting and precisely right. (I mention the bookcase because it's a big feature in *The Cherry Orchard*. You could go and buy one, of course, but it would have to look 100 years old in the early

1900's and that makes it an antique that will cost the world. Also, for this stage, where it is going to be seen from three sides of the theater at once, it is quite a mathematical problem which Guthrie himself worked out. I've never seen such a lovely job, and it's one of many. And when the play is through running it seems to me that bookcase should (if they can find the space for it) become a library. I've already got six books on design which have been donated to the theater, and we don't have a shelf to put them on.)

Again, to the actual work. Some of the things we need we find in Salvation Army shops. No artistry in that. You just, with luck, pick up something that will do. But for the most part, things are made here. And discovering all sorts of new plastics and synthetics . . . it's astonishing. I'm fooled half the time trying to tell the real from the synthetic. Last year, for instance, nobody in this building knew how to make armor satisfactorily. This year they've got some of the best armor I've seen on any stage in *Richard III*. They're using fiber glass, and a great deal of ingenuity and hard work, and it's a pleasure to behold.

Now, I can't do these things myself, and I'm impressed when other people can. But you can't learn and develop all these things in a workshop straight off. It is a place of development. You find out what's needed, then someone discovers how to do it and do it well. (Nobody here will stand for something only halfway good.) I can't go on much further about the workshop because it's so detailed and technical that I don't even know half of what goes on. I only know the result.

Take the fitting of costumes. The first fitting can be quite daunting unless you know your cutter, whose brain must work toward the same goal you have, though possibly by a different route. And the fittings, when the costumes begin to come together, are marvelous. You begin to see what it's all about because the actor is taking a hand in it, just by being alive and in the costume. The sketches are only the very early stages of what we're planning, but you have to have them or the actor and the director, the management and the tailor wouldn't have the faintest idea of what you're after.

N. What are the differences, or problems, distinguishing this stage from the more conventional proscenium stage?

MOISEIWITSCH: Speaking as a costume designer I would say that the problems are much the same, only the workmanship has to be that much more finished—bolder, perhaps. Maybe not so inhibited in length.

Say that you want someone to wear a train. On the open stage, where there is more space, and the actor provides his own background, a longer train will make a bigger and better picture. If the actor can manage it well, then it's a satisfactory idea. Coming nearer to the contemporary, in plays like *The Cherry Orchard* and *The Three Sisters*, and the audience has three walls to look through instead of one, it's a case of furnishing a room (not realistically) to make it suggest a real environment. The director has a big hand in it—he places the furniture in such a way that it suggests realistic movements, but if you really analyzed it you'd discover that it's as stagy as all get-out. And when we clear the stage as much as possible for the outdoor scene it became more illusionary than I expected because we played about with light. Shadows coming through the leaves of trees, as it were, which is as near to an illusionary effect as I've been allowed in this theater. I'm enjoying every minute of it—the actors coming and going in the light.

I don't think you can do this sort of thing in Shakespeare. It is essential to see and know who's speaking, and to keep track of the people.

N. Wait until you do *A Midsummer Night's Dream*.

MOISEIWITSCH: Wouldn't that be an adventure. But frankly, I have no idea of how different and how much more difficult it is to stage a play here rather than on a proscenium. Every play has certain problems to overcome, and you can regard them either as difficulties or as challenges. If you call them difficulties I think it would all end in despair, and one wouldn't want to do the play at all. So I'll try to fool myself and say they're just the expected structure and challenges which have to be dealt with.

N.   You've mentioned, frequently, the cooperative effort—

❧   MOISEIWITSCH : Yes. Generally, no one in the theater is working for himself or in a lonely, solitary position. I suppose that, in a way, someone who does monologues might think of himself as a solitary figure, but even he has contributions from the lighting department, and presumably he has to have some collaboration from the audience. He doesn't just speak to an empty theater.

It's all collaboration with the audience, of course, but before you meet the audience it's a collaboration amongst directors, actors, everyone who is here—even the management, who seem to live in another building. If you're alone on one side of the wall, and they're on the other, this theater wouldn't work. As it is we have a tremendous feeling of collaboration on all sides, from all departments. And we are in departments, or boxes, but with the doors open, held specifically open for the interchange of ideas. This doesn't mean it's a ragged sort of picnic, where everyone tosses in his bit without form. There is a definite form to everything one does, all fitting into the play and the director's view of the play.

"It's as though life begins and ends when you have your horn in your mouth."

GERRY MULLIGAN

Naming one's favorite jazz instrumentalist inevitably involves an ultimate sense of personal choice. For about fifteen years Gerry Mulligan has pleased me more than any other performer who comes to mind. He has style, dignity, intelligence, taste—an inventive and pleasingly cool approach to jazz as a medium. Any song he takes on becomes a case in point. At a time when it seems that we are not developing instrumental stylists it may well be that young Mr. Mulligan is really one of the last of the old-timers.

This is a very sad prospect. Electronic blather will never truly replace music.

MULLIGAN: I was born in New York in 1927. My father was an industrial engineer, and when I was one year old he became an executive in a company that manufactured power shovels and road rollers, so he took the family to Marion, Ohio, where I did a stretch from one to ten. But I liked Ohio.

After that I lived in a different town each year because his industrial engineering jobs kept him on the move, so I have as my home town Marion, Ohio; New York; Franklinville, New Jersey; Lockport, New York; Chicago; Kalamazoo; Ypsilanti; Detroit; Reading, Pennsylvania; Port Huron, Michigan; and

Philadelphia. As soon as I was old enough I left home and went on the road as a musician.

I started playing when I was in high school. Actually, I was interested in music long before then, but my family was not musically inclined so I can't say there was a great deal of encouragement. But I started taking lessons on the clarinet, then the saxophone, and when I was in high school I started working club dates around town (this was in Reading). I organized my own band—I had to, because there really was no music in the school I was attending, and I had to have some outlet. I wonder . . . if there'd been a school band and all that . . . if my career might not have been entirely different. As it was I became a bandleader while I was still in high school, and when it looked as though I had to go into the Army in 1945 I said, "I don't want to finish school. I want to go out and play with the band." As it turned out I didn't go into the Army because the whole idea of being shot at and shooting at someone frightened me so much that by the time I took the physical I was a trembling mass of fear. But to make a long story short I quit school and went on the road with a band and that's where I've been ever since.

I started as an arranger. My first job on the road was with Tommy Tucker's band. He had a very good band, actually. People think of the commercial bands as nothings, but there were very good musicians in his band and they put on a good show. I learned a great deal from them—and from Tommy.

At the time I was writing for the band there were two other men writing who were very fine musicians. One fellow named Ben Homer had written a few fine things—he was the fellow who wrote "The Mexican Hat Dance" for Les Brown. He'd done some even better things, including a couple of numbers for Tommy, so I couldn't help learning from simply being exposed to first-rate writers. So when people think of a band like that as being nothing but commercial mickey mouse they're wrong. It was very musical, and I was still a kid, wide open to learning and being influenced.

I hadn't been with the band too long when we settled down to a six or eight week stay in Chicago at the Stevens Hotel (now the Conrad Hilton). Every day I'd go around to the downtown theaters—the State-Lake and Chicago and Downtown—to catch the great bands that came through town. I heard Earl Hines and Billy Eckstine and Dizzy Gillespie—bands that were filled with great musicians—and my work for Tommy reflected more and more of what I heard from these other bands, and things got to the point where I really wasn't doing any good for the band at all—I was writing for myself. My contract with Tommy called for three ballad or two jump arrangements per week for $100. I suppose I was writing under scale, but I was on salary, and that made up for it. I lived up to that contract, which was remarkable considering that I was going on youthful energy and brass more than anything. (I could never hope to achieve an output like that, now.) But Tommy had told me that if I felt I'd like to leave to work in my own style I could, so when I realized that I wasn't doing Tommy any good anymore I took off.

I went back to Philadelphia—that was when Elliot Lawrence (now conducting the *Golden Boy* show) had taken over the studio orchestra at WCAU in Philadelphia, and I started to write for him. I wrote for his band for the better part of a year, and then I went on the road with Gene Krupa—as an arranger— when he had a big band.

Several times, when I was on the road with Krupa, I became a trouble-shooter for the band. You know, if there was a saxophone player missing I'd fill in . So when I left the band I came to New York because now I knew I wanted to play. I played a lot around here—jam sessions with contemporaries, friends. We chipped in our spare quarters and hired studios just to play. I still supported myself writing, but I wanted to play, and through the people I met I got involved in various projects. Gil Evans, Miles Davis, John Lewis, and some other very fine jazz musicians were around town, and we organized a nine-piece band which was essentially a rehearsal band, but we tried to come up with the most ideal instrumentations we could, giving maximum latitude to the writer. Sort of a one-of-each instrumentation—one trumpet, one trombone, one French horn, one tuba, one alto saxophone, one baritone saxophone—and it was inspiring to all of us. We put a great deal of energy into it and it was good instrumentation and it had a great deal of effect on orchestration. In fact, in all aspects of American music I hear echoes of what we did—in movie scores, television commercials, backgrounds for singers on records. All sorts of applications that never occurred to us. I'm afraid none of us had any sense about the money-making aspects of music.

After this I organized my own small band to work night clubs. We started off in New York, but things got so bad around here I hitch-hiked out to the Coast and stayed out there for a couple years and had a tremendous success. After I was out there for about a year I organized a quartet that was such a popular thing it enabled me to live like a human being—I didn't have to scrounge from one quarter to the next, one club date to the next. (This is what Sammy Davis called "paying your dues"—after you pay your dues and you have some return you feel as though you've earned it, but even after you've earned it you can't stop. You can't just sit back and enjoy the fruits of success. What you did ten years ago or ten minutes ago doesn't matter, because you have to live today and you have to play tomorrow. But a lot of us, even after we've paid our hard dues, and enjoyed some kind of success, have to keep on paying some kind of dues. This may be some sort of masochistic thing that I really don't understand in psychiatric terms, but I think it's bigger than that. I think that when you're involved in a creative art you have to keep putting something back—you can't just take from it and reach a point where it's easy for you. There are a lot of things now I can do with my left hand, so to speak, but I can't let myself do just those things.)

N.   What are your aims now, as far as career is concerned?

🌺   MULLIGAN: More than anything I want to write a Broadway show. You see, over a long period of time I've been finding out that what I really want to do is be a songwriter. I don't know if this is the *only* thing I want to do—I've gone through so many cycles of interest—orchestration, being a saxophone soloist, having a jazz band—but right now I'm at a point where the thing I really want to do is write songs. I've written a lot of them, and I wrote one show that was never produced. Maybe it will be, someday.

I love the theater. In a way I grew up in the theater—when I started playing in bands we used to work theaters all the time, and the vaudevillians who worked on the shows became good friends. I was closer to them than I was to the musicians. I felt more at home with them. So it's the whole attitude of theater that appeals to me—probably based on the enthusiasm for life that the vaudevillians had and the musicians didn't have.

The musicians were always complaining. They'd play the music, but when they weren't playing they were complaining and finding fault. The vaudevillians would come in on two-a-day and split weeks and work like hell but they'd make the dressing room look like home. They liked me and I liked them—we sort of understood each other.

You know, whatever you do there must be some kind of a way of life involved. The attitude these vaudevillians had involved an approach to life even at a time when their art was dying. They felt that every day you get up you must have an attitude toward that day. If it's a negative attitude the day is shot, and you undo yourself. You can't live with a negative attitude. In a way this sort of pushed me in the direction I'm going now, because I love the theater and the attitude people in theater have. I'm a latecomer to the theater, and the interest came about through my life in music, but through playing and writing I've learned a lot about theater. I still don't know precisely what I'll do—it's something I have to figure out.

N.　　　　How do you feel about popular music today? In terms of, say, the type of hit song produced now as contrasted with the hits of previous decades?

❧　　　　MULLIGAN: In a way America's popular music today is healthier than it was twenty years ago. It's more rhythmic, and I feel that we need the rhythmic outlet.

The music—the popular music—played twenty and thirty years ago was really quite unrhythmic. The tempos everyone wanted were slow, the songs were sentimental. Even before the war years, when the rage for overly sentimental music was understandable, we had this rigid, slow, dragging music. What is happening today has eliminated all of the intellectual from music. In other words, they've taken the beat, the rhythm, and they've finally learned the blues.

Now, this sounds like an incongruous statement, but American white people really didn't know the blues. Now they know them. Actually, we're talking about two different things at once. First, what popular music means to a nation as an outlet, and what it means to the musician in terms of taste. In terms of *my* taste, I think it's abominable. I can't stand these goddam loud guitars and electric basses. I can't understand the need for loud music blasting in your ears. It's terrible. But on the other hand, what the music means in terms of social significance, is another whole subject.

N.   Why do you think that American white people finally did learn the blues?

❧   MULLIGAN: I think it was helped through the integration fight, or vice versa. I think the day that blues became absorbed in our popular music was the day integration took place. There'll be marches and court fights and things like that, but the basic fight is won.

Now, when I say "blues" I mean the whole range of blues music—gutbucket, lowdown, refined. The point is, there's a freedom of expression in the blues that isn't necessarily a matter of crying—it's also shouting for joy. The blues is important. It's the basis of our American music, our whole idiom of music. Actually, jazz, just in my time, the past fifteen to twenty years, came from being the music of pariahs to being the diplomatic front for our country. This is because it is the voice for our country.

You can't even talk about jazz in terms that confine it to being one thing. It's not one thing. Jazz is the potential of individual expression, and the potential is great but our tradition is slim. Fellows my age—my contemporaries—are hanging onto that tradition because we love jazz, and we hope that musicians of oncoming generations will have some kind of feeling for it. I'm thinking, now, of some very good friends—men who happen to be very good jazz musicians, men who knew many of the guys who were really important in jazz—and their feeling is that jazz as we have known it and loved it is dead, or will die when we're gone, because the oncoming generations don't seem to have that veneration for what's gone before. What we were doing was deeply involved with developing a tradition. And there *must* be a tradition. Innovation is all well and good, but what lives is innovation based on tradition, and our jazz tradition is young and vulnerable. It can develop or it can die.

I'm talking jazz, specifically, but take a look at theater. That is something else, but in a way the theater in America is similar to the state of musicians' jazz. I heard you talking to Sammy Davis about Richard Burton's need to work a few more years in repertory. You're talking about a man who already has technique as an actor, the ability to make things come alive around him, the technical ability to project and command. Not only by virtue of technique but in terms of personal magnetism. And when you talk about repertory you're referring to a wonderful tradition of theater.

We don't have a tradition like that—not in our theater. You can't name five American actors who can stack up with the British actors in ability to portray and command many different parts. In the first place, we don't have any repertory to speak of. We have schools and attitudes that are so preoccupied with portraying inner feelings that they don't learn anything about technique. Watch some of the American actors do Shakespeare. It's embarrassing. So your criticism of Burton applies to Burton in England as a British actor on the stage.

Bring him to our country and try to apply that criticism—he simply racks all of our actors up when he's on Broadway. Now, maybe we are trying to build a tradition here. But must it be a tradition based on Brando's part in *Streetcar?*

As of now, our greatest contribution to theater is totally within the realm of musical theater. And I can't use all the fingers on one hand to count the men who are really first-rate in the musical theater of today. The man who can sing, project a song, and has the magnetism to be believable or commanding.

(We have more women than men, and I suppose that's true of our dramatic non-musical theater as well.)

But we don't have a tradition and it doesn't really look as though we're going to get one. Our writers seem to have no intention of giving us American characters of any depth or breadth. Take Shakespeare—he runs the gamut of possibilities of what a man can be at all ages. All the American characters on the stage are little boys who are afraid of their mothers, their wives, their sex, or the dark.

To develop a tradition we've got to portray our society. And the theater overlooks the fact that there are men in our society, and a majority at that, who are never really portrayed on the stage. The man who takes care of business, and the good man, simply aren't interesting to our playwrights. And as this goes on, and we avoid developing a tradition,. our actors get into deeper trouble.

Back to jazz (finally)—I'm afraid that the jazz traditions of my own generation are going to die out with us. There's a certain conceit in what I'm saying—and this may be a bit misleading—because jazz being what it is, encompassing the total gamut of human expression—the next generation could very well make it into something all their own. Fine. But now you're dealing with what jazz offers as an outlet, not what jazz is as a tradition.

I'm very concerned with what the men did before me. I love what they did. There were a lot of talented men, men of vision inside their own sphere and some 'way outside their sphere. This is what jazz offered these men—a place to portray their own vision. Well, even though succeeding generations ignore their tradition they can still use their means to portray their own vision. You can't take it away from them and you also can't say it isn't jazz. And what a man does in his twenties is apt to be quite different from what he does in his fifties—when a man is twenty he has no concept of being fifty, so the new cats can grow and change a whole lot. But right now this youth cult (and that's another whole subject) makes it seem that you're over the hill when you reach twenty-five. Maybe we need some of the Oriental veneration-of-ancestors.

There is one healthy note amidst the abominable taste the public shows in popular music. We've had some really marvelous talents write songs for us—Gershwin, Kern, Cole Porter— and they've enjoyed the fruits of their success. In their day they dealt with sophisticated audiences and their shows played to 2,000 people each night. By and large these shows were reviews—the songs could be lifted out of context and become very popular completely disassociated with the play.

Today's musical theater has terrible problems, the worst being outrageous production costs. Because costs are so high better songs should be written; by and large the songs are terrible. Most songwriters are trying to write two ways at once—for the popular audience and for the needs of the theater. But a great thing has happened with the few writers who are turning out good songs that are primarily written to knit tightly into the framework of the play, and it looks as though we've struck a brand new musical idiom—a sort of neo-Broadway opera, where the songs emphatically relate to the plot or the character.

West Side Story is a case in point. This was a combination of all elements of good theater, each element presented at its best by a man with talent and character. There really aren't too many first-rate talents in the theater, but they certainly got together on that show.

N.   To get back to you—what are your plans and ambitions from this point on?

❦   MULLIGAN : I want to keep on producing, of course. I love the theater—I want to be involved with the theater in any way I can. I want to write musicals and I want to direct.

I think I've learned a lot about direction. I've been around a lot of shows when they were being put together, I've seen a great many movies made, and I learn by observing. That's how I learned to write music and to play music.

As a matter of fact I have a feeling that I'll be a good director. Direction in itself should combine the qualities and experiences the director brings from the entire fabric of his life. You have to take care of business, and do your homework, and you must know what you're doing. You must know and tell everybody

everything. No confusion. This sounds simple, but it isn't—
there's often a terrible amount of confusion because nobody
took care of business. And you can't have people in various
departments vying with each other—the important thing is
what is happening on the stage. You must never let mechanical
necessities overrule the relationships between the people onstage.
This sounds simple and dogmatic, but I've seen shows destroyed
because of sloppy business handling or contesting egos.

I'm tired of being with a jazz band. I start other projects, get
involved with something, then I have to keep my band together
and go on the road and when I come back everything is changed
and I can't follow through on projects very dear to me. I'm not
available. So I've decided to stay in New York and figure out
ways of making a living. But I'm not going to be a bandleader
in night clubs any more.

This doesn't mean that I'm going to give up playing. I have
no intention of doing that. Actually, I think I'll have more
opportunities to play with different people I've wanted to play
with for years. But the responsibility of keeping a band together is too much. When I hire a bunch of guys I have a
responsibility to them. I must be sure they make a living. I'm
taking that weight off myself. I think things will work out
better musically. I'll be here, and when somebody says, "Hey,
call Gerry Mulligan," they'll be able to get hold of me.

N.   When you had your various jobs writing for bands
—then traveled with bands of your own—did you find it a
rather lonely life?

❀   MULLIGAN. Yes. Terribly lonely. In an odd way,
actually. You see, I'm the leader and I'm a personality and I
manage to make friends and have fun with people wherever I go,
but having fun with people is no substitute for work.

Life on the road for a musician—and I'm talking about a guy
playing with a band—is murder. It's as though life begins and
ends when you have your horn in your mouth. It's a hell of a
life for actors on tour, too, but for musicians it's worse. It's hard
to generalize, but it's like the loneliness of the long-distance

runner. But I suppose we're all lonely, in some fashion; it's an occupational hazard. A writer is even lonelier.

N.   Do you feel any definite sense of obligation as a musician?

MULLIGAN: My first obligation—no matter what circumstances I'm working in—is to satisfy myself. Then I can get to my obligation to the audience. I don't really feel that I have an obligation to entertain. In some circumstances I couldn't hold an audience if I played naked standing on my head. Other times I can win them over. An audience must be geared to you in some kind of way. They must have some preconceived attitude toward me or what the group is doing. They must react to us.

The groups I've worked with for the past ten or twelve years, and the music we've played, is a very cohesive musical entity that allows me a wide range of expression, but this wide range of expression means something only if the audience is for me. If I have to go out and win the audience over, then the quartet is no good. I'll go into one specific example that's so frustrating I hate to even talk about it. I've been working in a club in the Village opposite Dick Gregory. Dick gets an audience so wound up in one direction that by the time we get them they're in such a state of aggravation and turmoil that everything we do is a waste. The thing we do involves a great deal of love, sensitivity, interplay, the understanding of each other, and an audience that's all heated up about the racial issue isn't receptive to what we're trying to do. It's hell. We're not hitting anybody over the head; this simply isn't our musical approach, so we're dead. I walk on the stage into such an atmosphere of aggressive hostility that I don't know what to do. In a way this was the last straw for me; I just decided to hell with having a band. Being a performer—being an artist in any of the fields we've talked about—isn't easy. You have to learn techniques and grow and expand by adding to those techniques. You have to live your professional life and you have to live—or try, at least, to live—like a normal person. There are all sorts of occupational hazards.

I feel as though I've spent the last twenty years learning how to live. Now I feel as though I can function. Name me the situation and I'll figure out the way to cope with it.

That doesn't come easy.

"Suddenly, there I was on television doing all those wonderful, insane things."

PHYLLIS NEWMAN

Adolph Green is an incredibly fortunate man. He is talented, successful, and well-liked. Most importantly, he is married to Phyllis Newman, the funniest and most refreshing young actress in theater and television. Oddly, while most comedians confine the comic presence to performance time, Phyllis Newman is a rare and happy exception. She's as fresh and as witty in private life as she is before an audience—even when she's just emerged from a play that folded, her children are ill, and life is fraught with decisions to be made.

NEWMAN: I was born in New Jersey twelve years ago. (I've had a hard life, so I look considerably older.) I started performing when I was very little—I was four when I made my professional debut with Belle Baker. I've been in show business ever since, except for the period that began when I was twelve and went to high school and became a cheerleader and all that. I came back into the theater when I was in my first year in college. I answered an ad in the paper, auditioned, and got into *Wish You Were Here*.

I guess I was rather good at imitating Belle Baker; there weren't a lot of us around at the time and I sort of had the field to myself. She was a friend of my parents, but it wasn't all pull because I was very bright and precocious—I sang and danced and did everything as soon as I could toddle. I read when I was a year and a half old. I must have been insufferable. She heard me sing and felt that I was talented, so she took me under her wing and I did vaudeville and clubs, most of it totally professional, from the time I was five until I was nine. This was near the end of vaudeville, but New Jersey still had theaters where a child could work. (You couldn't work in New York at that time; a child could be in a play but you couldn't sing or dance in a musical. So whenever I appeared in New York it had to be set up as a guest appearance or a benefit.)

Considering all this Shirley Temple nonsense I've turned out miraculously well.

N.   Could you discuss the shows you've been in?

❦   NEWMAN: I'll start with my latest rather gargantuan turkey. You know, Adolph (Adolph Green is my husband) and I looked at the front page of *Variety* last Wednesday and saw that the biggest loss in theatrical history this year is the combined losses of *Fade Out, Fade In* and *Pleasures and Palaces*. Between us, my husband and I lost a million dollars of the investor's money. He just looked at me sort of numbly—he was depressed about all the misfortunes that happened to his show, and the whole thing really became insane with what happened to mine. He is not responsible for his, nor am I for mine, but nevertheless those were the shows we were involved in. I finally made the front page of *Variety*, though it wasn't in quite the way a young, tender, idealistic twelve-year-old girl dreams about. We'll see how much we can lose next year. On to bigger and better things. Like the poorhouse.

N.   What precisely happened with those two shows?

❦   NEWMAN: The history of *Fade Out, Fade In* is incredible. In fact, I'm after Adolph to write the story—Random House is publishing the play now. The saga of the show should be written as a preface to the play because there's nothing like it in the history of the theater. As soon as Carol

Burnett was signed for the show, and they combined the names of Comden, Green, Styne and Burnett, they had a million and a half dollars in advance. They no sooner set the opening date when Carol Burnett announced that she was pregnant and that they'd have to give back the million and a half in advance ticket sales. But she finally opened in it, and then she started being out of the show after the third or fourth week—she missed a great deal of time because of a neck injury and finally had to close the show. There were months of hearings at Equity and she said, "All right, I'll reopen the show." So she signed a paper saying she wasn't pregnant and they put $150,000 into the show to reopen it, this time without a dollar advance. This was a show that was doing standing room only business when it closed. It was a smash when she was there. She was out of the show after the second week. Two performances missed, then three--a cold, a virus or something, and finally she said, "I'm not coming in any more, I'm pregnant," and the show closed. So that counts up to a seven hundred thousand dollar loss—bigger than average because of the reopening and all. In five years or so it might seem funny. Right now Adolph is a potential suicide.

There was nothing quite as dramatic about *Pleasures and Palaces*, my flop. It just closed in Detroit, which is very unusual for a show Frank Loesser was connected with. All of the talent behind it was really top caliber, yet the show simply couldn't be brought off. Some of the score was marvelous, really, but there were so many things wrong with it that nobody knew where to start correcting it.

N.   What did you do in the recent years when you weren't losing a million and a half dollars?

NEWMAN: The last thing I did on Broadway was a show called *Subways Are For Sleeping*. I played a supporting part and got a Tony Award for it. I had a marvelous part—a very crazy southern girl, a Miss America loser, who was holed up in a hotel room and always trying to get guys to pay for this week's rent or the Chinese food. It was well done, in good taste. And funny.

I've loved doing *That Was the Week That Was*. It's fun because I can do something different every week. I never knew I could do all those imitations; I used to play around with them, all by myself in the bathroom, but suddenly there I was on television doing all these wonderful insane things. I'm going to go back and do the last show. I'll do a medley of my hits. I also, of course, do a panel show—*To Tell the Truth*—playing all the games. I love it because it's easy.

I met my husband (bet-a-million) Adolph, in *Bells Are Ringing*. I understudied Judy Holliday.

I guess I prefer comedy roles—and I may be the only comedienne in captivity with absolutely no ambition to do something very dramatic. Wouldn't I be ghastly in a serious role? During the heyday of dramatic television, when Philco and Kraft and all those long dramas were on, I worked a lot—especially for someone who is basically a lousy dramatic actress. I like to sing, and it's only lately that I've been allowed to sing very much. I just sort of stumble from one thing to the next. It would be nice to be in a position where I could pick and choose. (I do this, but nobody knows it; they always pick and choose someone else for the thing I picked and chose for myself. I'm very careful that way.)

N.   How do you produce *That Was the Week That Was?*

❧   NEWMAN : It's all very hectic. To begin with, it's the only really intelligent quality show left (except for the Bell Telephone show, which is a totally different sort of thing) .

The writers start working at the beginning of the week. They read newspapers madly and magazines just as madly and start cutting things out and getting ideas. I'm not around for any of that. On Sunday we come in and read the script and try to hear the good stuff. The writers discard the not-so-good and keep working on what has been selected. If there's a song we start working on that, and by Monday we have sort of a final version, but because news keeps coming in all the time things are taken out and put back and the writers are around us all the time, working in little rooms. Something comes in, some headline, and they come in and say, "Hey, is this funny? President Johnson just tripped," and we say, "Forget it."

Everyone listens to what's happening, and the day of the show is very hectic. It's one day of rehearsal and you're on the camera for an hour or two with changes all the time as the news comes in. There is one dress rehearsal in front of an audience and we try to weed out, again, what's really bad. It's all done on nervous energy, which is why the show is good. There have been wonderful moments on the show, and there have been bad ones. When it's bad it's excruciating because you know you're on live, everyone is watching you, and there's no turning back. I used to think, before every show, "I can't do it; I don't know what's going on," but somehow I'd get through it. I'm sorry it's going off; I think there's a place, and certainly a crying need, for that kind of television.

But I guess they won't stand for a half-hour of intelligence dropped into nine million hours of situation comedy. The show costs about a dollar—it's live, there's no big production, no guest stars. It should be kept on as a public service—though it's never lacked sponsors. The critics are rabid about it every week, as you know. Now they say, "Why do they take it off?" Yet all the time it's been on you couldn't drop a handkerchief on the show without all the papers saying, "The most tasteless thing I've ever seen." They're schizoid.

N.   How about *To Tell the Truth?*

NEWMAN : Well, this isn't performing. It has nothing to do with being a performer. It's a game, and I love games. It's stimulating, if you get an interesting guest, especially if the guest comes from a field you know something about. Then you can show off. I feel that I do the show well because I have sort of a garbage-can mind full of little facts. I remember a name here, a fact there, and sometimes I seem really profound. But if anybody *really* expert or profound came on I'd look like a gibbering idiot.

N.   How do you feel about television? The level of programming?

❧   NEWMAN : The level is dreadful. I honestly think that most of it is unwatchable. The situation comedy is painfully unfunny—I don't understand why the top-rated shows are even on. I must be from outer space, because millions of people turn on that drivel and seem to like it. With all the money that's spent I can't understand why there aren't more magical moments. Millions of dollars are literally thrown away.

N.   What about theater?

❧   NEWMAN : I'm sorry that it's such a difficult business to be in, and that so few shows succeed each year out of the many that are produced. The energy you put into it! I worked for ten weeks—worked hard—on *Pleasures and Palaces*. I put everything I had into it, and in one day it was over. It's not like doing a movie—even a lousy movie is shown, so you can at least see the fruits of your labors. If I had a lot of money I doubt that I'd invest it in theater. What a gamble for everyone associated with it!

N.   Why do you think the mortality rate is so high?

❧   NEWMAN : It probably is no higher than in any art.form. There are just so many good painters, so many good musicians, so many good writers. And the theater is such a collaborative effort that while one person's work can be good three or four others may contribute work that's not so good, and the whole thing goes down the drain. In case you haven't guessed the subliminal message going through this is, "Don't send your daughter on the stage."

N.   Were you aware, while you were working on *Pleasures and Palaces*, that the show was in bad shape?

❧   NEWMAN : Yes. At the first public performance you could tell that the audience did not respond. (With any show you're aware that certain things have to be fixed; this is a general problem.) But from the beginning of *Pleasures* to the end there was a general confusion as to what the play was about, what the style of the show was—very basic problems. It wasn't a scene here or a number there—it was the whole thing. I must say that my part was the best-written thing in the show, and that what I did worked. That was a great feeling, even in the midst of catastrophe. But I certainly didn't want to see the rest of it fail; all that work and all those talents wasted. But in a way it was gratifying to come onto the stage after things had been deathly quiet in the audience and hear laughter. To feel that the audience was involved, to have established some rapport. I'm not being very modest, but I know I did it, and it's a great satisfaction.

In fact, it sort of spurred me on to bigger and better things. Like never working again.

N.   How did you react to reviews?

NEWMAN: I absolutely adore any critic to death who has a positive word for me. It's great for the ego. It proves to you that maybe you are in the right business, after all, and that you do have talent, and that you shouldn't stay home and have eighteen children. Now, I did get good mention out of *Pleasures* even though the show was a flop, but there's something frightening about being in a massive failure. It really gives the ego a staggering blow. Right now I've got to decide about shows for fall, and I'm so bewildered after having this experience that I don't know what I should do next. I certainly don't want to go and have the same thing happen all over again.

In fact, I wonder if Adolph is game to have eighteen children.

N.   How do you prepare for a role you play? What does it take from you, what do you put into it?

NEWMAN: Well, I'm very slow working on a role. So slow I have everyone else slightly frantic. No one knows what I'm doing for the first three weeks. They all say, "She talks very softly; who is that girl?" I can't say that I'm conscious of what I'm doing—I don't have any rules—but I don't plunge into it. I just sort of let it happen, and most of it really happens when I come before an audience. I work hard, and think about the character and how she would react to the situations she's going through, and I try to make it as realistic as possible—even in a musical. But I throw all this away as soon as there's an audience. You do your homework then turn around and do anything at all for laughs. You forget the Stanislavski business completely and do anything—pull up your dress, anything at all—to get laughs. That's my version of Method. First you do the Stanislavski bit, then pull up your dress. *That's* going to go over great in your book. Want photographs?

N.   You did some motion picture work, too, didn't you?

❦   NEWMAN: I had quite a time being cut out of pictures. I'm the original face on the cutting room floor. I did two movies—the first one was *The Vagabond King*. I was in an off-Broadway show titled *I Feel Wonderful* which was written by Jerry Herman, my chum from New Jersey. We grew up together, and that was his first show, and I was his leading lady. Michael Curtiz, the director, came to see it and signed me for *The Vagabond King*. I read for him in his office and he cried. He really did. So I went out there and worked for four months in Hollywood and didn't know a soul and never got to meet anybody. I was stupid. Four insane months and I had one line left—"You haven't forgotten your Lulu"—that was it. The picture was cut to about forty minutes when it was released.

The next one was *Picnic* and I did it for Josh Logan. I worked for him in *Wish You Were Here*. That was my first show as an adult (of twelve, remember?) and when it came time to film *Picnic* he tested me for a small part in it. I got it and went to Hollywood again and then to Kansas to work for a month and then back to Hollywood. I still didn't know anybody or do anything—I was just there.

That picture came out and I went to the premiere and there I was: one line again in the whole thing.

Somehow I just don't think movies are my forte.

Then I made about nine million screen tests. I could put them together and make a feature-length film. Many of them were for *Marjorie Morningstar* and that turned out to be nothing but a big publicity stunt. No one could have told me that at the time, you know. I also tested for *The Helen Morgan Story*, which was also nothing but a publicity stunt. I was really so green I didn't know they did these things, and I had no idea they really didn't intend to use me at all.

I shy away from them now. I got one offer of a movie part about two years ago. I read the script and found I was to be the unattractive nurse friend of Sandra Dee. A real winner *that* would have been. So no thank you to Hollywood—not until they recognize my true worth. The chemistry's wrong, somehow.

There's no way of being in movies except being twenty and gorgeous and a star. It isn't like being in theater or television where you work, do your parts, and have some perspective and place.

N.　　　　What was your life like when you were a child performer?

　　　　NEWMAN: I don't remember much about it. I have a very bad memory about places and events and things. I'm a professional blotter-outer. I remember feeling much as I do now—loving the actual performing but hating everything else about it; the hours, the going back and forth, not being able to play with other kids. My parents were very good about it— they didn't push me, and life was normal. I went to bed at eight o'clock and led a reasonably normal life.

I think I'm somewhat the same now. I love singing and being on the stage but everything else makes me nervous. All the fuss about getting arrangements and having to see agents. I hate all this. I don't enjoy other actors, either. That sounds terrible, but I don't seek out other actors as friends. I don't like theater talk. I don't like talking about what I do and I'm bored with actors who talk about what they do. That kills my social life.

I don't think I'm show biz.

N.　　　　Could you pick out—say—a half dozen or so theater people you happen to admire, and why?

　　　　NEWMAN: I'll have to start with my husband. I've always admired Adolph Green, even before our marriage. I think he's talented and eccentric and has an enormously young and fresh view of the theater. He's like a kid, in a way, but a very bright kid. He gets very excited and he also gets very hurt by the wrong things that happen. Like losing a million dollars.

And, of course, my husband's beautiful and talented partner —Betty Comden. She looks like Garbo and is one of the few really sensational women in the whole world.

Then there are the talented composers—Leonard Bernstein, Richard Rodgers, Frank Loesser, Jule Styne, Steve Sondheim. They're all so filled with talent that even if a show they do is bad, glorious scores come out of them. This is one of our original art forms, you know, the musical comedy. It's really American and we've made enormous contributions. These composers turn out show after show, each with memorable songs, and the songs keep adding to our culture. Jazz and musical comedy theater are ours.

I think Judy Holliday is enormously talented. She's a unique actress as well as being a wonderful, intelligent and unique woman.

Anyone who gives me a good job means a lot to me. I like them a lot. In fact, anyone who likes me, I like.

Mike Nichols is certainly someone I admire. He means a great deal to the theater because he has a whole new fresh, honest approach. He levels with actors, he levels with everyone he deals with, and this is a refreshing commodity in theater. He's a great performer, as well.

I think Beatrice Lillie is the funniest woman I've ever seen. I went to see her in *High Spirits* last year and Adolph claims that I made the show a success. It was opening night and one of those typical bellwether opening night audiences and we were sitting in the front row. When I saw this vision come onto the stage with bicycle clips holding her dress together and an insane hat and little bunny slippers I screamed. Until then the audience hadn't been laughing, but I was so taken with her, and screamed so much, that Adolph insists I made the show a hit. She kills me.

Alan Arkin in *Luv* was just marvelous. He's an eccentric who can make you laugh at anything. He gets laughs on the straight lines. He's an original. I guess what I like most is eccentricity, or the rare gift of originality. I don't like all-around good professional talented people. They're good but they're boring. I like the nuts.

But I'm impressionable. (At twelve one is, you know.) I like whoever it is I saw last night.

And I can't forget Sophia Loren. When Adolph and I went to see *Marriage Italian Style* I decided to go back to *my* old style. I thought to myself, "Why do I worry about being thin and always dieting and fretting about looking like models and being quiet and ladylike?" after I saw this movie with this woman who is so full of life and not afraid to commit herself. American girls sort of pigeonhole themselves, you know, and here's this glorious creature, Loren, who might talk too loud one moment or be too vulgar the next. She's almost constantly in a state of excess, but she's so magnificent. She also has huge hips. I'm going to go back to having huge hips, too.

N. If you were to offer advice to the talented young actress who really wants a constructive career, what would that advice be?

NEWMAN: Stay out of the business. I'm not interested in young actresses or anybody who's aspiring. Don't write to me for advice because I'm not interested in you. Stay home and get married or go to work in a steel mill. I've got enough competition.

N. With all the things you do—theater and a heavy television schedule—how do you stay so organized?

NEWMAN: I don't know. I'm totally and impossibly vague. I never think about anything until the moment arrives. I'm unplanned and uncalculating. I don't think about what tomorrow is and I don't think about yesterday, so you have to catch me when I'm in the middle of it.

My husband always marvels at my vagueness. He did a piece about me for *Show* magazine. They said, "You've got to explain to us what it's like to live with someone who is so busy." (At the time I did eight television shows a week, and I have two children and this huge rather dirty apartment.) They said,

"How does she organize it all and stay so cheerful all the time?"

Poor Adolph thought about it and all he could tell them is this: "Whenever I come home she's lying on the bed with Hershey Bars and magazines."

I'm very lucky I married someone like Adolph. I'd drive a more average man out of his mind. Take today. I've been up since ten o'clock but don't ask me what I've done. Two sick children and hundreds of things going on in my life, hundreds of decisions to be made, and all I've done is wander about the place. I pulled myself together for you. I put on eye makeup and everything—two seconds before you came in. And I've talked for an hour and given you a big fat nothing.

"*I was a director. I felt as if I had come home.*"

MIKE NICHOLS

I first saw Mike Nichols, in person, in a Chicago night club. He was so extraordinarily good I knew he wouldn't stay in the Midwest long. (We have a way of losing people.)

The next time I saw him was in his justly publicized apartment in New York—the penthouse so elegantly and tastefully appointed that it is best described by Phyllis Newman who says, "It's the one place in the world that any girl in her right mind would enter, look at, and scream, 'Yes!' "

Mike Nichols hasn't changed, really; he is still unassuming, gracious, and seemingly unaware of the enormous talent that has made him the most electric and fascinating man in show business.

Whoever said, "Nice guys don't win ball games," didn't know what he was talking about. The versatile Mr. Nichols has played, now, in every major type of ball game, and he's won 'em all.

❦   NICHOLS: I was born in Berlin in 1931. My father was Russian, my mother is German. My father came to the United States in 1938, my brother and I came in 1939, and my mother came in 1940. (The different times of arrival came about because my father came first to establish his practice so he would be able to support us when we came over. My mother was sick, confined to a hospital with a lung disease. When things began getting sticky, in 1939, they decided to send us kids on ahead. My mother still couldn't travel, so my brother and I were sent by boat, watched over by a steward. She was fortunate enough to be released from the hospital in time to catch the last boat to the United States before the beginning of the war.)

We lived in New York. My father died in 1944. Then, in 1948, I went away to college at the University of Chicago. I was planning to enter pre-medical school (my father and grandfather had both been doctors) but I wasn't very good at anything that had to do with medicine.

Actually, I got into the theater by mistake. I joined University Theatre to see if I could meet some girls, and then a bunch of us got together a group—sort of an off-Broadway theater far off Broadway. *Very* far off Broadway. And I got a job as an announcer on radio—I was sort of a classical disc jockey. But I felt that something was wrong—I guess everything was wrong —so I came to New York to study with Strasberg, which I did for two years. Now, I still didn't know whether or not I wanted to be in the theater, but I knew I could never hold an office job and I wasn't going to get to medical school. Everything was minus, in other words—I knew what I couldn't do but I didn't know what I was going to do. I was drifting, but I liked studying with Strasberg, so the drifting wasn't bad. Then some friends back in Chicago told me that they were starting a cabaret, improvisional cabaret, and they wanted me to join them. I went with sort of a heavy heart. The one saving factor was that Elaine was there, and I knew her well enough to want to work with her. Still, I didn't want to leave New York and I wasn't sure I wanted to perform.

We started the Compass thing and I began to like it. I didn't perform too well at first, but then Elaine and I started developing material. I didn't think this work pointed to any sort of career—we were doing it for our $60 a week—but I began to enjoy it. We did some good work, but there was some bad stuff, too, and when it was really bad we'd all run out the back door and down the street to jump in Lake Michigan.

But we lived a nice life.

This broke up, after three years, because the business wasn't well-run. (These things have a life of their own.) I didn't know what to do next, so Elaine and I came to New York. We were young—23 or 24—and since we thought we should make a living we auditioned at the Blue Angel, not as a gag, but with a sort of "let's see if we can work into a night club for a while to pick up some money" motive. We auditioned on a Friday, started work the next Monday, and suddenly, without having planned it, we were a night club act. Then we went on television and into a lot more night clubs. In other words, much to our surprise we were in show business. Our manager was making plans for us to go to Las Vegas, we were to have our own TV series and some television specials—and Elaine and I were the only ones who knew the secret, which was that we weren't meant to be there at all. We felt they had the wrong idea and had taken us by mistake.

It was fun. We made a much better living than we ever thought we could, and we had fun together, but it was always a temporary thing, as though we were visiting in night clubs and pretty soon they'd catch on that we didn't belong there. So after a while, when they still didn't catch on, we said "All right, now let's try it in the theater" and we did. It went over very well. Then Elaine got tired of all this. Somehow, it was a greater strain on her than it was on me. I think this was because she's really more of a performer. I could do it rather casually, but she worked harder and it took more out of her. So we called it quits.

N.   I was always surprised that you and Elaine didn't marry—

✿   NICHOLS: It's very hard to understand why we didn't—and incidentally, everyone asks us *why* we didn't. We kept marrying a lot of other people. Perhaps, if we'd married, the tax problem would have been impossible.

N.   How did you begin your career as a director?

❧   NICHOLS : I got into directing in the same casual sort of way. Saint Subber said "Would you like to direct this play, 'Barefoot in the Park'?". I said "What a strange idea." Now, I had thought a lot about directing (doesn't everyone?) and I thought I might have some ideas, so I said "All right, let's try. Let's do it in the summer, and if I'm no good you don't have to keep me, and if I don't like the play I don't have to do it in the fall."

We went into it this way, and I liked it and they liked it and the play was all right and I was a director.

I felt as though I had come home. I do feel that way when I'm directing—it seems more right for me than anything else. I no longer feel that I'm in the wrong place. (It's strange, the way one gets to do the things one does; things don't happen in a haphazard way, exactly, but it's not done by a master plan, either. Just as I'm a comedy director, now, but only because I was given comedies to direct. If I had been given serious plays to direct I'd be a director of serious plays. Now I will be a movie director, and it's a little by chance that that came about, but it is comfortable to find yourself in a position where you can try all the things you want to do.)

N.   I'd like to ask you about the incredibly good material you and Elaine May used. How was it written, rehearsed, and developed?

❧   NICHOLS : It was never written and it was never rehearsed. It was developed in front of an audience. It was always improvisation, either from an idea that came from the audience or from one of us. I once said "Let's do a scene about adultery in three countries" and she said "What countries?" and I said "Oh, I don't know, America, England and France" and that was it—that was all we said to each other. And we did it in front of an audience in Chicago, and we would do it again and again, and we wouldn't talk about it much—we'd just let it build and erode and take place, all by itself, and after a few months it was set.

She once said to me "Let's do a scene about two teen-agers" and I said "Oh, good, two teen-agers in the back seat of a car."

That was all we said, and these things built themselves over a number of performances. This is the way we turned out everything we've done.

N. I'd like to turn to your upcoming debut as a movie director. How did you happen to choose "Who's Afraid of Virginia Woolf?"

NICHOLS: Well, I thought then—when I took on the assignment—as I do now—when I'm working on the material—that something like *Who's Afraid of Virginia Woolf?* is written very rarely. There are people who don't like it and people who think it's the greatest play written in the last fifty years, but whichever position you take you've got to admit that its a powerful piece of material to deal with. It draws me. The things that happen in it draw me. I think I've learned something about the life those particular college people live— and the broader life it represents, for which it is a microcosm, since it really isn't about college people at all.

It intrigues me. People always say things are a challenge and now I know what they mean. I also know what that wonderful word "challenge" means. It means that if you fail trying to do it it's still more interesting and more worth trying to do than tossing off something light and simple that doesn't call for much of an attempt.

This is what attracts me to *Virginia Woolf*. It's a great big formidable thing to take on, and that's why it's worth a try, and perhaps it can be done well.

N. What were your first impressions of "Virginia Woolf" as a play? How did you respond to the idea of directing it, once it was proposed to you?

NICHOLS: It's an odd story. I remember the first time I heard about *Virginia Woolf* I was in Philadelphia with Elaine's play. (It was a disaster, as you may know. Not the play—which I still love—but the production. Altogether it was a terrible experience. And it's terrible to be in Philadelphia when things aren't going right.) Anyway, the girl I was playing with said "Oh, I can't wait to see Edward's play. It's going to open the night after we do, and I hear it's wonderful."

Well, we *closed* in Philadelphia, and I went to New York, happy to be free, and I saw *Virginia Woolf* shortly after it opened. I was so excited by it that I went back a few more times. I loved the play. It seemed frighteningly real—and something happens to me when I like a play or a movie very much : I don't pick at it. (I'm always somewhat impressed with people who come out from a play and say "Yes, I loved the first and third acts, but halfway through the second act there was a ten-minute stretch I didn't like, but on the eleventh minute it picked up again." I either go with something or I don't. When I don't go with something I might go so far as to qualify the negative with "Yes, but that girl was very good," or something like that, but I'm no good at dissection.)

I bought *Virginia Woolf* and sent friends to see it. It was just a terrific play. I didn't think about it as a movie. I did think "Boy, I'd like to have directed it!"—Schneider did a hell of a good job. It was a brilliant production.

After that I did some plays, then signed to do the movie "The Public Eye." After this a friend who lives in Hollywood told me they were doing *Virginia Woolf* as a picture, and I said "Interesting; who's going to play Martha?" and he said "Well, it's a big secret. Nobody has been told, but it's going to be Elizabeth Taylor." And I said "What a great idea!" because I really did see it right away. I thought Elizabeth would be great.

Then I forgot about it until I talked to John Springer one day, and said "You know, *Virginia Woolf* would be some movie to direct. I'd be interested in doing it." He told me that Elizabeth had mentioned me, but apparently the studio or someone felt that they should have an experienced film director. I said "Who can blame them?" Months later they called me when I was in Jamaica, sent me the screen play, and I read it. I had some disagreements and some ideas. I began to think, immediately, "What would you do with this scene, or how would you manage that, or what place does this have . . ." and I talked to Ernie Lehman. We agreed on almost everything, and I said "Okay, I'll do it," and I've lived happily ever after.

N.   How are you going to handle the age disparity between the heroine's number of years totted up and Elizabeth Taylor's?

ꕤ   NICHOLS: Obviously, Elizabeth Taylor can't be 52 years old. But strangely enough, that is the least important element in the play. They can't be people in their early thirties, but neither do they have to be people in their middle fifties. There is a ground in between, and the play is not about their age. In fact, the literal facts of age are not terribly important to the play

N.   Can you see any fundamental differences that will exist between *Virginia Woolf* as a play and as a movie?

ꕤ   NICHOLS: I can't talk too much about what we're going to do in the movie—we haven't done it yet, you know, and theory and reality are usually quite different. Actually, I think it would be a mistake to talk about the differences rather than the similarities. I hope it will be a movie, not a play, and the differences are obvious and inherent. It won't take place behind a proscenium, it needn't take place in one room, and the points will be made differently in some instances because it is a movie, yet the points will be the same as in the play because Edward Albee wrote it. He envisioned it and created it and set it up and what Albee has done rather dictates what we will do.

The successful movies that have been made from plays—such as *The Little Foxes*, for example—were not so radically different from the plays. They were simply motion picture versions of the play—less confined, of course, as far as sets were concerned, and all the exteriors one could want to work in. They did go *out* of the theater.

In a movie you see one thing at a time rather than the whole picture. You see a woman's face, or a hand picking something up, or someone reacting very specifically to something set up by the director, and you see nothing else. This is the essential difference between movies and plays: the director chooses what the audience looks at. (He does this in a play, too, but in a much more general way.)

But the similarities between *Virginia Woolf* as a play and as a movie are what count. The characters will be the same. The event will be the same, the things that happen will be the same. It will still be Albee's *Virginia Woolf*.

N.   This is a general question, but what do you find significant—in either or both of a negative and positive way—in American theater today?

❦   NICHOLS: Well, in the category of encouraging things there are two factors that seem to count. The first is the really enormously talented people like Jerome Robbins who—every year—do extraordinary things. People like Lillian Hellman. (It's stupid to say "people like Lillian" because there's no one else like her.) But every year there are great things—there was *Virginia Woolf*, there is *Fiddler on the Roof* the way Robbins has done it. The established people of talent who continue to astound us give theater excitement.

The second factor is the new and exciting thing that is characterized by, say, the presence of LeRoi Jones and James Baldwin. The Negro rights movement is the most vital and important thing happening within our country, for us and to us, and it's come into the theater so impressively that I think we'll see a great deal more of it. When I see a Jones play or the Baldwin play I feel that one essential function of the theater—of being concerned with something deeply important and of shocking people with reality—is contained in these plays. Our theater has slipped a great deal in this function, and it's good to see values being restored. Negro actors are beginning to take their place in our theater. There's Al Freeman Jr. (I am enormously impressed with him, and hope we can work together). Diana Sands is wonderful, and Bea Richards, and many others.

It's fortunate for the theater that people like these are working now rather than fifteen years ago. (Fortunate for them, too, I might add. Fifteen years ago they would have played butlers and maids and been swallowed up the way Negro actors have always been.)

I think that plays concerning real issues, and the influx of important Negro actors, added to the remarkable work we can expect from people like Robbins and Albee and Hellman and Williams, is going to be the life of the American theater. It makes theater important.

N.　　　As a director—and I'm referring to your theater experiences primarily for the present—what obligation, if any, do you feel?

NICHOLS: I have only one obligation, and it is to the playwright. If I have chosen to do the play it means that I like the play or find something interesting or challenging in it (or both) and by discharging my obligation to the playwright I will take care of the audience at the same time.

You see, the very act of choosing the play contains the assumption that it is something the audience will want to see. Then it's up to you, as the director, to try to achieve the play for the playwright in the way that the playwright has suggested both openly, in his words, and in the more subtle and mysterious things contained in the play. The playwright has the right to expect you to find and explore those elements that aren't simply and clearly indicated. And when you achieve— as it were—all of the potentialities and possibilities inherent in what the playwright has done, then you've done the job.

N.　　　Mr. Albee has stated that once the director takes over it's *his* play, and that he steps away.

NICHOLS: They are two separate functions. But we've got to assume that the playwright is blessed with a director he has faith in.

N.　　　Now, with the plays you've directed thus far I wonder if you could single out the things that have pleased you most or problems or disappointments associated with them?

NICHOLS: I can look at any or all of them and say, sometimes, "Yes, I have served them well" and at other times "Oh, I could have done this better, look what I left out there." When I say "I" I'm referring to failings that I recognize as mine,

One of the pleasures of working in the theater with good people —which I've always been fortunate enough to do—is the way everyone looks at the work and finds his own mistake. I've experienced this with the three writers I've worked with thus far in theater, and with the designers and most of the actors. The actors are, of course, in a special situation because they can't sit back to look at the play; they're in it, so they have to trust the rest of us to a great extent. But these are some of my favorite experiences; all rather like a good marriage because the collaboration is very real but at the same time individual areas of responsibility are very real.

This analysis isn't just a polite thing that comes over you. You simply see what you should have done. The writer says "Oh, I've got to redo that" or "I didn't make this clear." I enjoy this because it's the real way to do a play. When you see chronicles of disaster in the theater you often find that the give-and-take element of rapport was missing. You had people saying "You must do this" and the writer saying "No, if it were performed properly it would work" and the director saying "But if you change it it will work" and the actor saying "You must give me other material" and the writer again saying "But if you acted it properly . . ." Now, there's probably nothing wrong with this as a point of view, except that it doesn't accomplish any work. It doesn't produce a better play.

But I've been lucky.

The other good thing about it is that if you do have this attitude and you're free you can say very happily to the author "Look what you did here; it stinks" or he can say "You've done this all wrong" and you're very apt to say "Yes, I see where I did it wrong; thank you." The pleasure of being told the truth (which can only be told if the atmosphere is right) is a great pleasure indeed.

As for problems—each play presents different problems; some are immediate, some take longer to work out. But when you've finished you forget what those problems were. Not completely, of course, but so far that you don't come up with "favorite" plays. The plays you direct are like your children— you don't like to discriminate amongst them, at least publicly.

You do have favorites, the things you're proudest of, but to everyone else all I can say is "There they are."

N.   What do you think of theater criticism in New York? Both as to the power of the critics and the obligation discharged or undischarged?

         NICHOLS : People always complain about the power of the critics, and how unfortunate it is. I'm not so sure it's unfortunate. I might feel differently if they'd been rough on me; I hope not. I think that their power is inescapable. They're the six men that see the play and report on it to the rest of the world. As far as discharging their obligation—I think it was Walter Kerr who pointed out that the power of the critics is not *that* great. The critics can say "This is a very good play" as they did, for example, with *The Subject Was Roses*. Yet we don't see long lines at the box office. They can say, as they have about plays recently, "It's not much, but it's very funny" or "It's not very good but the star is very talented and exciting" or in some notable cases they can simply say "It's not very good" and there are long, long lines at the box office.

It's not as cut and dried as people like to make out. What *is* becoming apparent is that musicals and light comedy are much more popular with the New York theater-going audience. *Waiting for Godot* ran, I think, four weeks in New York. There are not long lines at the Baldwin play or at the Jones plays. *Who's Afraid of Virgina Woolf?* was just under selling out all the time it ran.

Now, you can't blame the critics for this. It's the public that deserves the blame. The people who have the money to spend and can go through the whole thing that's required in the theater—the dress, the hairdo, the dinner, the sitter, and all— prefer to see light comedies and musicals.

Actually, the theater has a life of its own, and in art it has never been true that the most popular things were the best or that the best things were the most popular. Things endure and things change the course of the theater that may not have been smash hits when they were first presented. (Smash hits can be totally forgotten a year after they've closed except what they may have been as commercial phenomena.) But the play that was excellent, that may not have done terribly well, will be remembered.

Theater stands with a foot on one horse, a foot on another. On the one hand (or foot) it's a business. On the other, it's an art practiced by a few people. I don't applaud the playwright who turns out a minor play that makes two million dollars. But I don't feel sorry for the playwright who's turned out a great play that does *not* make two million dollars. Each gets his own reward—the one now and rather fleetingly, the other with some rather splendid fame and immortality.

N.   To move on from the astonishing number of things you've accomplished in a short time, what other ambitions or plans or desires do you have?

❦   NICHOLS: I'd like to do—I guess you'd call them "old plays." There are some classic plays I'd like to direct—some Chekhov, one or two Greek comedies. Right now I'm fixed on movies. I'd like to make many kinds of movies, strange ones, and it looks as if I'll get the chance.

I've been in love with movies all my life—directing them is like getting to marry this girl you followed around for years and years. I worry to some extent about what will happen after *Virginia Woolf* because I feel I will rarely get such marvelous material to work with. This is the experience of working with Ernie Lehman, with Elizabeth and Richard and Sandy and George, with lines and scenes that shock and challenge you.

But that's all part of getting this girl you've followed. There'll be good times, and some not quite so good, but it's up to me to do my best. So on this final bromidic note, with the sun sinking slowly in the west, farewell.

On filming "Lawrence": "Sand, heat, and a ridiculous amount of exercise . . ."

PETER O'TOOLE

Since he is one of the great and exciting actors of our time, it would logically be anticipated that Peter O'Toole would be an impressive personality to meet. We might even expect flashes of the determination that characterized *Lawrence of Arabia*, the vigor of *Lord Jim*, the thoughtfulness of *Becket*, the rollicking humor of *What's New, Pussycat?* We would expect him to be intelligent, urbane, mercurial, witty and forthright. In four hours' time I discovered that O'Toole not only lives up to all expectations; he exceeds them.

O'TOOLE: I've been asked about origins and early experiences so often I've almost forgotten what the real answers are, now. It's all the more blurred because I feel as though I was really born when I was twenty, but people won't stand for this. You have to be born somewhere and grow up somewhere—they won't let you crack out of an egg, aged twenty, at the point where you begin to *mean* something to yourself and others.

Well. I was born in Ireland of totally Irish parentage, except for my mother who had made a slight mistake. Her great grandmother, I believe, was Scots. We came to England when I was very young—a baby, in fact—so I can't really claim to be a soil-reared Irishman. I'm more free- than battery-running. I was brought up in Yorkshire, which is in the north of England, and in Lincolnshire. (I was evacuated to this very agricultural area during the war.)

But you see, all these things are only glimmers—I just remember scattered things before I got out of the Navy when I was twenty. I left school when I was thirteen and went to work in a warehouse. *That* I remember bloody well. A Catholic priest named Leo Welch, who was and is a great friend of mine, more or less helped me out of the warehouse and got me a job on a newspaper. (This became my education; I have very little formal education, only about two years in all, so I'm deeply grateful to the newspaper.) I met people who were, as it were, in the world—who had horizons I didn't have, horizons I didn't know existed. And it was very important that Leeds, where I was brought up, had three operating theaters, including a Yiddish theatre, and it became part of my duties as a fourteen-year-old boy to carry a camera case or run with copy from the theaters.

I began to love the theater, wholly and indiscriminately, and I attended it more and more frequently, and finally got involved playing little bits and pieces in the BBC and in repertory theaters in the area.

Yet I think this affinity with theater started before that. I think my origins in theater were perhaps the origins of theater itself—I was extremely grave and earnest, and a very good altar boy at the cathedral, and the entire ceremony of the Mass used to intrigue me enormously—the Latin, a language I learned, and the whole transubstantiation, the turning of the wine into blood and the bread into the body, the whole (not mystic) but almost magic—it was almost conjuring. And the robe, the ceremony, the audience (or congregation—they didn't pay money for their seats, but really they *were* in audience)—I think things like this, the Church, was the real origin. Also, my mother was an extremely well-versed woman who would recite poetry and stories to me.

As I mentioned, these are vague things, but they must have meant something.

So I went to the theater a lot when I was a boy. The first play I saw was *Rose Marie*, and I fell hopelessly, irredeemably in love with "Hard Boiled Herman."

But the real beginning came when I was twenty, when I got out of the Navy, and a painter friend of mine, Patrick Oliver, came with me on a Grand Tour of sorts. It was my actual entrée into theater—and a rather funny story.

You see, I'd done a bit of professional work before the Navy, and a great deal of amateur work, dueling and plugging away at little things, so I felt some affinity for the theater. But now I thought, "All right, I have to make a start." I had a few pounds, demobilization money, and as I mentioned Patrick and I went on this Grand Tour. He was going to dedicate his life to painting, and I was going to dedicate mine to the theater, and we thought we'd have a fling before we got totally dedicated. So we toured the British Isles. (As a matter of fact Patrick and I were taken for brothers. We are, even now. We're very tall, very thin, the pair of us.) But we toured in terms of hitting the theater towns—hitchhiking, bumming, all the way into Scotland. When we got to Stratford Michael Redgrave was doing Lear, and we had just enough money left to buy two back stall seats. Then we had to sleep wherever we could find space, free space, so we went out into the fields and found what we thought was a haystack. Pat went crunching off to sleep. (He always did this, and he was marvelous in the morning, light and thrusting. I'm good late at night and in the morning I'm distraught and crucified.) So I tossed around in the hay, building a little house of it and making a bivouac, and in the process of building I discovered it wasn't a haystack, after all, but a dung heap covered with hay to keep it nice and warm and alive.

The following morning we went to London, and I can assure you that no one crowded too close to us or even spoke. We got a lorry ride and we dropped off at Euston Station—we were coming to London primarily to put the arm on my sister for a few shillings because we were so broke. Anyway, we were walking from the station to the YMCA, which is in Tottenham Court Road, and on the way we went through Gower Street which is a parallel and passed the Royal Academy of Dramatic

Art. So I said to Pat, "I think I'll pop in here to see if they'll have me." I was wearing all sorts of beards and sweaters and things, and he stayed outside and sat on his knapsack while I went in and said, "Look, I've just been demobilized from the Navy and I'm wondering if I could possibly apply for a scholarship to your establishment." The lady said, "Well, we've had all the oral and written examinations for this year. I'm very sorry, but we can take your name for next term."

I'm desperate, of course, and I sort of keep the subject open.

At this point Sir Kenneth Barnes, God rest his soul (he is now dead), the principal, came walking through and said, "Well, what is it?" and I told him the whole story. What an extraordinary man he was. He had his foot planted right in the Victorian theater, you know—Terry and Tree and Irving. He said, "Come into my office." So I went into his office. I did an oral exam, and a written one, and he said, "You're very promising; come back in about two hours and we'll admit you to the Academy. We'll give you a scholarship test."

So I went on to the YMCA with Pat, and I said, "I think I'm in at the Royal Academy, but we haven't got any money and I'm to go back in two hours to do a further test." I went to the head of the YMCA, told him the story, and said, "Look, I haven't got any proper clothes and what I have on don't smell good." I borrowed a blazer, shirt, tie, and a pair of trousers, and went into the lavatory, the gents', to shave. Pat went into a little cubicle. I finished my shave, shouted to him, "I'll see you later," and went off.

At the Academy I did my test in front of a load of people—I don't know who they were to this day—and sat biting my nails for an hour and a half until Kenneth finally came out and said, "Congratulations." I'd gotten a scholarship, which meant that my fees were paid, and I was given a grant of five pounds a week (four pounds ten, to be exact). So there it was; my life had changed completely.

I went back to the YMCA, as jubilant as you might imagine, and went back to the gents' to take off my borrowed plumes and give them back to the YMCA Secretary. While I was getting into my rather odorous original clothing a little door opened and out of the cubicle came Patrick—he'd been asleep on the pot, and his face looked like a piece of crumpled newspaper, and his legs wouldn't work and his arm had gone to sleep and his face was all screwed up. He'd slept the whole of the time I was back at the Academy starting my bit of history.

The first year at the Academy—well, I was a bit of a child, and the whole idea of London rather stunned me, and the only thing I remember of that first year is gin and giggles. It was nice, wandering around wearing a duffle coat with all those pretty ladies around. I really didn't prosper at all as a student until the second year.

I love all academies. They're funny places, where you either do a great deal of work or none at all. I was very immature, really, and I was very lucky. You know, I think an education depends upon A PERSONALITY who can inspire you. Who can spark you off, as it were, and I was very fortunate. During my second year at the Academy I was in the hard-labor period, playing in the public parks. Dreadful. Good God, Russell Square . . . Imagine doing *The Trial of Mary Dougan* in Russell Square, where you can't hear the dialogue for the noise of the taxis and buses taking people to the theater. We were doing one of these productions, and I was playing a small part, coming on at the beginning or the end. And I was grumbling one day about my pitiful allotment of two lines when a man named Hugh Miller tore into me—at the time it sounded like the knell of doom. He said, "There are no small parts, only small players, small people," and he gave me the thrashing of my life in front of everybody. He pulled me out of myself, somehow, and I started working with him. Strangely enough, he's been with me ever since. He does dialogue coaching and one thing or other, and he's seventy-six now. In fact, Omar Sharif has inherited Hugh from me. Hugh is working with Omar on *Dr. Zhivago*.

But you know, you meet certain people, and something happens. They don't inject anything in you, but they lay bare a nerve of great enthusiasm, a prism of revelation, something that makes you crunch.

The next important thing was—again, it's always personalities, always people—an audition at the Old Vic, a public audition (they have to have them because it is or was a subsidized company) and they hold public auditions twice a year, with four or five hundred people trying out. I was up on the third day, the 405th or so, and I got half-way through my little bit and the man said, "Come here." So I went there. He said, "You're the first actor, real actor, I've seen this morning." I said, "Thank you." He said, "Are you Irish?" I said, "Yes." He said, "Do you drink?" I said, "Yes, in moderation." He said, "Let's go down and have one now." So we had one. And he said, "Look, I'd like to offer you work at the Old Vic, but I've got nothing—we've only got one thing open and that's in the way of prompting, and you could stoke the boiler. Would you like to do that?" and I said, "I'd love to do that."

This was the beginning of my Old Vic career. There was a man named Nat Brenner, who is now the principal of the Old Vic Theatre School. He was Number Two, then, and now he's down here, doing some extra lighting on the play. Nat, I love him—he's one of the few administrative geniuses I know. He's not an actor, he's not a director, he's not a producer, he's not a lighter, he's not a manager—he's just an administrator. He can marry the person to the fact. He knows about mental arithmetic, menopauses and menstruation—you know, headaches and things. There are bloody few like him. In fact, he may be the original . . .

I went with the Old Vic company in Bristol and I was there for three years. I played over fifty parts—two years as leading man, playing everything. Bristol was the turning point—perhaps one night was the turning point.

Nat came to see me before the opening night of *Waiting for Godot*. I had gone in an hour and a half early—a thing I hadn't done before. (I used to go in a half hour before, make up quickly, and go on.) That night Nat told me to lie down and put on eye pads and pretend I was a foetus. (I play a foetus in the play tonight, at one point, a suspension of age, a nullifying of experience, an erasure of personality.) At any rate, that very night something began to click, and I realized what it was all about—me, *Waiting for Godot*. It was a rebirth, probably.

Now I always have to be there an hour and a half or two hours early, even when I'm making a film, and I put on eye pads and become a foetus. And that happened in Bristol—God, so many things happened to me in Bristol I could talk all night. Three years of incident.

The play you'll see tonight is a first play by Mr. Mercer, and it is flawed, but it's also, I think, the greatest first play I've ever read or been in. Mercer is a triumphant writer, and this play is so densely packed with his genitals and his stomach that he may have lost some objectivity, but he is a man who writes prose like Swift, who writes character like— (Oh, what comparison? There is none!). He's unique. There's no simile. He is one of the major voices in the theater, certainly of our time.

Well, this play is about a rebirth. It happened to me in Bristol, this play, but no one came to reclaim me as they do on this stage. In Bristol it all happened. I fell apart, and found my own little pieces and put them together again. My own private little jigsaw puzzle, as it were.

We did this play in Bristol, before we opened in London. My first time back at the alma mater since 1958, and we played for a week. A very strange feeling for me—very strange. Bristol became my home; I was accepted there, and it's where I became *me*. You see, when I left Bristol I was famous, and the city haunted me. I'd go back—well, I gave up driving because of Bristol because I used to get the car out, sometimes at two o'clock in the morning, drunk, and drive to Bristol. It is the most beautiful city in Great Britain, and the last time I was in Bristol, driving a car like a bloody lunatic at four o'clock in the morning, I hit—of all things—a police car full of sleeping policemen. They woke up.

But it was strange to go back to Bristol with this play, and it was good, as well. Nothing had changed, really. (The only thing that really changed was a friend who runs a pub which was about the best pub in Great Britain. It was a sawdust pub, kept by a family of wrestlers and prize fighters, a royal family of the West Country strongmen. He had cancer or something and he'd gone from eighteen stone to about eight stone and had "Finis" written all over him, and this was sad because he should have endured like the Theater.) You know, the ships come right to the stage door of the theater in Bristol. It's a jewel of a theater, a little 1760 affair built without a façade, built in a corn merchant's house. The Puritans had closed theater, but with the issue of a little silver coin you entered into magic. You would go through the corn merchant's front door, then his bedroom, and after that—Paradise. The paradise the Puritans tried to forbid. It was built by one Thomas Sanderson, who was the master carpenter at Drury Lane. It's the most beautiful theater in the world. But I'm rambling.

Such a *fixée* for me, Bristol is. But in going back—well, on opening night I was all right until about twenty-five minutes before curtain call. Then the phone rang, and it was a friend of mine calling to wish me luck. He said, "I thought I'd better ring you, you're probably feeling a bit funny." I said, "I'm feeling all right." He said, "I just thought you might be feeling funny, coming home." So I promptly felt funny.

N.   What happened after your three years in Bristol?

❧   O'TOOLE: I had been to London during the stretch in Bristol. I had played *Major Barbara* in London. And I played *Oh, My Papa*, a musical—my first West End play—but these were with the Bristol company. So I came on to London in earnest, then, and the first thing I did was a play in which I met my wife, called *The Holiday*. We played brother and sister—a very Greek relationship *that* turned out to be, after a couple of weeks. Then I did a television show which I co-wrote on the life of a fine sculptor—this attracted the attention of a few people. Then I did a play called *The Long, Short and the Tall*, which was a huge success. In fact, everybody in the cast was unknown, at the time—the only one who was known was Robert Shaw, but he wasn't all that successful then. He's since become a major actor and novelist. Eddie Judd, Alfie Lynch (a hit both here and on Broadway), David Andrews (now a director), Brian Pringle, who is a big thing here, Ronnie Fraser, and me. We've all done terribly well from it, including Willis Hall, who was the author.

After that I started my film career, and a very distinguished

fucking film career it was. It all worked out, everything—
worked out totally wrong. The first thing I was going to do was
The Long, Short and the Tall as a film, then they told me I
wasn't—Laurence Harvey was doing it. It went on from there,
and I did one film that was a disaster. Then I was out of work for
six months. I was doing something Hugh Miller told me never to
do—I was playing checkers with my career. Finally I was
asked to do another big film, which would be a lifesaver, and I
was all set to do it when I got an offer from Peter Hall to play a
season at Stratford, including Shylock. I couldn't resist it. I was
twenty-six. Big challenge, so on to Stratford. (Or Okefenokee-
on-Avon, as they call it. It's a swamp, the most ghastly place in
the world, and when people ask me how I happened to survive
Lawrence and those two years in Arabia I tell them that anyone who can survive Stratford can survive anything. And it
really is the culture drome. It's Mother's Day at Lourdes. But
you can't get away from the scripts—they're pretty well-
written.)

During the course of that season at Stratford I met David
Lean and Sam Spiegel and I agreed to do *Lawrence of Arabia*.
From then on I think I'm a rather open book.

N.   Was filming *Lawrence* as demanding a venture as it
seems?

❦   o'toole: It was hard, extremely hard work. Sand,
heat, and a ridiculous amount of exercise. You see, I'm rather an
indoor fellow. I don't like the sun, I don't like the fresh air—I
don't hate them, but I prefer the indoors, stale air and smoke.

The most unnerving thing about *Lawrence* was the time
element—it took so bloody long. I'll give you an example. In
one scene with Omar—one of the first scenes we shot—some
cutting had to be done later on. So at the end of shooting the
picture, to bridge the cut, they shot another close-up of me, this
time in Morocco, against the blue sky. (Skies don't vary much
in Arabia.) When I saw the scene—quite apart from the general
horror of seeing myself—I found that it started with a shot of
my head when I'm twenty-seven, cuts to Omar, cuts back to me
when I'm twenty-nine, cuts to Omar, and back to me and I'm

twenty-seven again. Believe me, that's a shock—two years of my life passed in eight seconds.

N.   How did the filming of *Becket* go?

❧   O'TOOLE : *Becket*, as far as the sum total of living is concerned, was the happiest professional experience I've ever had.

We worked like dogs, all of us—Richard, Peter, Gielgud, myself—we labored like lunatics. I never laughed so much in my life, nor cried so much. I never worked so hard, nor enjoyed myself so much. We did it in thirteen weeks, you know. We shot it off the cuff—and it was really something to put me in amongst those pros. We shot the play, really, we didn't change it at all. Anouilh should have got an Academy Award. Bryant made those wonderful sets—we tried to put a style on it. Like Olivier did in the film play he made, *Henry V*. He imposed his own style because he made his set.

We could have shot *Becket* in France, in dusty old dilapidated decaying castles. But the Cathedral in Canterbury in the 12th century was brand, spanking new—those bricks were red—so we helped put a style on it by putting up cardboard realities. God, *Becket* was fun. Richard Burton, to play with, to be with, is not a man—he's an experience. Total generosity. If I said something to him in a scene he took it—like the tennis match which delayed me a little tonight—and gave everything back. Fascinating. Endless genius.

N.   *Lord Jim* must have been another vivid experience.

❧   O'TOOLE : That was a brute. We shot it near Vietnam, in fact we were right on the border, and a lot of the film takes place in the jungle. As I said, I'm not very fond of Stratford, so you can imagine me in the jungle. Hopping, leathery things landing in your eyeballs every few minutes, snakes, beasts of all descriptions—and the weather hot, sticky and nasty.

Even more disturbing was the pulse of violence all about us. We were employing the army in some of the scenes, and the soldiers all had loaded weapons. There they were, with their fowling pieces. They hated us, hated all the Americans and English. (Look what's going on now.) About this time they started burning down embassies. They burned the American, then the British. It was exceedingly nerve-wracking—we spent the last four days hiding in the lavatories.

As to the film—well, I've only seen bits of it, but I think that one of the faults it had (in those bits I saw) was that it lost simplicity. I don't know who was responsible, but at one point it was a very simple narrative yarn, but it got rather overstated. I don't know how it happened—Richard Brooks is an extraordinary man.

Wait until you see me in *The Bible* for John Huston. I've only seen thirty-five minutes of it, but it's something else, something extraordinary—a symphony. It must be extraordinary because I play God three times. I'm a pre-echo of the Trinity. I'm O'Toole playing Trinity in the Sodom and Gomorrah sequence. (You know, the stranger, the one who is God, and I play all three strangers and all of them are God.) There's such an Irish slant to the picture I decided it should be called "Sodom and Begorrah." Richard Harris plays Cain. John Huston, Ireland's most prominent citizen, is the director. It's the Gospel According to Mick. But what I've seen is beautifully done. John hasn't gone to that awful pastiche—"Have you met my sister Salome?"—none of that. I think you'll get the shock of your life.

Huston is an involved, dedicated man, and he sticks his chin out, but he's got a good slant on this picture. He treats it as myth into legend into pre-history and then ends. The only statement he makes is *that*.

He said, in my presence, that you would find something in the picture whether you followed the Bible, the Talmud, the Koran, whether you were Buddhist or Shintoist or whatever.

Myth into legend into pre-history and The End.

N.   When you assume a role, and most of yours are demanding ones in whichever medium you choose, are you conscious of an obligation to anyone in particular? Whom do you try to please, primarily?

❧   O'TOOLE: The only person I have to satisfy is myself because I see myself as the author's advocate. (I never achieve total satisfaction, however.) I think acting is making words flesh. But I'm also a performer, an entertainer, and this assumes a relationship with the public.

But in terms of satisfying—I would say that the big objective is to make myself less discontent. Actors are often accused for not being writers, for some strange reason. I don't know why that should be, but they are. As I said, being the author's advocate is the big thing on my mind.

N.   In a contemporary play like the one you're doing now, do you find that audiences vary enough to affect your performance?

❧   O'TOOLE: Every audience is an experience, really, but they don't affect the play in—for example, terms of pace. I'll give you an idea. (I'm a bit of an old Puritan, you see.) These are the running times of the play. I keep them every night. You'll find that we varied a half a minute—in a three-hour play a ninety-second variation isn't bad, is it? It's all a matter of adjustment, you see.

A very distinguished (I won't mention his name; he wouldn't like me to) pianist once talked to me about audiences, different audiences. I told him I had this thing with audiences—some are yuckie, some are dull and I've got to stir them up. I'm within and I have to fight, control, shepherd them, if you like, and I told him how wonderful it must be just to have the interpretation in the tips of the fingers without recourse to alternatives. He said, "Don't kid yourself; when they are there I know exactly what's going on, what's selling and what isn't." But in terms of pace, you make up. This play is so carefully orchestrated by Mr. Fleming, our director, and myself, that we can adjust—what I mean is, in the second act you'll find that it's a poetic play, that things recur in various degrees of intensification, and that this careful orchestration is needed to keep its poetic balance.

Laughs are a big problem—what a thing to say! Laughs a

problem! But the play, and the interplay between us and the audience, must be carefully balanced.

N.   To turn to the personal side. A great deal has been written about you in these past few years, and a portion of it has centered about your problems with marriage, the Church, and Ireland, and another portion portrays you as a troubled and insecure person. Frankly, I don't find you troubled or insecure, but I wonder how you view yourself in relation to the things which have been written.

O'TOOLE: Troubled and insecure . . . and you think I'm not . . . My God! If someone tells me I'm neurotic I want to shout, "I'm not!" and now you say I'm adjusted and bland and I want to shout, "I'm not!" This word bland—it sounds like a diet for an ulcer.

N.   You're *not* bland.

O'TOOLE: No, you're right, these things have come up.

Marriage—there should be no fuss, no bother, because it should be common knowledge that Siân and I are happily married. Oh, yes, now I know . . . I was accused, by one of your newspaper reporters, of leaving Siân and going to live with Rudolf Nureyev. I almost sued; I would have sued the bastard, but I was told I couldn't win. I wouldn't have sued for any moral reason or to get money out of him, just to make the ass look as absurd as he was. But I've got a wonderful wife, and the only dreadful thing about our marriage is that she understands me too bloody well.

The Church, I'll admit, is a bit of a strain. But I'm very old, now. It used to be a much greater problem, but now it doesn't bother me intellectually, at all, but emotionally it still does. I still feel things too much in terms of the Church, but I suppose this is a cross—see? That bloody cross again. I'm a left thief.

Ireland—it's the usual wild rubbish. I'm not a New Yorker, so I don't feel the intensified Irishness they have there, but it is a little thing that trickles around in me. I go there a lot. I love Ireland. I've ancestors who were terribly prominent in the

Movements, and I'm still asked to help in the fight to remove the ignoble partition. Things like that. Being Irish is a unique thing; I don't think that Jews feel toward Israel the way the bulk of the Irish feel toward the Ould Sod. I reject it, but it's still there. Never, never, completely subdued. Perhaps I wouldn't want it to be.

Siân, you know, is Welsh, and my first daughter was born in Stratford-on-Avon, poor child, and the second was born in Dublin. There was Siân, who is really Mother Wales—she is the Welsh national heroine, dripping with every honor and degree the Welsh can afford. She had to learn to speak English. But there she was in Ireland. They don't have any of this highly sterilized, pampered systems of birth for the mother. None of your childless pain-birth. They're not put in glass tanks while some great, moustached lady bullies them into having no pain. There are things like contractions, and they say "pain." There's no brute leering at you, telling you to relax. Some old yokel from Connemara stands with the sweaty mother's head in her arms, holding her and wiping off the sweat and saying, "Come on, girl, I know it hurts, I know what it's about, come on, girl." And when that little thing sticks its head out they slap a whole bunch of cotton wool soaked with chloroform over the mother's physogue and out she goes and somebody yanks the damn' baby out.

Well, Siân was going under the chloroform and the doctor, who had once played rugby for Ireland, was pulling the baby out, and Siân suddenly started singing the unofficial Welsh anthem as she was going under.

The poor doctor—having played against Wales, where this thing is sung all the time at every game—felt as though he was in a rugby match, putting a ball out of the scrum. He nearly passed my second one on to the matron. But wasn't this a marvelous unconscious protest against being in Ireland?

N.   To turn back to your career . . . can you sum up your objectives as an actor?

❧   O'TOOLE : The answer is as prosaic and banal as can be. I simply want to be a good actor. That's all. There are to be more movies, naturally—good ones, I hope. If they aren't good it will be my fault, because I'm choosing them, even producing some of them, so if they fail the finger can be pointed only in my direction.

I want good parts, big parts, some of *the* big parts, of course. The play I'm in now is satisfying—I'm in a very fortunate position, you see, because I can pick and choose. I've had the classical training, done many of those parts, performed big roles in excellent plays. (This is safe, in a way; you can't say *She Stoops to Conquer* is a bad play. You're there already, if you know what I mean.) But now I can fiddle around and look for new writers. Choose things that interest me. Like *Baal*—I did Brecht's first play. Nobody would have done *Baal* if I hadn't done it, and it fascinated me to see what the beginnings of Brecht really were.

I felt greedy about Mercer. I wanted to be in his first play because he's going to do enormous things. He hasn't learned his business, yet—this is his first play, his first stage play.

I want to play Lear. I have, God knows, done *Hamlet*—all the Hamlet I want to do for a lifetime. I opened, mind you, the National Theatre with *Hamlet*. Larry Olivier, who directed it, is a very distinguished Hamlet himself. Michael Redgrave, who played the King, was also a very distinguished Hamlet. There must have been at least nine great Hamlets in the cast on that opening night (and they'd attempted to open the National Theatre from the 17th century on). Well, Larry asked me to open it, and I happily refused, though I was flattered in a childlike way. I didn't want to do Hamlet, I don't like it, I did it but didn't enjoy it, and I said, "No." But have you ever tried to argue with Olivier? He's the most charming, persuasive bastard ever to draw a breath. I said, "No," but then I said, "Yes." Then I said I wanted to play it in a very cut version—"I'll only do two and a half hours," I told Larry. A week later I was doing the uncut version which takes five hours. Then I wanted to play it with a beard because I said why should I be the only man in Elsinore with a razor blade. Three weeks later I'm standing on the stage clean shaven with my hair dyed white in a Peter Pan suit.

Such is the power of Olivier. Hamlet again—never.

But Lear I am dying to play—I think Lear is the greatest artifact in our world. It's the supreme play, the supreme challenge to any actor. I haven't got the apparatus, the breath, the voice, to do him yet. But I will have.

N.   How do you feel about both the power and the quality of critics?

❧   O'TOOLE: Critics I do not and will not discuss. I'll just say this: They do not matter. They do not matter a damn.

N.   Why is it that the British Isles produce so many outstanding and accomplished actors? The English theater almost always has a surplus, and in America we seem to have trouble producing enough of them?

❧   O'TOOLE: I don't know. I really don't know. There are many. Of course, not all of them are English. Olivier is French, Gielgud is a Hungarian Jew, Scofield is Jewish. Perhaps it's the English tongue that makes England's actors what they are. But there are, as you say, so many. . . .

But give your English-speaking actors time—in America, Australia, Canada, New Zealand. They haven't a tradition, yet. America has some fine actors, some extraordinary actors, but they haven't the opportunity to develop as we can. We're very fortunate. We've got our bred-in-the-bone tradition.

Spencer Tracy, for example, is one of the really great actors of all time. And I wish Marlon Brando hadn't given up the stage. God knows what he would have done, how far he'd have gone. I think he's dissatisfied with his present work, and perhaps he'll return. He's a tower—he's so funny—he's got it all. He's only about thirty-eight, still a baby (Laughton didn't *start* until he was thirty-five).

But I wish Brando would go back to the theater, I really do. I admire him enormously; he's got every single thing a great actor needs.

N.   The final question: If you were to give advice to the neophyte, the assumedly talented aspiring actor, what would that advice be?

❦ O'TOOLE: You've gone and done it. I've been dreading that bloody question all my life. I'm not a young actor any more, you see; now I'm called upon to give advice.

N. I meant the real fledgling—

❦ O'TOOLE: That bloody question. Listen, I've got a poem from a friend of mine, a very distinguished poet named R. C. Scriven. He's blind and he's deaf and lives in Leeds, or near Leeds, and for some reason he heard I was in town. (He doesn't really know what's going on because, as I say, he's incommunicado in the normal sense of the word—perhaps, today, we should call it the abnormal sense of the word.) It comes from Forner, which is a little village in the West Riding of Yorkshire and he says: "Dar Peter: Heard you were in town today, moaning about how old you are. My condolences herewith. Whitelocks (that's a pub) is busy these days. I do my drinking in The Muckles in Harrowgate."

Then he dedicated a little poem to me titled "What Genius I Had Then."

> "To Peter O'Toole, bemoaning his old age!
> What, still alive at thirty-three?
> no genius can afford to be.
> When fame arrived at twenty-two
> you rushed to give (you idiot, you!)
> the damning details to Who's Who!"

Advise any young actor—Christ! I'm so conscious of my own age. I adored being the youngest. I was always the youngest. I was the youngest leading man at Stratford, the youngest—and now I'm not. I've reached old age, and I wish to build a cage for myself in which to mope.

Advice? Take it in your stride. Have courage—that's what I'd say—have courage to be bad.

"I have a reputation for being able to keep spirits up, and it isn't a chore."

✻

ROBERT PRESTON

It is a shock to see your most dependable second male lead, the assistant-stalwart of many a panoramic outdoor adventure, turn into The Music Man and Ben Franklin, reigning over the competitive world of Broadway as he never positioned himself in Hollywood. But it is reassuring to realize that an actor with talent and courage can break a mold in which he has been unjustly confined, and attain the stardom promised but never delivered through all those plodding years.

And it couldn't have happened to a nicer guy.

✻ PRESTON : I was born on June 8, 1918, in Boston— actually outside of Boston, in a town called Newton Highlands.

N. You and Jack Lemmon—

✻ PRESTON : Yes, and Bobby Morse, and I think that's about as far as we can go. But I left Newton Highlands at the age of two, and they hung on a bit longer and became very Ivy League about it all.

At any rate, when I was two my family moved to California, so both my brother (who was then only six months old) and I were raised in Los Angeles. In our section of town the motion picture business was simply part of the way of life. When we saw a company shooting on location we didn't even bother to see who was in it. When they were using the zoo (and we were always sneaking in) we'd be annoyed because we wanted to see the animals. And driving to the beach, down the bridle trail on Sunset Boulevard, we'd see Hobart Bosworth on his white horse, and all the famous picture stars of the era, and we weren't really impressed by any of them.

Of course, this was before I was ten years old, before I did my first work in the theater. How this came about I don't know—I've tried to clear it up with three or four biographers, but I really can't specifically state how I got interested in acting. It seems now that I've always done it, and that I've always been in a position where something in the neighborhood was going on that called for my—in quotes—"services." In grammar school my brother and I were the only two in the school who were not Mexican; ours was a Mexican neighborhood. This gave us a language advantage in school (everything was taught in English) and we skipped along merrily. This wasn't too good for us in later years because we skipped all the basics in English grammar and mathematics and we had to go back and pick up quite a bit. But in high school, at that tender age, I was blessed with a marvelous coach, E. J. Wenig. (He's retired, now, in the Ojai Valley, where most of the teachers in the Los Angeles City School District go—it's a beautiful place for them to retire.)

E. J.'s great love was Shakespeare. I don't think that up to and including Laurence Olivier there is any man fonder of Shakespeare than E. J. He was also a frustrated actor—by his own admission not a very good one. But he was a marvelous teacher and he instilled his own enthusiasm in you. He also made his own costumes. (I remember visiting his little apartment on the other side of town. There was just room enough for a bathroom and his bare cot—the rest of the place was taken up with hangers full of costumes.) He could do almost any of the chronicle plays from the costumes he had on hand. He had an old German friend named Hegner who helped him with the work and the wife would sew on the beads. He was a legitimate makeup man, too; that's how we learned professional makeup as kids.

It seemed that we were always in rehearsal. Most high schools at that time would do one major play a year, but E. J. had an entirely different setup. We would do a Shakespearean play each semester, which meant two major productions a year, and the rest of the time we did what I suppose the other schools were doing—A. A. Milne and stuff like that. It was all quite extensive for high school, even for a school in the Los Angeles area.

Along with all that I did some extracurricular work in pageants and a couple of variety shows that played in downtown Los Angeles. Because of this extra work it took me five years to graduate. Just before I turned sixteen, E. J. took me down to the Musart Theatre where the Patia Power Repertory Company was doing some casting. I read for them and was immediately made part of the company, and I played with them until it broke up. I guess I did quite a few other local things, too—once your name gets around certain circles, and they know you're willing to work for nothing or next to nothing, you're called upon by everyone. For me it was good. I lived at home, had no need to make any more money than a boy that age should, so I did a variety of plays. Some of them even had a political content—I played them long before I realized what my politics was going to be. Then, suddenly, there came an end to all this and I had to make an honest living. I went to work at the Santa Anita Race Track, and while I was there I ran into a group of fellows working there in the daytime and at the Pasadena Playhouse at night. (The Pasadena Playhouse, aside from the few and far between touring shows that came to the downtown Biltmore in Los Angeles, was just about the only place where theater was going on at the time.) I was aware of the Playhouse because so often they needed supernumeraries or people to say one or two lines—and they'd call upon E. J. to send over his prize students. So I'd worked in things like *Judgment Day* and *Cavalcade* and *Old Heidelberg*. (I remember that one, particularly, because John Conte, Ernie Sarrocino and myself were all in it.) Anyway, I went to the Playhouse and read at the open readings they had on Sunday nights. I got the part I read for, and became a regular at the Playhouse. At that time there were four or five theaters available to the Playhouse, and you worked in them all, which meant that not a day went by that you weren't rehearsing or playing or both. Aside from the main stage—their big theater—they had two laboratory stages. Gilmor Brown's wonderful little pet project was the Playbox, the house where Southern California saw its first theater in the round (or in the square or in the triangle, whatever the show adapted itself to, since the theater was so adaptable. You could move the stage around to wherever you wanted it—put it in the center or in one corner. Sometimes the audience would swing their chairs around because one act would be played over here and one over there.)

I did forty-two plays at the Playhouse, and the variety was astonishing—from contemporary things in the laboratory theater Gilmor used to give young playwrights a boost, to the entire range of the classics. They had five or six marvelous directors to work with; the last week or so of rehearsal Gilmor himself would take over, and I learned more about acting from him than from any other man.

In a group like that you really learn the most important thing of all—the thing that's got to guide your professional life: utter and absolute devotion to the job you're doing, the profession you've entered. They give you respect for your work. I think a great many actors feel guilty about acting, particularly when they start making money at it. But when you have pride in your work, in the profession, you're halfway home. I think this is what I got from these people. I got over the absolute kid kind of fun very early in life, and began to have adult fun.

Then I did a production of *Idiot's Delight*. I played the Alfred Lunt role. I was between eighteen and nineteen at the time, quite young for that role, but I had attained my size. (I don't think I've grown much, physically, since then.) My voice had matured, so no one was aware that I was really that terribly young, and from that production Paramount signed me to a contract. I signed it against Gilmor's advice. Gilmor wanted me to continue in the theater, but Paramount offered money that was hard to turn down. (It was the tail-end of the depression years; my father, I think, was on the WPA at the time.) So for the next twelve years—with time off for war—I did everything they threw at me at Paramount. I was a bit more choosy after I got out of service—in fact, I spent one entire year on suspension for turning down scripts.

It seemed the only good things I got to do—the really decent parts in good pictures—were away from the studio, but I think this often happens when they get you so young. They found out, very shortly after they had signed me, that I was only nineteen, and they took me down to court and had my contract validated legally, which tied me to them. (This is an offshoot of the terrible thing that happened in Jackie Coogan's life, when he became a man entitled to all the money that had been held in trust for him and discovered there was nothing left.) So the court became the trust, which is a good thing, and it's gone that way in Hollywood ever since.

Fortunately for me—as far as training and development were concerned—the gang I'd known around the Pasadena Playhouse was still a close-knit bunch, and loved the theater as much as I did, and we were all working in motion pictures. (Had to make a living.) I'm speaking of a group that consisted of a wonderful director and actor, Morri Ankrum, who died last year, Victor Jory, Dana Andrews, Charles Lane, Don Porter (who's working on Broadway in *Any Wednesday* right now) and many others. They formed a group called "Eighteen Actors"—it started out as a nucleus of nine actors and their wives. All the wives, as it turned out, were actresses. (Including my wife, Catherine, whom I'd met at the Pasadena Playhouse; she later had a contract with Paramount also.) We got a subscription audience of about 1500 people in the Los Angeles environs—Altadena, La Crescenta, Pasadena, etc.—an audience that had been familiar with us for years. They accepted anything we gave them, so we could experiment all we wanted, and Moroni Olson (a member of our group, a wonderful director who once had a great stock company of his own) was a Strindberg lover. Raymond Massey did Strindberg's *The Father* on Broadway, and it folded after a very few performances, so

Moroni wanted to do a production to see why. And with our limited funds and capabilities we did a better job than they'd done on Broadway.

We would perform each play four consecutive weekends on Saturday and Sunday nights, until our subscription audience was exhausted (in more ways than one). We'd follow a heavy play with something farcical, like *The Play's the Thing*, or a complete variety show, but we still kept up our gym training. (You get so accustomed to acting only from the shoulders up when you're in movies that you have to get out there and stand naked in front of an audience again to keep yourself mobile.) When I got out from under the contract at Paramount I made a picture on my own in London, and the theater bug bit me again. The picture itself wasn't very good—it wasn't too bad, but it could scarcely be called great—but the thing it did for me was to expose me to working with English performers. I found out why—down to the smallest bit players—they are so much better prepared as actors than we are. It was an episodic type of picture, so I was with an almost entirely different cast every day, and almost without exception at the end of the shooting day these actors would go to their theater in the West End. I realized, full force, that we are the only nation of any size in the world where the capital of the motion picture industry and the capital of the theater are 3,000 miles apart. In France, in Germany, and in Italy, as well as in England, they adapt the shooting schedule of a movie to the schedule of the man who's performing in the theater that night.

So I came back to the United States with my eyes opened, and luckily, things fell into place. I heard that Jose Ferrer was looking for someone to replace him in *Twentieth Century*, which he was playing with Gloria Swanson. As fate would have it, he wanted to leave the play to go to my old home—Paramount—to film *Anything Can Happen*. So without giving the matter a second thought I said, "Yes, quick, let's draw up a contract I can sign before I change my mind."

I was determined not to go back and fall into the same pattern I had established in California. I knew that I could make a very good living playing all the second men in the big pictures and leading roles in the smaller ones. I had established this pattern for myself, but it was very unsatisfying. I knew I was better than the stuff I was doing, but there was no way to prove it, not even to myself, without going someplace to really do something. So instead of taking the summer stock route, or one of the other routes open to the Hollywood personality who wants stage experience, I jumped onto Broadway with both big feet.

It worked. I played the part, and played it well, and when the run finished I went back to make another movie. They were still unaware that I had proved myself to anyone but myself, and while I was in California, finishing up the movie, Elliot Nugent called me. They were going to get together a revival of *The Male Animal* at City Center, and they were trying to get as many of the members of the original cast as they could, but Leon Ames, who had played Whirling Joe Ferguson in the original company had just finished a year's tour with *The Moon is Blue* and didn't want to leave home again. He had to stay in California to tend his automobile business. So Elliot asked me if I would play Joe. Well, it's the kind of show I'd seen as a young man (and you're crazy if you don't love that sort of comedy—frankly, I'm still waiting for someone to come along to replace James Thurber) and I grabbed the chance. The whole thing was good for me; it gave me my first out-of-town tryout—two weeks in Washington—and then we came to New York for two weeks at City Center. It was a smash hit—we had a wonderful cast and hit a very arid season on Broadway. (If my memory serves me right there were only six shows running at the time, four straight and two musicals, and even one of the musicals was a revival, *Pal Joey*.) So for very little money we were able to move the production downtown to the Music Box, and we ran longer than the original run.

So by then I was firmly established in my own mind—and in a few of the critics' minds—as an actor who could appear on Broadway.

Shortly afterward I had my first flop. This is something an actor must experience (perhaps as quickly as possible) to prove that it isn't all glory. I came on in a thing titled *Men of Distinction* which closed in four turgid performances. It was my first experience since those early days in the laboratory theater at the Pasadena Playhouse of taking a brand new play from scratch—my first experience, with the pros, in what can happen, and what might not happen, in the pattern of birth pangs and tryouts and doctorings and the fateful presentation. But *my* pattern was more or less established. My heart was really wrapped up in what I could do on Broadway, but when I had the time, and a picture was available to me, I'd go out and do it, and when a summer would come along that didn't find me on Broadway I'd work in summer stock in plays like *Detective Story* and *Inherit the Wind*. This went on for ten or twelve years, and I was doing what I had sworn to myself I would do: play a variety of roles. It's like the baseball player who swings the leaded bat. Do something that is over your head and the next thing that comes along is easy.

One summer Marty Ritz, who's now a motion picture director, had been given carte blanche to do four plays at Fairmont Park in Philadelphia. There's a whole great new plant there, now, but at that time it was like a circus tent—full of colors and in the round. I did *Front Page* and *Boy Meets Girl* for him, and Marty was having a ball. It was his first experience with theater in the round and he staged it like a carousel. It happened that we were being followed by Morton de Costa with his production of *The Little Hut* with Barbara Bel Geddes, so he was there while we were doing our shows, and Kermit Bloomgarten, who sees almost everything, was there. So the following season, when they were looking for someone to play *The Music Man*, and they decided to stop looking for a musical comedy star and take an actor who could get away with the singing and dancing, they remembered having seen me in these two productions. So they called me and gave me what they considered to be the toughest song to audition—"Trouble." (It's the easiest, actually; it's a song you can't fall off of once you learn it if you can learn it.)

I auditioned and they signed me. The understanding was— because we were all friends—that if, during the first or second week of rehearsal, we saw that it wasn't going to work, we would part company and no one would be hurt in the feelings. But it

worked—it started to work immediately—and as someone said,
"the rest is history."

Now, we knew we had a character the audience would buy,
but no one expected it to be the hit it was. Rex Harrison had
done *My Fair Lady* the year before, but that was a different
thing—no one was too surprised because the best man to play
Professor Higgins was Rex Harrison, whether patter, song and
movement was or was not involved.

I think that *The Music Man* marked the first time a straight
actor stepped into the musical comedy field and got away with
it, so the show was newsworthy. It was fun to do, and so
infinitely rewarding . . . I never expected the jet-propulsion
burst that came to my career. It was wonderful. But after I
played *The Music Man* for over two years I realized that I had
to get something different—that if I wasn't careful I'd end up
like O'Neill's father, who was the Count of Monte Cristo all his
life. I certainly didn't want to be the Music Man all my life.

So I did a few movies at Warner Brothers, one very different
from *The Music Man*. The reason I did them at Warners was
because they'd bought *The Music Man* and I was determined
that if it was at all possible (and I knew I was flying in the face
of all worldly precedent) I was going to play Harold Hill in
the picture. So finally, after they had exhausted every possible
male, they settled on me, and I got the part. I was pleased with
it, thoroughly pleased, but I realized that now—more than
ever—I must do something different.

A man brought me a libretto based on the character of Pancho
Villa, and I fell in love with it—the music and the personality
of Villa. I thought it would be the best thing I had done in my
life, but it never came to New York. We couldn't lick the second
act, so we closed it for repairs, but somehow or other everyone
associated with it scattered to the four winds and we never got it
together again. I hope someday we will because it's a character
worthy of a top show, and a joy for me.

Yet I had made my first big step in getting away from *The
Music Man,* and since then I've tried to do a variety of roles.
There's the tragic husband in *All the Way Home* and the next
season the heel in *Nobody Loves an Albatross* and now Ben

Franklin. I have a character for next season that will again be a marvelous departure. I can't tell you more about it at this time; it's a well-written costume comedy (a phrase that producers hate and dread). High comedy of the great old style S. N. Behrman used to do so beautifully. I think audiences are ready for this again, ready to come full circle away from this long cycle of domestic comedy. Unless you get a smash like *The Odd Couple* (a smash simply because two geniuses are involved, plus two genius actors) Broadway will fall into the trap of following suit and trying to come up with another *Any Wednesday*. But wherever you go as the actor, you have to be the one who makes the decisions. If you fall into a type-casting trap it's your own fault—I found this out years ago, fortunately. I allowed myself to fall into it in Hollywood because I was too young to protect myself. At that age I relied on the studio for bread and butter, and looked up on the executive as Dad. I'm over that, I must say.

And that, my friend, covers (at too great a length) the story of my life.

N.   How much are you enjoying your Ben Franklin role?

❦   PRESTON: I enjoyed it tremendously for the first seven months, but now I've fallen prey to the terrible thing that has happened to Broadway. Except for the three smash hits that are booked in advance—and booked so solidly you have to use your ticket the night it says or no show—every other show is doing what *Ben Franklin* is doing right now: playing three or four times a week to standing audiences, the rest of the week to half-houses. The audience just isn't around. People have trained themselves to want to see the status symbol, the talked-about hit, and they're just not shopping around for anything less than the most-talked-about show.

I'm not singing the blues about Ben because I've had a ball with him. The fact is, I'd just as soon go somewhere now and grow hair, but I do hold a brief for the wonderful shows like *Poor Bitos* and *The Severed Head*, all the shows that (if it were economically feasible) should stick around and find their audience if their audience would find them. But our audience has lost its daring.

I suppose the easy way out is to blame television. But I think there's a great deal of truth in the fact that the public has hypnotized itself with that TV set—Monday night whozis' show is on, Tuesday is for whatzat, etc.—so they stay home and watch some pretty wretched stuff. We saw it last season, though we did very well the first six months with *Albatross*. Everyone thought that when the World's Fair came to New York it would be a tremendous break for theater, because all those out-of-towners (and not the stultified New Yorkers) would want to see some New York theater. We found this was not the case. After they had seen what they wanted of the Fair they rushed to their hotels and turned on their television. I'd like to go through hotel rooms with a little ax, the way Carry Nation used to swing through saloons, and end part of the TV menace. The trouble with so many viewers is the way they just watch—not caring what they're watching. And if kids grow up conditioned to the idiot box as the sole entertainment medium, think of the trouble we're in.

Speaking of kids, I'm happy to report that the kids around the country are in pretty good shape. I was sorry to see an article the other day—an article based on an interview a woman did with me—in which I seemed to take the blackest possible view of the entire coming generation. Actually, I was just taking a dim view of one particular segment of our coming generation; I've met many, many kids who are going to grow up all right, and I hope they're the ones who end up governing this country and running the show, not the crazy kids I pictured as walking around with a transistor set growing out of their little heads.

N.　　　How do you feel about New York critics and their influence upon the theater?

　　　PRESTON: I wish they *had* an influence upon theater. As far as I'm concerned I've always agreed with what the critics have said about me—almost always, anyway—because it's usually applied quite accurately to my limitations or the limitations of the play. I've had my share of flops and hits.

Take Walter Kerr, for example. I know I hear a play through his ear, I hear what I'm saying through his ear, because I trust his ear. And when he comes up with a line about me in his critiques I say to him the next time I see him "I knew I wasn't going to fool you on that line."

The influence the critics can have is out-of-town rather than in town. Of course they do, right now, make or break a show—yet this isn't entirely true. The word was out about *The Odd Couple* and I saw lines standing in front of that theater two weeks before the critics ever said a word about it. There are certain plays you cannot keep from being hits—but I've been in plays that have had seven unanimous rave reviews (when we have seven critics here) that have flopped. I can think of one, *The Hidden River,* the last Ruth and Augustus Goetz collaboration—a marvelous play. Not only did the critics give it seven unanimous raves, but it made the Ten Best of the year and got one of the big prizes. We ran for fourteen money-losing weeks. So although the critics may be able to kill you they can't help you if it's something the public doesn't want to see. The critics function best, for my purposes, out of town. I always love to go to Boston because Elliot Norton sits with you, the writer, and the director, and gives you the constructed critique. By the time you get to New York it's too late. I know certain directors who work on a show after the opening, but they're rare; and quite often, even though they make major changes that may have made the show a big smash on opening night, people won't come to see it once it's been "labeled" by the opening-night reviews.

Years ago I read a bit of research that pointed out that (as far as movies are concerned) critiques affected only 5 percent of the audience. People go to see a motion picture they think they'll like, with people in it they do like, directed by someone they like, and these names are magic. This is the way it should be in the theater. It would be very difficult for Mr. Lunt and Miss Fontanne to come in with something that would close quickly because too many people want to see them, but we have few such stars anymore.

The only way I can define a star is this: a star, to me, is someone who, when they do not play, there is no show. We have very few of them now. I've never known of an understudy going on for Lunt or Fontanne. Even Helen Hayes has understudies go on for her, now, without having the entire audience walk out. So it gets down basically to the play being the thing, and we're not going to get that audience back into the theater until our old playwrights and our young playwrights find something in between the pap and the theater of the absurd. There *is* something between these two extremes; as a matter of fact this is what intrigues me about the play I'm going to do next season; this new young playwright has found it.

Once again it will be up to the critics. I may find that I've read something they don't think is there, but an experienced actor rarely misses that widely.

To talk about my flops. Quite often I would do a play simply because I liked the role—it offered me something different. I had no guarantee in my own mind that the play was going to run any longer than it did, and no disappointment when it didn't because I'd gotten out of it what I wanted.

I remember Edna Best—one season she'd done three or four shows. And there I was. I had folded quickly in *Men of Distinction* and was playing with Celeste Holm in *His and Hers* (at the end of the tenth week we knew it was going to close). The same director wanted me to do a play we were all interested in titled *The Magic and the Loss*. Now, I didn't know if it would be very wise for someone who was just making a name for himself in the theater to do three flops in one season (I had no guarantee the last one wouldn't flop). Edna Best came to see a matinee of *His and Hers* and I said to her, "Edna, you did three or four shows that failed last season, and now they want me to follow two flops with another play that might fail. Should I?" and she said, "Do you like the part?" and I said, "Yes," and she said, "Do it!"

She was right. The actor very seldom (unless he's absolutely to blame) bears any stigma for a show flopping. But if he's played a part he wanted to play he's gained, whether the critics like the show or not, whether people come to see it or not.

N.   How do you approach a character you play? What kind of study goes into it, what kind of preparation on your part?

❦   PRESTON : This is something I decided never to put into words for myself or for anyone else. If you put it into words they're there in your mind and you're stuck with a pattern. And you may inflict the pattern on someone else. You're wrong, in both cases, because there's no one way for the same actor to approach a variety of roles, and there's no way in which one actor can use another actor's approach.

Something clicks with the first reading—the first time you read the play to yourself. Something else clicks the first time you hear it aloud when you do it with a cast. And during the very first week of rehearsal the pattern of what you're going to do and the way you're going to do it becomes clear to you. You suddenly find out how this fellow moves (and everyone moves differently) and the brain starts working with the feet. Your whole body starts to work on this character. It's a conscious, an unconscious, a subconscious (all three) process. If you ever do it too consciously, however, then I think you're in trouble; it's like listening to the sound of your own voice. I can always tell when an actor's doing that—it sounds great to him but it puts you to sleep.

I guess you can get into a discussion of what has become known as the Method. Well, the people who talk about the Method at great length are the people who are involved—for the most part—in what I call the abuse of the Method. They're the people who look for the sickness in a role, not for the health, and this is not what sick people do; sick people look for the health. (Like when you play a drunk you try to play a sober man because that's what a drunk is trying to do.) Right now I'm playing Ben Franklin as a sixty-nine-year old man, but I'm not thinking him old because Ben thought young. Now, he moves a little more slowly than Harold Hill did, but his mind is just as young as Harold's was, so you put on the accoutrements of age but you think young. I've said that if Walter Huston had been around when this part came along I would never have got it; Walter, at the same age as Ben, had the vigor and the lustiness necessary for the role.

But I'm digressing.

I'll give you an example of how things happen with a part. When we started rehearsing *The Music Man* all I knew about Harold Hill was what I saw on paper. Now, we get into the rehearsal hall early in the day and I change into my rehearsal clothes. (This is something you don't do for an ordinary rehearsal. I'll never rehearse with a jacket on if I'm not going to wear a jacket in the scene onstage; the jacket becomes one extra bit of protection or crutch between you and the audience you're not going to have. Similarly, I'll never smoke a cigarette in rehearsal if I'm not going to be smoking at that point in the play. You don't use anything that won't be available to you at the actual performance. You should be able to stand there and do it naked.)

Well, I changed into these clothes because I had to run from the rehearsal of the book to the rehearsal of the music to the rehearsal of the choreography, and to be sensible about it I wore a sweatsuit and tennis shoes. In the middle of the second week of rehearsal Pete said to me, "Bob, when we start talking costumes we've got to get you shoes that don't inhibit the way Harold's starting to move." And that's the first moment I became aware of what I was doing, what Harold was doing, and we established that fancy footwork routine simply because I was rehearsing in tennis shoes. This became Harold's characterization—light-footed, bouncy, always ready to hop the freight for the next town. It happened that unconsciously.

Also, there's an underlying rhythm that's identifiable in a musical. (There's also an underlying rhythm in a straight play and you try to find it, to get the pulse of the audience beating with yours.) We found the rhythm in *The Music Man* and that's why the audience never failed to applaud in rhythm at the final curtain-call.

But it's the same with comedy. There's a rhythm to a joke. Bob Hope can make you laugh at something that isn't funny, and he goes on to his next joke so quickly you're not aware that you laughed at nothing. He's rhythmed you into it.

N.   How about the audience? Does it vary from night to night? Do its reactions have an effect on you?

❧   PRESTON: It varies greatly—and it has a great effect on me. I guess the only universal show I've done was *The Music Man.* That's the only time audiences never varied, even when we did benefits, which are our death, you know.

Now, with *Ben,* every audience is entirely different. Your approach to them is different. It's a subconscious thing. You don't say, "Oh, oh, that's the kind they are tonight, so this is what I'll do." You make your adjustment to them very shortly after that curtain goes up because they tell you something. I don't know what it is, any more than Howard Lindsay can tell you how it is that no one has ever coughed on a word of his.

A heartbreaking thing for the actor is when he tells his best joke and somebody coughs on the punch word. I've seen Howard pause in mid-sentence, let that cough come out, then finish; he's known for never having had a line of his coughed on. I've said, "Please, Howard, tell me your secret," and he could no more tell me that particular secret than I can tell you how you adjust for an audience.

N.   What do you call "adjustment"?

❧   PRESTON: Sometimes it's as simple as picking up the tempo a little bit. And the tempo of an audience varies throughout the week. A Monday night audience is different from a Saturday night audience; these people have had their weekend. Friday night audiences are the optimum audience—not only is it the beginning of a weekend, and you find a great many responsive college students in your audience, but it's also not the rousing, fun-loving audience of Saturday night who maybe have had a bit too much to eat and drink. On Friday the audience is hip and witty, ready for everything, every subtlety, and the lines that never get a laugh the rest of the week will deliver for you on Friday. It's very gratifying. But as you play your Saturday (a bit rougher) and take your Sunday off, you have to adjust to Monday again.

I suppose it's something in the actor, too. Regardless of how we proclaim, "There will be no second-night letdown, there will be no letdown from Saturday to Monday," the fact remains that we're human beings and are bound to have differences in mood and feeling.

I use Olivier as a case in point for the thing I try to do very carefully. (Marlon Brando was known as an actor who would give two fantastic performances a week and six mediocre ones. That's his makeup. An actor's argument can be that Brando on a given night can be better than Olivier, but there's always room for argument as to whether he could or could not.) Whether it's a swinging night or an ordinary night for Sir Laurence there is a level of perfection beneath which he will not fall. You can do this consciously. In other words, whether it's voluntary or not, you always try to do your best.

When I start musicals, and you're working with gangs of people (as opposed to *Two For the Seesaw* or *The Fourposter*) I take a sort of special interest in the young kids. The chorus kids of today are far different from what they used to be in the days when they were kept in penthouse apartments and all that. They're studying, they go from their rehearsal to a dancing class, then go to their singing class, and they're taking acting lessons somewhere else. But they get discouraged—it's hard not to get discouraged when you don't have as much to do as I have, and you have to spend a lot of time in the dressing room—and I keep telling them, "Look, you have to be here for the next two and one-half hours whether you like it or not, so you might as well like it."

It's so much easier to have fun. I have a reputation for being able to keep spirits up, and it isn't a chore. It takes a great deal out of you to mope. God knows during the break-in and the trial and the rehearsal period you have low moments, but that's part of the game. It's nothing new to me that I'm going to be depressed now and then, but you can't allow things to get you down. This is a business of highs and lows, and the person who can't bounce right back from the lows should get out of it.

But I got a long way from your question about adjusting to the audience.

N. What—if any conscious—obligation do you feel, as an actor toward playwright, role, audience, and profession?

❧ PRESTON: This goes back to what I said earlier in this interview about self-respect and pride. We've come a long way from the time when an actor was called a vagabond and wasn't allowed to sit at the same table with the gentry. If we're going to call acting an art or a profession (and we do throw those words around) we must feel that way about our work. We cannot engender respect for our profession if we don't have a great deal of self-respect.

Our obligations are part of this one picture, and they begin with our attitudes toward each other. Take the director. He's your teacher for that term, and speaking of any method you use, you by and large find yourself falling into the method the director uses; you're seldom aware of your own particular method of working because you adjust to him. (I work with a variety of directors, and there are certain ones with whom I know how much I myself will have to bring, and others I'm going to get a great deal from. There are directors you can bring any question in the world, and others you shy like the devil from ever asking anything. The reason you work with the latter man is because he has a good play.)

Actually, your obligation is primarily to the audience. This is why, even on closing nights, I don't like to see kids playing around on the stage, having fun the audience isn't in on. That isn't for us to do. We can have all the fun we need during rehearsals, but when we do the show it must be the show. In a certain play Lunt and Fontanne had been doing for a long time he actually called a rehearsal to clean up something on closing night. That's the way it should be done.

N. If you were to give the aspiring actor advice, what would it be?

❧ PRESTON: I keep harking back to Olivier, but what actor doesn't? He did an interview for *Life* magazine not too long ago, and I think any kid who wants to act should go back to get a copy. They should read it and reread it—I reread it every time I have a problem. He states the case for the young actor so beautifully. He even gives some tips on what to do.

How do you keep in shape? Well, your work is keeping you in shape. How do you stay young? You stay as young as the people you're with and the roles you play. I've never known an actor's age. I've never been aware of it, I've never cared. Physical fitness is something Olivier touches upon heavily in this article.

He also goes quite deeply into the attitude a kid must have. If he thinks it's going to be easy, if he wants to act because he might meet Elizabeth Taylor or drive a Rolls Royce, he doesn't belong in the profession.

I know fine actors who have not, to this day, made it big. They will, however, because their attitude is right. This business of being in the right place at the right time is a truism only because it's so true. And I've been fortunate. Every move I've made in my life has somehow or other been related to being in the right place at the right time. However, I've been able to deliver—if an actor can't deliver, all the right place-right time opportunities will be wasted. The actor has to be ready—physically, psychologically, artistically—at all times.

I hate to come back to me, all the time, but I'm the actor I know best and can relate to. I know, for example, that I'm learning every time I work. Better than that, I'm learning every time I perform. I would like to find out from someone whose judgment I trust—from Walter Kerr, for example—just how much my portrayal of Ben Franklin has improved (or worsened) in the seven or eight months I've been playing it. I find new things every night, even when I'm not looking for them—they just happen.

One of the best things ever said to me came from one of the great directors I've worked with, Michael Gordon. I was on the witness stand, making this simple statement: "Then we went to a restaurant and had some chop suey." Mike stopped me and said, "Bob, how do you feel about chop suey?" and I said, "What?" He said, "Well, when you read that line I couldn't tell whether you liked chop suey or not." I said, "Oh, yeah," and he said, "Oh, yeah; always have an attitude about anything you say." Which is true. If I listened to a playback of this tape I could tell you, just by the inflections in my voice, which subjects interested me most.

Well, Ben finds different attitudes toward different things every night. The play of color is marvelous.

N.　　　　　The final question—and I think you've half-answered it already, in scattered statements—is this: What do you look for in a role? Have you a preconceived idea of a role you want?

❦　　　　　PRESTON: I don't know that I'm looking for any tangible thing. The only time I've ever consciously looked for something is when I say, "That role is much too similar to the one I just got through playing." But if that's a good role you say, "Please hold it off for a few seasons; I'd like to do it then."

I guess what I look for is variety, variety that offers joy and growth, but beyond that the play finds you. I'm constantly reading things. I didn't know what I was looking for, as far as next season is concerned, until I read the costume comedy I spoke of before—but when I read it the play hit me right between the eyes and I *had* to do it. (As a matter of fact I was looking for something quite different from that role.) I have no guarantee that it will run for four performances, but it has class and appeal and as I said before, we work for joy and growth.

I feel sorry for the actor who finds himself in something he's not very fond of playing, something he doesn't like, just because he has to work. It's been a long time since I've done anything in any field simply because I had to work. The dollar part of the business stopped frightening me, thank God. It would be terrible to work in any field if you didn't enjoy your work.

I know good actors who never rose above bit-status in Hollywood, yet they're very well-known to millions of people because they've been seen thousands of times. Now you, as a lead, have the whole script, but the bit actor comes in and he's given just two pages, enough to cover his day or two of shooting. He doesn't know who I am, his relationship with the story, or where he is in time. Often these people go to a movie and suddenly see themselves, after watching five reels without knowing they were in the picture. But the good ones make up a beginning for themselves and follow through, and in their own minds they give themselves a flow and continuity. They have a reason for being there, which is what one must do. It's simply an extension of what I do in playing a lead role. Now, I know Ben Franklin as a boy even though none of his boyhood is involved in the show. I know the kind of childhood he had. This is unconscious—I haven't Stanislavski'd myself into anything (consciously, that is).

There is a certain amount of small-m "method" in that work, but anything else can be hog-tieing. An actor can hog-tie himself by knowing more than the author intended him to know. That is, when he feels obliged to tell the audience more than *it* has to know. Spencer Tracy once said—and you can't convince me he did this, however—that you should "Do nothing in a closeup; just stand there. The audience is following the story, so just stand there and let them photograph you. They'll think what you want them to think."

I found great joy in working, several times, with Gary Cooper. Now, Cooper doesn't have the reputation as a great actor except with us who knew him as an actor. But he was great. People used to comment on what they called his idiosyncrasies, his little foibles. But Coop never made a move that wasn't thoroughly thought out and planned. He is probably the finest motion picture actor I ever worked with. . . .

I guess he, in his career, summed up everything I feel about the profession, anything I look and hope for, any advice I give: you've got to know what you're doing.

Schultz's Charlie Brown said it better—"Security is knowing all your lines."

"Money, taste, the ability to handle the right people—that is the producer's job."

HAROLD S. PRINCE

What is it like to direct or produce, or to direct *and* produce, a Broadway show? Why does any mortal man tempt such invitation to ulcer and coronary? How does it feel to take that big pile of money, attach it to that vulnerable little script and all those fallible people who emote or sing or dance? Then wait for the applause, then for the notices, that tell you whether that big pile of money has been irretrievably lost or will be graciously compounded?

Who would know the answers to these questions better than Hal Prince?

PRINCE: I was born in New York City in 1928 and reared here. My father is on Wall Street; he's a member of the Stock Exchange. My mother is a housewife who likes the theater—thus I was exposed to theater at a very early age at Saturday matinees, etc. I remember seeing *Julius Caesar* with Orson Welles when he was twenty-one. Lord knows he's a lot older than I am, so I must have been idiotically young to attend that, but I did.

I saw a great deal of theater. I went to a private school in New York—one school all the time—from the age of four until I was ready to go to college. (The Franklin School.) Then I went to

the University of Pennsylvania, graduated in 1947, and at the
end of that year I came back to New York to look for work. I
didn't find work right away and was told that I had no credits
and wasn't too employable. So I lied. I made up a whole list of
credits as a director, though I had never directed anything but a
few plays when I was in college (college casts) and a great deal
of radio. (During college I worked with some other people in
starting the University radio station, part of a university network, which turned out to be very successful because we went
commercial. We broadcasted in the West Philadelphia area, near
the University, and it really did give me a lot of experience. I
even did the play-by-play on our football games, along with
another fellow.)

Then I came here and made up this dossier of phony credits
of plays I had directed. (I must say I was acquainted with the
plays; I used to read them instead of novels. I think I've read
every damned published play that came along before I became
a producer. Now I read only unproduced plays, often a dreary
business.)

With phony dossier in hand I walked into the office of a
rather famous agent, Chamberlain Brown. Brown had the
biggest name in the business back in the day of Fritzi Scheff—
that's a long time ago. All the old ladies and gentlemen knew
him. So I walked in and it just happened that this very old
gentleman was looking for someone to direct a season of stock in
New Jersey, and there I was—a director for someone's dreams.
"This boy is marvelous," he said over the phone to somebody.
This company was in terrible trouble; they'd lost their director
and had a season scheduled. So I went down and directed a show
every week, starting with *John Loves Mary* and *Angel Street*.
We were sold out every single night, and the owner of the place
was pleased, but I wasn't. I told him that I really didn't want to
direct this tired stuff—I wanted to do something real, like *Sunup*
in the round, and I wanted to do *Mr. Pim Passes By* and some
fresh stuff that nobody else was doing in stock. He said, "You do
four good plays that sell out and I'll let you do what you
want." So I did, and we sold out for four weeks and went
bankrupt in the next two when I was doing *Mr. Pim Passes By*.

I was left stranded in the wilds of Sussex County, New Jersey, and hitch-hiked back to New York two weeks sooner than I'd anticipated.

I started to write. I wrote some television stuff. (I forgot to mention that I'd written a few plays in college, too.) I wrote out an idea for a television series and sent it to George Abbott, who had a small television operation here in his office. (Happens to be the office we're sitting in, now.) This was in 1948, and someone here at Abbott's read the presentation and asked me to come up. During the course of the interview I said, "Look, I need a job. I'm lucky enough to be able to support myself without a salary, and I can't think of why anyone would give me a nickel a week, so why don't you let me find out if I can be of any value? The hardest thing for you will be having someone around you're not paying; you're going to feel guilty. But the likelihood of that someone not working out is rather great, so why don't we see how it plays?"

I worked ardently, and after about two months they gave me $25 a week, then raised me to $50, and finally the television thing went kaput. That was when George said, "I don't think this is amounting to very much." By then I had followed George in writing and directing a television show on NBC titled "The Hugh Martin Show"—Joan McCracken was on it, and Kaye Ballard, and Hugh Martin plus thirteen singers, and the credit read "Written and directed by Harold Prince." It came on at 7 o'clock on Sunday night, and I got all of $50 a week. We also put three other new shows on television, including the first of those charade-type shows (ours had Tom Ewell). I forgot what it was called.

That was the operation, but I was out of work one Friday when George said, "I think it's a time-consuming money-loser." I pulled all my stuff out of the office and very unhappily went back home. But on Monday he called me. George had a stage manager named Bobby Griffith, and they had been discussing me, and George said, "What you really wanted to do was to be in the theater, wasn't it?" and I said, "Yes," and he said, "Well, Bobby has talked me into firing an inept assistant stage manager on one of his shows—*Touch and Go*, written by

Walter and Jean Kerr." So I grabbed the job at the munificent sum of $75 a week and I was on my way in theater. I've been either backstage or out in front ever since, and never out of work for a minute since the end of 1948 (drawing a blank on two years in the Army of course.) Can I tell you a Kerr story? The other night I climbed out of a cab to see *Judith* and there were the Kerrs. It was opening night and my wife and I dared her advanced pregnancy to go, and I said, "Oops, look who's standing there!" for there were both Kerrs in the flesh. Well, Walter Kerr has been giving me bum reviews for such a long time I can't remember when he gave me a good one, and people are whispering in my ear that he has something against me (which I doubt) but 'way back since *West Side Story* his reviews have been terrible. He just doesn't like anything I do. Anyway, as we got out of the cab the Kerrs turned their backs on me. I was quite ready to say, "Hello," very cheerfully and go on into the theater.

I think it's just some odd feeling they have that if they give people bad reviews those people hate them or some damned thing, and maybe I'm supposed to, but the shows run and they're very successful and I have a nice feeling that Walter Kerr doesn't matter. And it doesn't hurt to be friendly. I don't know why they're so sulky. I sat next to them on opening night of *Do I Hear a Waltz?* and they wouldn't talk to me. We used to be friends. Now he's giving me bad reviews and they won't talk to me. *You* figure that out.

After *Touch and Go* I went on to another show called *Tickets, Please* that Paul and Grace Hartman were in. Then I went over to Leland Hayward's office to do the casting of *Call Me Madam*. (George sort of loaned me out to Leland because Leland's casting man was in Europe working on something else.)

Then I got drafted (this was the time of the Korean business) and went to Germany.

I got out of the Army and hadn't even climbed out of my uniform when I went to the opening night of a show George was producing with Jule Styne titled *In Any Language*. Bobby Griffith and George were sitting on the stage and I walked in. George is not a letter-writer—he is, actually, but he wasn't to me during the two-year stretch—his secretary would write to me occasionally to let me know the office presumed I was still alive—but otherwise I felt very much out of things, as though my career had been rolling and was suddenly and irreparably stopped dead. I was a sorehead about it.

Anyway, I had no real assurance that I was going to get my job back, and there I was at the Cort with George saying, "Are you here on furlough?" I said, "No, I'm out," and he said, "What, already?" and I said, "Yes," and he said, "Two years —it seems like two days!" But he recovered and said, "Anyway, it's fine, and you go into rehearsal next week with Rosalind Russell on a musical." So a week later I started to work on *Wonderful Town*. When I think of the trouble I could have saved myself had I known how it would turn out—but I suppose it *was* character-building.

During *Wonderful Town* Bobby Griffith and I decided we could be pretty good producers, and what happened our first time up was a pie-in-the-sky affair that maybe could never happen again, but would it be as much fun?

We found a book called *7½ Cents*. (The story is pretty well documented.) We bought it, and talked George into directing it. We acquired a third partner, Freddie Brisson. Then we tried to find a writer, but we were turned down by everyone including Richard Bissell, the author of the book. Then we tried to find someone to do the score, but nobody would touch that, so we hired two new fellows named Adler and Ross. Then no choreographer would touch it, so we hired Bobby Fosse who had never choreographed. Then we got a bunch of actors nobody was hiring and put everything together and called it *The Pajama Game*. We had one hell of a time raising the money—went through auditions, where I used to tell potential backers the story—a strictly fraudulent story. (The first time up I told the truth, about this being a strike at a pajama factory, and scared them off.) Later I talked all about a Romeo and Juliet romance in Iowa, a romance which didn't have a thing to do with *Pajama Game*. We had to reorganize the score completely to fit my invented plot, but we raised $250,000, and the show went on.

From then on we didn't have trouble raising money. *Damn Yankees* came on its heels, then a lot of other shows.

N.   How does it feel to produce a success? Especially one that's a bit of a surprise, as far as critics and public are concerned?

❧   PRINCE: *Pajama Game* cost $169,000, and the show paid off in twelve weeks—which is an absurdly short time. It was a smash, and the lines were beautiful to see. In fact, I haven't had a hit like it until *Fiddler on the Roof* came along this season.

Overnight we were fellows with a big hit, two of us with no money; we used up any money we had in just getting the show on. We were the stage managers of that show, and we worked backstage on opening night. (Bobby never actually saw the show until it was on Broadway three months. I was his assistant, so I used to go out and look at it once in a while and he'd have somebody spell me.) So on opening night we were in black ties with flashlights in our hip pockets and we ran the show. We talked to each other over the intercom every time something stopped the show, and *everything* stopped the show that night. It was quite the biggest opening night I've ever had. We just kept saying, "Listen!" and "Great!" and "Whee!" and "I think we're in!" The excitement never stopped. At this time all our income was our stage manager salary; Bobby was getting $250 a week and I was getting half that.

And it was wonderful the way the kids in the show were with us. They stood in the wings and kept grabbing us every time something worked, and everything worked. I don't think anyone could describe the excitement of having a Broadway opening night that big.

The next morning at nine thirty we stood watching 750 people waiting patiently to purchase tickets. For us, of course, there'd be no extra money until it paid off, so I was still living on my $125 a week and getting a lot of back-slapping and quips like, "Hey, lend me a hundred thousand, will you, buddie?" I had all of $400 in the bank. But it was a hell of a thing. I knew it had happened, all right, but I didn't know whether it would ever happen again. I didn't know how much luck had to do with it, and, frankly, I didn't really feel *in* the theater from one show. I didn't feel in the theater, professionally, until long after other people assumed I was in. It took me through *West Side Story* to give me a sense of continuity of real self-assurance, and by then we'd done five hits in a row, which is being damned lucky.

N.   What were those five hits?

          PRINCE: *Pajama Game, Damn Yankees, New Girl in Town, West Side Story* and *Fiorello.* We had some flops right after that—*Tenderloin* and *A Call on Kuprin.* In fact, I'd been wondering what would happen when I had a flop (and you have to have one sometime). I wondered if I could live with a flop, what the whole feeling would be like. Well, it happened, and I found that it wasn't very hard to take. In fact, it was a relief to have gone through it.

N.   Do you ever recognize a flop in the process of getting it to Broadway?

          PRINCE: Only once. We all pitched ourselves into *Tenderloin* because we had had such fun doing *Fiorello,* but I had grave misgivings about it shortly after we started rehearsing. It didn't come together, somehow, but we kept hoping it would.

N.   *West Side Story* must have been a great experience.

          PRINCE: It was. It's the only show I've ever worked on that underwent virtually no substantial changes from the first public performance in Washington.

But then it was so especially Jerry Robbins' concept—Arthur Laurents' book, Bernstein and Sondheim's score—so particularly right for what Jerry had in his head that I think—we all knew—it would either work or it wouldn't, with no in-between.

Every other show I've worked on has undergone a great deal of change. (Between the out-of-town performances and the Broadway opening.) *A Funny Thing Happened on the Way to the Forum* was dismally received in Washington—it was a disaster. We came to New York and we were a hit. Down there we played to empty houses night after night after night, and people kept telling us to close it. Perle Mesta said, "Such a nice young man. I've liked everything you've done, and I don't know how you could produce this dirty show. It was all I could do to sit through it opening night." I said, rather arrogantly, "But it's going to be a smash, you know," and she said, "I don't think so." I don't know whether or not I really believed it would be a smash, but generally I'm an optimistic fellow. I think you have to be optimistic to be in theater. I think you have to love what you're doing each time and I think you must be inspired.

Look at it this way. The gradations in the levels of talent in the theater are enormous. There are extremely talented people and very mediocre ones. The mediocre people very often have a big success. The thing that makes their work successful is the fact that they do the best they can, inspire themselves.

On the other hand some extremely talented people in the theater often work on something they don't really care for. They get cajoled into it, but they don't really believe in it. They want the money or to be busy. And you can spot this lack of enthusiasm, the missing dynamism. It's one fellow's worst against another fellow's best, and the other fellow's best, even though he's much less talented, wins out.

N.   What are the exact duties of the producer of a Broadway show?

❧   PRINCE : To find a project, to have taste.

I think it would be better for me to define qualifications than duties because the duties are within the easy reach of almost everyone, which is why so many bad producers exist and why so many production offices open and close. There isn't much continuity in the theater among production firms beyond a handful of people. The qualifications : taste is vital. Somehow he must have the ability to raise money. And the ability to talk to writers—and, in the case of musicals, to talk to composers and choreographers, too, and mold them into the happy package called a successful collaboration.

The producer has to keep everything on a fairly even keel, yet push for success. But to know precisely what will make a success is the hardest thing. To know what to push for, and when to say, "No, I will not give you $2,000 for that ridiculous scenic effect," or "Yes, the $2,000 is worth it; I can see where it will make the difference." This takes talent and taste, and it's in this area that most producers stumble. It isn't enough just to back a play. It isn't enough to be a good enough salesman, to talk good people into working with you. You also have to know how to push and *when* to push—*that* so few of them know—and cajole a project along. But not to nag—never to nag.

I've never produced a play that hasn't come to one point or another when I feared it wouldn't come off because something had gone seriously wrong. There's always been a crucial day when it seemed that unless we could get over a particular hurdle the show wouldn't go on. And the thing that people don't realize is that for every show I do that gets to Broadway there's another that never makes it. The fact that I may have put my own money into it, and worked on it for a year or two, makes no difference: it just doesn't jell.

Money, taste, the ability to handle the right people—this is the producer's job. The director has the actual artistic control of the show.

N.   Could you define the director's role?

          PRINCE: The director is the artistic controller, a guide, the liaison between the many collaborators. It's a more immediate, a more specific role with the actors and with the production. Frankly, I find it more interesting.

However, I have found producing interesting because I have deliberately avoided working with anyone who felt the way "the boys" felt in the old days—that the producer was just the businessman, so divorced from the show that when the creative department meets the producer isn't present. I've never had this disassociated association with George Abbott or Jerome Robbins. I wouldn't want it with anyone. I have to know what is going on. I'm sure that many producers stay clear of the actual production, figuring it's all in the laps of the gods the day the show goes into rehearsal. I stay with it.

N.   You go out on the road?

❧   PRINCE : I go out on the road and I don't come back to New York until the show opens. I'm with it every minute, present at every meeting. This is the only way I can do it, and I have a very good time. It's a lot of fun—not because it's glamorous, but because most of the people who work in theater consistently simply know how to have a good time even when they're working desperately hard. I forgot, before, to say that another part of the producer's role is to know something about promoting. Pitifully few of us do. I don't consider myself among those who know much about it, either. I'm a little lost at how you sell something that people don't want, whereas, thank the Lord, if you have something they *do* want there aren't very many problems involved in selling it. I go the usual route in publicity. I normally don't spend as much on publicity as other producers do because I'd rather not throw money away on something I don't quite understand, and I don't quite understand how you sell theater tickets.

One of the great problems of the theater is that not many people *do* know how to sell tickets. It's an industry-wide problem, not an individual problem. It's one that's occupying a great deal of my time, right now, as Director of the League of New York Theatres.

N.   How has the great rise of costs affected the theater?

❧   PRINCE : For one thing, I keep being told that raising money is very difficult. It must be. I don't have any difficulty, which is good, because I hate asking for money. In fact, the raising of money in this office over the last three years has become my secretary's function. She sends out the letters, she talks to the investors. I really can't talk about it. The moment someone says, "Do you really think this one will be a hit?" I'm embarrassed—embarrassed for them for asking me, and for me having to answer. I'm a very good businessman by default. I have given them a good return on their money.

Earlier this year *The Wall Street Journal* figured out that the return on the investment made with this office is consistently higher than with any other office in the theater. They figured out that in all of the years I've been in the theater the average profit returned on a dollar invested in my shows is 62 cents plus—and that was before *Fiddler on the Roof*. *Fiddler* will have probably raised that to 75 cents or maybe even more.

I think it comes from my willingness to say "No" and to watch costs. But (as I've mentioned before) a great deal of it comes from that indefinable thing called "taste." From knowing where to cut corners that don't show, by knowing when not to let people indulge themselves. The artistic, the creative tendency is to spend money—to indulge the creative mind with dollars. I worked for too many years for George Abbott to respect that kind of madness. Creating isn't spending at all, as a matter of fact. The spur to Broadway, the strongest element of Broadway theater, the thing that keeps theater alive and will keep it alive, is the fact that it's a hungry industry. Beware of the fatted calves—they're in trouble. This is what happened to Hollywood not too long ago and why movies are in better shape today. This is why television has such a paucity of decent creative material. (They're grand at putting a camera on a news event, but they're in deep trouble when they have a creative itch.) Both the movie and television industries got so rich and so lazy they figured they didn't have to be creative. But Broadway is poor, always was poor. Every time, with every new show, you go to bat for the first time with no score on your side.

Now, Richard Rodgers probably has the biggest name in theater, but when his new show opened the other night he was up at bat for the first time. On Broadway you've got to be good every time. This isn't true of television or the movies. You can slide along for years on a good movie you made eons ago, pulling down a top salary all the while. Theater doesn't pay salaries. We work on spec all the time, and until the show is a hit we don't make any money.

N. What do you think of the power of New York critics?

PRINCE: I don't know how powerful they are. I don't think they're as powerful as they used to be because of the television critics; they're getting to be very important.

On the other hand I'm more concerned with the responsibility of the New York critics than I am with their power. I don't think they've done very much to help, or even recognize, the drama, what we call "serious" theater. I happen to be lucky. I'm in the musical comedy business, and that's where the audience is— people come to see light comedies and musical comedies. It didn't occur to me until the other day, when we were discussing theater in someone's living room, that this isn't even the theater I like. I rarely like a musical and I almost never enjoy the highly touted comedies; what interest me, when I go to the theater, are the dramas. We go to far more dramas—my wife and I—than we do comedies, and we usually come away satisfied or at least provoked. One of my favorite evenings in the theater this year was *Slow Dance on a Killing Ground*. I enjoyed *Tiny Alice*—not entirely, but I found it interesting. I saw *Judith* the other night and thought it brilliant, whereas when I go to a musical (and most of them are ordinary) or the comedies (which are so slight) I come away hungry.

The question is, what is the job of the press? Are those men there simply as critics? If they are they're doing their job— they're telling us what they thought of the play. But it's going to be a steadily narrowing sampling they're going to get if they don't make things more exciting in their reviews. It's easy to say you fell off your chair laughing, but dramas demand more of reviewers.

I had an interesting thing happen recently. We did *Poor Bitos*, which got pretty good reviews. The week before it opened, with no advance, it picked up $22,000 at the box office. We played two weeks of previews, our business was great, the word was good and people had a wonderful time. Just before we were set to open I said to my business manager, "Isn't it a shame we have to open? We could run twelve weeks easily this way, at these grosses, without ever getting reviewed. The audience wants to see it and we're getting the right audience."

We opened, and the reviews came out, and while they were good they were dull and we had no audience. We closed in two weeks. There's a lesson here, somewhere, but I doubt that the critics are about to learn it.

N.   What about *Fiddler on the Roof?* How did you get involved in it?

PRINCE: It first came to my attention about four years ago. Bock and Harnick and Stein were working on it, and they brought it to me and I said I thought they should wait a year before they went near it because there was a whole flock of Jewish plays on Broadway and I didn't think it should get confused with any of that other material.

In the meantime we did *She Loves Me* (which they also wrote) and after we got that on they came back and asked me to direct *Fiddler*. I said, "No, I can't—I'm not the right fellow. There's only one man for that show, Jerome Robbins," and they said, "But he's doing *Funny Girl*," and I replied, "Which is a good reason for not doing *Fiddler* at this time." So they went away again, they got a new producer, Robbins became available, and then they all came back to me. I happily involved myself with *Fiddler* then because it was all I had hoped it would be.

N.   What is your next project?

PRINCE: We're opening out of town next week with a show titled *Flora, the Red Menace*. It's fun, it's about something that interests me. It's a case in point about the years sometimes having to pass before you get a property in production. I bought a book titled *Love is Just Around the Corner* two years ago, maybe a bit longer, from galleys. I've been all this time trying to get it off the ground properly, and I think it's going to be good. It's a different kind of show.

N.   In a general sense—considering your career as a whole—could you state your aims?

PRINCE: I'm by no means satisfied. I think that what I'd like to do would be to direct and produce, as I'm doing, and I'd like to direct for other people and have other people direct for me. What I really want to do is to open up all possibilities—this is why I wanted to be able to do *Baker Street*. I wanted to make it very clear that I could work for someone, that I was up for hire, that I wasn't abandoning this office, that if someone came to me with a play and I wasn't the right director for it I would still like to produce it. I don't want to categorize myself or limit myself. I like it all too much

At the moment I seem to have achieved the dual roles; now it's a matter of seeing what comes up, and as it comes up, doing it. Because the producing end requires an office and a staff and substantial fixed expenses, I always have to be sure I have something coming out of this headquarters.

I'd like to direct movies, too. Good movies are as good as good stage plays. I have no desire to work in television, however, or in any other field.

What's so good about this sort of career, of course, is the fact that there's no end to it. Each play presents its own new set of problems you have to solve, so there's never a lack of stimulation and there's nothing to get comfortable about. I like the fact that every time we go to bat it's the first time. They say it ages you, but I don't think so—I think you stay young and alert longer. Abbott's proof of that. Then, too, the more chances you take, the greater the rewards.

N.   How would you assess the general health of the theater?

❧   PRINCE: I wish we were healthier economically. We have problems, but perhaps that's for the best. When you have economic problems you come up with more ideas, and that may happen to us. Broadway is still the artistic center of the theater and always will be; people have to make a living and they've got to attain prestige. I'm respectful, but a little bored, with all that publicity the nonprofit subsidized theater's been getting. It's a wonderful movement, but it's not the creative center of theater. It helps build audiences and develop talent, but it's not an end in itself. New playwrights by the dozens will cut their teeth, perhaps, and new actors will be seen, but they'll want to do their real work here.

I'll digress to the situation in England because it has bearing upon what's happening here. Interesting and terrible things have happened to the professional theater in England over the past few years. I don't know how they're going to solve their problems; I don't know the setup that well. But I do know this: with the advent of a national theater, subsidized theater, they virtually killed off independent commercial management. I don't think anyone knows how to resolve the problems. The great actors don't want to sign now with a commercial manager for more than eight or twelve weeks; the great playwrights are right behind them because, naturally, they'll follow the actors they depend upon. They don't have to because they can do *Othello* or the avant garde or anything else they want in the national theater for a limited length of time. They can indulge themselves on a three-month basis, then make movies (and real money!) almost simultaneously because London is the center of the motion-picture industry in England.

Where does this leave the producers and managers and everyone who's not being spoonfed by subsidized theater? Last month (and the same was true of the preceding month) there was only one play in rehearsal in London. (In this country that couldn't happen unless the movie industry was moved to New York, and nobody seems to want this.) So we'll always be able to sign our actors for eighteen months and then they can go make their movies. But at least we're not going to be subsidized out of business—our actors have to make a living in the theater.

I feel confident, obviously, that we're going to be all right. Right now we're overemphasizing the value of regional theater. Bricks and mortar and not enough concern for plays and players. Still the Government is planning to spend ten million dollars on subsidy and if it stimulates live theater then it will have served us well. But we've got to put everything in its proper perspective because the best directors, the best actors, the best scenic designers, the best choreographers are here, and the best that come up through the regional route will soon come here. And who knows—we might even develop more critics who help make the theater exciting to a larger audience.

"Many people have said to me: 'I don't know why you ever leave a part like Auntie Mame.'"

ROSALIND RUSSELL

I first became aware of Rosalind Russell when she played a serious role opposite Robert Donat in *The Citadel*. Some time later she stole that brilliant film, *The Women*, from the industry's heaviest competition. Since then she's been Eileen's protective sister, Electra, Sister Kenny, and—of course—Auntie Mame. Plus many other notable women we temporarily overlook because of the way she dominated these big roles.

The word "incomparable" has been attached to persons as various as Max Beerbohm and Hildegarde. It also belongs to Rosalind Russell.

RUSSELL: In asking for autobiographical data you've asked for something that could take six tomes. I can't say how good those tomes would be, however.

My start in the theatrical world was forced upon me in a strange way. My father passed away while I was in college. He was a remarkable man, a great believer in education. I'm one of seven children, and perhaps he knew he didn't have too long to live, because he left a will in which all of his children would receive no money of any kind after they had been graduated from college—after they had been educated. In other words, they could go to school as long as they wanted to, take up anything. I always say that I had one sister who finally had to give up at the age of thirty-seven. She came down to smiling lessons. (She also crocheted quite well and collected nice stamps.)

My father believed that we should go out and earn a living after we were educated. He had a great fear that his four girls were going to sit around and play bridge and drink cocktails and wait for husbands. But there I was, out of college, equipped to teach. It was during the depression when new teachers were paid about $30 a week, and this frightened me. I thought that I had to have a few more hats and baubles than that salary could possibly purchase, and wondered what I could to to make money. "Oh," I said to myself, "actresses make lots of money."

Little did I know. But I went to my mother and frightened the poor woman half to death by telling her that I had always wanted to go to The American Academy of Dramatic Arts in New York. She said, "What on earth for?" and I said, "To teach dramatic art." That pacified her because I had a bit of a flare in that direction, having done all the plays in every school I was in (an endless number of them) so she gave her consent and off I went. I was there only two or three months when the head of the school sent for me to come to the office and told me that I should leave. Having spent most of my time in the Dean's offices of most colleges I said, "What have I done?" and he said, "Well, we feel that you should get experience, that you are quite well advanced in the work in many ways. We think you ought to go to some stock company and get a job." I said, "You can't throw me out of here—I've paid my tuition." A convincing argument, so they kept me.

At that time, from the two or three hundred students at the school, they selected what they considered the fifteen best boys and girls they believed could have a career on the professional stage. I was one of those, and as a result I got to play a lead in one play. (We did about fifteen plays during a year, at the Lyceum Theatre, performed on Friday afternoons.) Well, I did a play titled *The Last Mrs. Chaney*. You were supposed to ask your theatrical friends to come to see you. I didn't have any theatrical friends, but I was spotted, so to speak, in the play. The day I was graduated a man came backstage (again at the Lyceum; Edward G. Robinson made the address—he was a graduate of the American Academy) and as I was picking up my wrap in the dressing room he said, "You're Miss Russell and I would like you to come to Greenwich this summer and work in our stock company." I was so flabbergasted at being offered the job in front of my mother, various aunts and uncles, student friends, and all, that I didn't know what on earth to say. I finally stammered out, "How much do you pay?" and he said "We pay $150 a week." I almost fell off the chair with that, but I was even more nervous and in order to sound professional (I had a purely nonsensical idea of the theatrical world and its financial machinations) I looked at him and said, "That's not enough."

He backed right out of the room, staring at me as though I was quite mad (indeed, I was). Needless to say I lost that job.

However, that very day my mother had a little tea for me with the relatives and she went all around the room telling everybody that I had been offered a job in the professional theater for $150, so I knew then that she was quite impressed and would not be too upset if I went into the theater. She allowed me to stay in New York to look for a job, and after I was there for four days she phoned me from Waterbury, Connecticut (our home), and said, "Rosalind, I think you'd better come home." "Why, mother?" And she said, "Well, it's obvious, after four days, that you're not wanted in the theater." I must admit that I got a job on the fifth day. I was very fortunate— remember, this *was* the depression. At that time I knew of only two places to look for work. One was the Shubert office, the great powerful syndicate of the theater; they cast and produced many plays in those days and in addition owned or controlled most legitimate theaters. The other was an office called the Chamberlain Brown Office, an agency. I used to go between the two to sit and listen and wait, hoping to be interviewed. I was not interviewed. One day, in the Brown office, I heard some actors talking, and was stopped by one of them saying, "He doesn't cast that company until May." This was late March. So I got

up, went over and said, "Excuse me, but what man is that?"
With rather an annoyed, dirty look he said, "Oh, a man named
Casey." I said, "Where is Mr. Casey?" and got the terse reply,
"He lives on Long Island and he's *not* casting now."

I ran downstairs (I can still hear my heels clicking on the
marble) and looked through the Long Island phone book and
found a man at Forest Hills named Edward Casey. And sure
enough when I called he said he did have a company in Saranac
Lake, New York, but he wasn't casting, so I said, "Well, Mr.
Casey, I'm going away; when are you coming to New York?"
(I was going home to mother, if the truth be known.) He said,
"I'm coming in tomorrow to see my dentist, but that doesn't
have anything to do with you," but I pleaded with him to see
me, and finally I wore him down and he agreed to meet me at
the Astor Hotel.

There I was, sitting by one of those potted palms, when a
very nice, attractive young man, twenty-seven or twenty-
eight years old, came in. We met and talked and he finally
said, "What do you play?" I was terrified to say I played bits
or anything, so I said, "I'm a second woman." I didn't dare say
I was an ingenue because I was always tall and didn't look a bit
like an ingenue; I had to play many ingenue parts later, in
stock, and I was always ghastly in them. Anyway, he said,
"We don't need a second woman, we need a leading woman,"
and I promptly assured him that I really was a leading woman,
that I thought he'd have one signed. A stock company pretty
much consisted of a leading woman, a second woman, an ingenue and a character woman (plus a leading man, juvenile
etc.) and though I was much too young to play character parts
at that time I was willing to do anything including sweeping
floors and building scenery. I assured him again that I really
was a leading woman and he told me that his wife was coming to
meet me. She came, they ducked behind the potted palm, and
after a long talk he came back and said, "Well, I like you and
my wife likes you but my partner has another woman in mind,
a girl he's seen. You want $150 a week and we can get the other
girl for minimum." Then he asked me what experience I'd had,
and I had to tell gray lies. I told him I'd worked in Pittsburgh

(it seemed so safely far away) and in Hartford (I thought my oldest brother could call Parsons Theatre and tell them to say his sister had worked there). He didn't inquire, however, and finally said, "We'll take the chance and sign you, but I'm going to be in trouble with my partner." So I dragged him to Actor's Equity that very moment and made him sign the contract. In June I took the train to Saranac and I was met by the entire company. I stepped off the train hoping I looked like a leading lady—dressed ravishingly in black with a hat over one eye and carrying my dog—when this terrible, anguished scream came from one of them. A strange man pointed at me and said, "That's the girl—that's the one I told you we could get for minimum!" He'd seen me at the Academy, and I was caught in my gray lies, but they were perfectly wonderful about it all. They paid me my full salary, though they used to tease me by putting the $35 minimum in my pay envelope, giving me the rest on the side. And that's how I got my start in theater.

N.   What roles did you play?

❦   RUSSELL : I played two leads a week—it was marvelous experience because we played for thirteen weeks. That was twenty-six plays, altogether. The plays weren't the greatest— we didn't pay much royalty for them—and there were times when I had to play ingenues; in that era many plays were written for ingenues. I always felt embarrassed, leaping onto the leading man's lap and being coy, but I gained wonderful experience. (Not in lap-leaping, but in acting!)

I went from there to Boston with E. E. Clive and played in a company that was very famous for many years, the Copley Players. It was English, and when I was interviewed by Clive I was British, so British you couldn't understand what I was saying. But I got that job and then went back to Saranac a year later for the experience. Two leads a week is a lot of sides to learn, and there's scarcely an old play you can name that I haven't played in stock.

Later, in stock, I worked for a company that actually did pay minimum—the subway circuit, more or less around New

York. We went as far as Washington and Baltimóre, Philadelphia and Newark, and that's where I was spotted for pictures. (I wouldn't work for minimum, however; I made them pay me $5 more. Then I'd ride back to New York with a man named Mr. Leventhal who owned the company I worked for and play pinochle with him. I earned more money playing cards with him than I earned acting for him, but now that I look back I realize that he let me win many times.) Oddly enough, I went to Hollywood without a successful Broadway role. I remember being interviewed by a man in New York to play a part on Broadway and he asked for my experience and I told him about stock in Boston, Philadelphia, and so on, but he merely said, "You haven't done anything on Broadway." I tried to explain to him that I'd done a lot more work than if I'd played two or three bits on Broadway, which was true—I'd carried heavy work, high and slapstick comedy, all types of drama, everything. But he wouldn't even let me read for the part, and to this day I can't think of this shortsighted individual as being any favorite of mine.

N.   How did you get to Hollywood?

❧   RUSSELL: As I mentioned, I was "discovered," you might say, on the subway circuit and brought out to Hollywood by Universal. I was there for two weeks when Metro sent for me to make a test. I was frightened of the medium, but felt I had quite a bit of experience for someone who'd been in theater only three and one-half years so I quelled the fright.

My first movie was with Bill Powell and Myrna Loy in a picture titled *Evelyn Prentiss*—I was the second woman. I was always "the threat," you see, to all the great women stars at Metro and they certainly were legion. For example, I was the second woman in two or three Jean Harlow movies, and you can imagine the audience worrying its head about *me* taking Clark Gable away from Jean Harlow. It was ludicrous. I was always rather stuffy—Lady Mary or Lady Sylvia. I used to roar with laughter about it, but I think I did learn a great deal. The techniques were totally different from theater and I worked with good people. I played second leads with Joan Crawford and

Bob Montgomery and Clark Gable and every other star on the lot. At first I was doing three pictures at a time and I'd be wearing a bathing suit and they'd say, "No, no, it should be the evening dress. You're over on Stage Nine. Come back to Stage Seventeen at half-past four and be sure you have the coat on and the hat without the gloves." Oh, dear. But we made many more pictures in those days. Each company—at least the six or seven major studios—tried to do fifty-two pictures a year, one a week for the theaters. It seems to me I was in *all* of them at once.

I got my first lead in what was called a B Picture—we don't have them anymore. Sometimes we had very good B Pictures, and certainly a great deal of talent was developed through them. (Now, of course, that talent is more or less developed through television.) My first lead was with Paul Lucas, a most attractive man, and then I went into a number of leads. *Craig's Wife* was a very big break for me. I must have been about twenty-four at the time and the wife was an older and very unsympathetic woman. As a result I was put in dramas. (We had very little to say, then, about our parts, but now that I look back on it all I'm glad it happened.)

I did *Night Must Fall* with Bob Montgomery—a wonderful picture, and *The Citadel*. In that one I had to be English, and English I was, frightfully so, and I worked with Robert Donat —a great actor. And there were a few people in *The Citadel*, playing bit parts, we've heard from since. A fellow named Rex Harrison had a small role, and another named Emlyn Williams, and a third, Ralph Richardson.

But the big break, the really big break, came with *The Women*. I wanted the part of Sylvia very badly and I knew they had someone else for the part, so I went out to the producer (Hunt Stromberg—I'd worked for him in *Night Must Fall*) to ask him why he didn't test me. He said, "Roz, we thought of you but" and here I almost choked ". . . you're too beauti-ful." I laughed and said I'd never been told *that*. "We want somebody very odd looking." I crossed my eyes and assured him that I would go to the makeup department for a wart or two. He said, "No, you're essentially a dramatic actress" and I said,

"Some of my friends get a laugh out of me." We chatted. And chatted. And I felt I'd gotten nowhere.

Then I came home and the phone was ringing. It was Stromberg. "I though over what you said, and I want you to test for it. Tomorrow." I had only an overnight session of preparation but I went in the next day and played it several ways, with the emphasis on drawing-room comedy. The last way I played it was in an extreme fashion for the director, George Cukor.

The following day, when the film had been developed, they called me. I could hear them laughing in the projection room. Hunt and George called me over and told me I had the part.

On the first day of filming I played it high-comedy and George was aghast. "No, no—you play like you played that final way!" he shouted. I was shocked and said, "Oh, George, that's terrible, that's extreme, the critics will murder me!" and he said "Now, Roz, you have a very big following at the Plaza Theatre in New York, but in Waukegan they've never heard of you." He was very sweet, and he explained to me why I must play it the broad way. He said, "You must not be the heavy; you break up a marriage here and there's a child involved. You must be the potpourri of all the gossips, of all the women who make trouble. When a man says, 'I'm going down to buy a cigar,' you're the redhead at the cigar store that makes the wife say, 'I'll go with you.' You're a freak." He gave me the courage to do it that way, and the picture made a tremendous difference in my career.

N.   You stole *The Women*.

❧   RUSSELL: It was a wonderful part. I had great fun doing it—I could go wild. George just said "Do it broad—don't hold back." The cattiness, even the extreme bitchiness, is human (perhaps all too human). You know, the nice, "Oh, you're here!" followed by the lowered-voice "Who the hell is that?" and the "Dahling, how are you?" followed by "Look what she's got on!" George thought the best scene in it was the fight scene Paulette and I staged—plus the scene following, the one I remember as the Bad Temper. (I suppose a gossip like Sylvia is rather like a child, and she was so in character when she broke all the plates and said, "I won't! I won't!" and stamped her foot.)

But the fight with Paulette was a riot. We only took one take, and I always had to reassure George that Paulette and I really did like each other; in fact we were rather good friends. Paulette was on the horse, and I had to pull her off the horse and swing at her. Well, I pulled her off the horse all right, but when I swung I hit the rear of the horse instead of her. Then she flipped up my shirt front; I had on a stiff shirt front (like men used to wear with dinner-coats) and that hit me in the face. Then she took my straw·hat and pulled it down, then we rolled about, two or three cameras trained on the scene, and the finale was that I sat in the dirt and she had won and I looked over and spotted her little boots, bare legs and shorts, and crawled over to bite her in the mid-calf. Well, I was so happy that we got through the fight the first time around, that it was natural and we'd hit the right camera points, that I crawled over and *really* bit. Poor Paulette . . . she let out a yell and she should have; my cups and saucers on her leg didn't disappear for days. (This first-person pronoun is driving me mad; it's all I-I-I but I don't suppose I can refer to myself as "she" or "that woman," can I?)

I had a fine break, too, with *His Girl Friday* with Cary Grant. He was a joy to work with. Then, for years and years and years I became a career woman. I played—I think it was twenty-three—career women. I've been every kind of executive and I've owned everything—factories and advertising agencies and pharmaceutical houses. I've been a psychiatrist, every kind of doctor, and Sister Kenny. (I can operate if you'll sharpen the knife.) But they were fun, these comedies.

In fact, a very nice award was given me by the Business Women's Club of America, which has millions of members, and they had a large convention up in San Francisco and I spoke to them. I didn't know exactly what to talk about but I decided that since they were executive-type women I'd compare *my* executive role with theirs. We had fun because I asked them how many phones they had on their desks (two or three) compared to my twelve. Then, too, I always opened my office on the fortieth floor of Radio City, then went to lunch, then to my summer home, then to my penthouse. They never saw me in the office again. (Doris Day does these comedies today, and they're allowed a little more sex than we had.)

Shortly after *The Women* and *His Girl Friday* I went free-lancing. I knew I was going to be married to Freddie and I had hoped to have a large family and I wanted more free time.

N.   *Sister Kenny* was a radical departure for you, wasn't it?

❧   RUSSELL: I felt I had to get away from executive women parts because I wasn't growing in any direction. So I deliberately did *Sister Kenny*. I knew her, and I'd always been interested in orthopedic work and worked at the Orthopedic Hospital here with the League for Crippled Children. That's how the script came to me; then I met Sister, was fascinated, and just had to do it. I did *Electra* the same way—trying to get away from comedy. I enjoy comedy more than dramatic work, but look at it this way: The longer you have a career the more challenging the work you do must be. You cannot remain in a rut; you have to take a gamble, and many times you fail, but it's better to have tried and failed than not to have tried. (Original, that one, though I think it had something to do with amour the first time around.) This is the way I feel about it, and it's proved right for me. When the challenge works, it's delicious.

Many people have said to me "I don't know why you ever leave a part like *Auntie Mame*. It's so perfect for you, etc." I have done everything possible to get away from Auntie Mame. For instance, doing *A Majority of One*—I play a far older woman than I am, of the Jewish faith, with a Jewish accent, all padded (like Sister Kenny). I am of the Catholic faith, have been around the orders a great deal, and I'm looking forward to a picture called *Life With Mother Superior* that Columbia is about to start. Then, on the other extreme, I'm doing *Oh, Dad, Poor Dad, Mama Hung You in the Closet and I'm Feeling So Sad*. That one's avant garde, extreme as all get-out. I keep accepting challenges. It's stimulating.

N.   I'd like to ask you about two roles you are strongly identified with: *My Sister Eileen* and *Auntie Mame*. Did you enjoy creating these roles? and, Did you enjoy, or not enjoy, your identification with them?

         RUSSELL: I played *My Sister Eileen* as a film, and for years Joe Fields, one of the authors, used to beg me to do a musical based on it, and I would simply roar with laughter and explain that I cannot sing a note. But one night at a party I did two numbers (nonsense numbers; Cary Grant taught me both of them one day on the set) and Joe came over to the piano and said, "Have lunch with me tomorrow," and I said, "If you want to buy me a nice, expensive lunch, all right." He's a nice friend and he pleaded the *Eileen* business again and I said, "No, Joe, I'm not doing any such thing."

Then I went East to make a film in Virginia with my husband—*Never Wave at a WAC*—and Joe asked me if I would see George Abbott. Mr. Abbott has always fascinated any actress or actor, and I was pleased to meet him, so I did. Again—*Eileen*. Again—Not interested. I was supposed to see George before going back West, but I was so afraid of being pinned down that I flew back from Washington instead of coming through New York. Then the producers started sending me telegrams and one day I told my husband that I was going East ". . . to tell them that I'm not going to do that play." He asked me why I just couldn't spend three dollars on the phone instead of flying to New York, but I felt I had to talk to them personally. I went East and said, "No" again. (Really, it wasn't my virtue being questioned; just my wisdom.) But finally I consented to do it and I was very, very thrilled that I did.

A remarkable group of people were connected with *Wonderful Town*. George Abbott directed, Leonard Bernstein did the music, and Adolph Green and Betty Comden did the lyrics. Jerome Robbins and Don Walker did the choreography and musical direction. So I was in good hands. I adored doing it—I'm far from being a musician, but I love music. (I *can* keep time;

I've been around music all my life.) But we all worked together and there it was, a wonderful thing.

You can be dog-tired at curtain time, but when you hear that orchestra go into the overture you literally fly onto the stage. Doing a musical is like going into another world. Again, the techniques are different, and you're learning something all the time. Fortunately for the show (and for me) I am athletic, so I loved doing the conga number. (People used to say, "Don't do that lift—Nora Kaye wouldn't do it; it's dangerous!" and I'd say, "Don't tell me if it's dangerous because I wouldn't know whether it is or not. Just let me fly up there.")

Then, again, Mame was a character I loved, and with whom I had rapport. She was a joy to play. When you're in the theater you don't have to wait until Friday nights to get paid; you get paid through the audience. People ask you if you tire—

N.   That was going to be my next question, in fact.

❦   RUSSELL: You don't tire, not at all. Of course I was a very lucky actress—I had two smash hits. (There's such a difference between a "hit" and a "smash hit." A "hit" is something everybody gets their money back on; a "smash hit" is something that makes everybody rich. Not only financially, but careerwise. A "smash hit" has excitement, news; it discovers people. When you come into a theater every night where people are screaming to get tickets and they're standing twenty feet deep to see it it's a wonderful feeling.

It takes many, many people to put a smash hit, or even a hit, together. One never does it alone. It's a timing, a jelling, an expiation. There's blood with it, all over the stage. The show is composed of so many personalities, gifted people that want the hit but are nervous about it, tense, overtired. When you work with a man like Abbott you're fortunate because he keeps the balance.

But being around talent is always interesting. Any kind of talent. I don't care if it's the man putting the plaster on the wall—if he does it well there's something exciting about it. And when you get the kind of group together—the kind I had with

Wonderful Town and again with *Auntie Mame*—you are blessed.

N.   How have you reacted to critics and criticism?

RUSSELL: There was a director here—I didn't work for him—named Boleslavsky. He said two things I've never forgotten. The first: "I never have trouble with actors because I make them comfortable and I credit them with a little intelligence." (Anytime a director says, "What do you think," about a scene you can die for him; he may not do a thing you suggest, but you're so grateful that he asked.) The second: "The day you start believing your publicity is the day you should quit." This means in either affirmative or negative direction. You can't let either affect you emotionally.

Criticism, after all, is a good thing. You can't do without it and you shouldn't. All in all, the press has been more than generous in my behalf, and when I've had a few (shall we say) "crispy" remarks tossed my way they've been quite accurate. There are some things you try that you shouldn't have tried, or things within your scope you didn't do well.

N.   Is there any advice you could give a youngster who wants a career as an actor?

RUSSELL: Many people ask me how I became a star, and immediately follow the remark with, "My teacher says I have great talent, my mother was a dancer and I've studied etc. etc."

Well, talent is the least of it. The number one thing is vitality, health. Then you must have self-discipline, but if you have good heath you will have self-discipline.

I've worked with many an actor who had more talent in his little finger than I have in my entire anatomy but he couldn't be heard in the third row; he could not project, even with a mike, on film. No vitality.

You must also learn to fail and overcome failure, not allowing it to destroy you. You're bound to fail temporarily in any business, so why is it exceptional in ours? Especially when you're in it over a protracted period of time—like my thirty-year period? You get over fright, like anything else. Young people are so frightened of failure. Often, in this business, I've seen youngsters who've had two failures in a row become paralyzed. They shouldn't. You go by the track record and you learn from failure.

Then you've got to have a willingness to work and to learn and to continue to work and to learn. (I sound as though I'm a model on Olympus; I don't mean to be arbitrary about this.) But if a yountster really has these qualities, and talent in addition, he's got the whipped cream and cherry on top. Talent can be developed; I'm certain of that.

N.   Do you feel a sense of obligation regarding your roles? To yourself, the part, the writer, the audience?

❧   RUSSELL: There's a definite sense of obligation in every direction. It begins with the author—you owe him so much. Some think that they could do it alone, absolutely alone, but that isn't true. What you're doing has come from someone's innards, and the more you understand that, the more you try to find what the author is really trying to say, the better. To destroy these main arteries is a cruel and a stupid thing to do. Tennessee Williams, for example, knows what he's trying to say.

I feel the same way about an audience. As a young girl in Waterbury I went to the local stock company, paid my quarter for a gallery seat, and got mighty angry when I couldn't hear. Now, I'm rather a shouter in the theater. You can hear me. But an actor *must* be heard.

You should, of course, give your best performance at every performance. In the theater I have very little time to spend with the cast during rehearsal. With the changing it's a difficult and busy period; then you go on the road and you're changing, changing, changing. This goes on night and day because you rehearse all day, you perform at night, and often you rehearse again after the performance. But once we are a "hit" I have a short speech to make. (There's no sense making a speech if we're a flop. You thank everybody and kiss them goodbye.) But in the speech I thank them, sincerely, but add this: "Never fool with me on the stage. No jokes, no 'inside' jokes. No asides. No nothing. No 'Look who's outside!' under your breath, or 'Noel Coward's sitting there.' And you must perform as you did last night. Every performance is your best."

I resent going to New York to see a hit play that's been running for a while to discover that the players have become sloppy. I think this is insulting and stupid.

N. Does audience reaction—or lack of reaction—disturb you? Particularly when you're doing a comedy?

❧ RUSSELL: You bet it does. You get mad. But what you're mad at is yourself, because when they sit on their hands it's your fault.

For instance, lack of concentration. Now, I can't see too well but I can hear like a demon. I used to send my maid out—I'd say, "In the tenth row there are four people who aren't with us. What's going on?"—and she'd go out and look and come back and say "Well, one of them is slightly inebriated, one is trying to wake him up and the ladies are a little upset." Now, I probably can't do much about that delightful quartet except hope they get the alcoholic friend up and away.

But when you see those programs going. Even on the hottest night I don't like any programs going. You're in trouble; you've got to make them stop wig-wagging to concentrate on what's going on up on the stage. They must, in a sense, be part of you, but to get them to come to you you must go to them. You become a unit, a family, a mutually involved group. The programs have to stop, and the only way to do it is to climb right back into that character. You can't just become louder or more flamboyant; you've got to remember that you lost them because you didn't convince them you were that character. If you're successful the programs will stop wagging, the feet will stop shuffling, the coughs will die down.

You know, my only regret at this point of the interview is the way I sound so all-fired serious and grim. I'm not that way, really; I enjoy my work and I enjoy the people I work with and I have a lot of fun, and I hope to continue to do so.

"I have . . . four months after finishing playing a part . . . found myself thinking about it and saying, 'My goodness, of course this is what that meant!'"

JESSICA TANDY

There are performances in the theater which are land-
marks—rare occasions when the actor and the part
come together in a marriage so brilliant the audience
thereafter identifies *that* role with *that* actor. It's true,
however, that the part must be a great one to begin
with—a Hamlet, for instance, to create partisans for
Gielgud, Barrymore, Olivier or Burton. There is no
such controversy about the identity of Blanche in *A
Streetcar Named Desire*, nor (for those who attended
the third season at the Guthrie Theatre) the perfect
Madame Ranevskaya in *The Cherry Orchard*.

Enter, Jessica Tandy.

TANDY: I was born in London. My mother was a
schoolteacher and my father was engaged in the manufacture
and sale of rope. My family has no theatrical background at
all, but I think my two brothers and I were remarkably fortunate in our mother who had an enormous interest in theater. We
were taken to any performance of consequence, sometimes
spending hours in a queue to get into the gallery, hours full of
delicious anticipation. There we were introduced to Shakespeare
and the best that Shaftsbury Avenue (the Broadway of Lon-

don) had to offer. We were transported by the magic of the theater and reveled in it.

I also think my religious training has something to do with our love of theater. On every seventh day, my mother and brothers and I participated in a ceremony of great vocal and musical beauty. The peaceful atmosphere of the church, the Crusader's Tomb, the stained glass windows, the deep roll of the organ accompanying the purity of the voices in the choir (among them that of my elder brother) and the uninhibited singing of the congregation where mother, my other brother and I were doing our best, the chanted responses, each one given its full meaning by change of tempo, music and feeling; and then the rich and well modulated voice of the rector during the sermon; these sights and sounds together with the grandeur and poetry of the language had a quality of theatricality about them. No less reverent for that and infinitely satisfying. I am not at all sure that this recurrent experience didn't prepare me in some measure for my profession.

I was the youngest of three children. My elder brother Michael had, I think, an enormous theatrical talent, and during the holidays he would encourage my other brother and I to give performances of all kinds at home. Usually of things we really couldn't fully have understood. The last program when I was ten was a potted version of the *Mikado* with my brother Tully and I singing all parts while Michael pounded the piano, and the last act of Cyrano de Bergerac somewhat rearranged so that Tully could play Cyrano and I could play Roxanne, a part enlarged so that all pertinent lines of other characters could be added to my part; together with old favorites, poetry speaking, comic songs, etc., until the audience was exhausted. Pretty protean.

My brother Michael was my first director and I never had a more exacting one. When he went up to Oxford he did great things in the O.U.D.S. and professional theater people were interested in him as a potential actor, but he decided on a career in the foreign office. When it became apparent that I wanted to be an actress he persuaded my mother to let me leave school at the age of fifteen and train for the theater. I had already been attending classes in Shakespeare and verse speaking for two years.

This brings me to education, which between my fifth to tenth and thirteenth to fifteenth years was formal and educational, and between the tenth and thirteenth was decidedly spotty due to illness. So at the age of fifteen, having had two years of unbroken good health with no backsliding, two medals for poetry reading, and an absolute determination to be an actress, I was allowed to leave school and attend a dramatic school from 10 A.M. to 4 P.M. every day with the understanding that I would stay for three years. There, I was exposed to the various techniques of speaking, singing, dancing, and acting as well as French and English literature. My education was continued in this specialized form until I was eighteen. I owe an enormous debt to Lillian Simpson, who ran that school, for all her patient and impatient, encouraging and demanding, teaching. To the yearly student performances I invited the people who had been so impressed with Michael at Oxford and whom I hoped might look kindly on his sister, among them the manager of the Birmingham Repertory Theatre. At that time the best in the country. He did help me after I had finished my training with letters of introduction and recommendation which brought me odd jobs and special performances and finally about eight months later a marvelous part at the Birmingham Repertory Theatre, the child in Richard Hughes' *The Comedy of Good and Evil*. It was played for three weeks, the usual run, then I stayed for the next play, J. M. Barrie's *Alice Sit by the Fire*, then toured for six months with the same company in *Yellow Sands*, playing the ingenue. I was launched! The next eight or ten years were spent mostly in London, with one season at the Festival Theatre in Cambridge, playing a different play every week for twelve weeks—a musical revue, Shakespeare, Elmer Rice, John Masefield, and so on. Frankly, I don't know how I did it. It was extremely hard work, but I found it tremendously stimulating. In London, subsequently, there was *Autumn Crocus*, my first long run, Manuela in *Children in Uniform* (I have a review by Alexander Woollcott which I treasure), Ophelia to John Gielgud's *Hamlet*, *Noah*, *Antony and Anna*, *French*

without Tears, Twelfth Night and *Henry V* with Laurence
Olivier, Cordelia in *King Lear*, and Miranda in the *Tempest*
with John Gielgud. These last four all at the Old Vic.

I first came to America in 1930 with an English company
headed by Constance Collier in G. B. Stern's *The Matriarch*. It
was short lived but six months later, I returned with another
English company in a play which had been very successful in
London, but which the American management so cut, rewrote,
and redirected, that it was unrecognizable, and frankly awful.
Let us draw a veil. Seven years passed busily back in London
before I returned here in J. B. Priestley's *Time and the Con-
ways*, a short run but well worth doing. The following year, I
returned alone to play with an American company *The White
Steed* by Paul Vincent Carroll, a fascinating play by a very
interesting writer. Then at the beginning of the war I toured
Canada with an English company and came with them to New
York in G. B. Shaw's *Geneva*. It rather misfired. It was already
a little out of date. It wasn't fun to poke fun at the dictators
anymore, though when it was written a few years earlier it had
been a wonderful way to awaken people to the gathering storm.
But it wasn't very successful. Back to London for my last two
productions at the Old Vic, *King Lear* and *The Tempest*, then on
to New York for A. J. Cronin's *Jupiter Laughs*. Then Emlyn
William's *Yesterday's Magic* with Paul Muni. Then I went to
Hollywood; really because I was married to Hume by this time
and he went to Hollywood. I made a few movies in the five
years that I was there, but actually I went to have babies and be
married to Hume. But I found that wasn't quite enough. I have
to function concurrently as an actress. Some of the things I did
in Hollywood I found absolutely fascinating—*The Seventh
Cross* in particular. It was my first picture and it was the first
major picture by Fred Zinneman who is a stimulating director
to work with. He understood the importance of rehearsals in
quietness before we got to the costume and makeup stage when
technicians were running around making sure the lights were
right, etc. We would rehearse in his office the evening before we
were scheduled to shoot and as a result when we came on to the
sound stage our performances were at least somewhat prepared.

Usually one learns the lines alone at home, sometimes without even knowing with whom one is to act. The costume is fitted with great care, the makeup is put on with great care, one arrives fully accoutred. There are costume tests, makeup tests, hairdressing tests, finally you arrive on the set, say "how do you do" to the other actors, wait while every technical snag is ironed out, then off you go with a minimum of rehearsal and there it is on film forever and ever. Not my favorite way of working. Nevertheless, I learned a great deal from those years in Hollywood. It is as important to be able to give a performance quickly, to respond to and execute a director's demands expeditiously as to rehearse for weeks and weeks, perfecting a performance bit by bit. I am very glad that I had the opportunity to profit by this experience in Hollywood. But there came a point when I felt that I just had to act in a play again. Hume, knowing my need said, "All right, let's go to the Actor's Lab where you can work at whatever you want. Why not do *Portrait of the Madonna* by Tennessee Williams?" Well, I did. Hume directed me in it, and it was tremendously successful, leading to my being cast as Blanche in *A Streetcar Named Desire*.

N.   What are the basic differences between the processes and the satisfactions of acting on the stage and in motion pictures?

TANDY: Well, one great reward is denied the actor in the film—the direct contact with the audience. Then, I have always found it less satisfying to memorize the dialogue by myself and then just rehearse the scene with the other actors a half an hour or so before the camera records it forever and ever.

The rehearsal period of a play is a most interesting time. So much is learned from everyone else, so many people contribute to the whole. Performances evolve; one has time to experiment and make mistakes—that is not time wasted. However, I understand in Hollywood now it is becoming more usual to rehearse a script a week or two before the camera turns.

N.   Could you choose a few of your strongest roles— say, Blanche in *A Streetcar Named Desire* and Madame Ranevskaya in *The Cherry Orchard*—and explain your preparation for the parts, your homework?

❧   TANDY: Basically, the preparation is the same for both parts except that *Streetcar* was being prepared for the first time, whereas *Cherry Orchard* I had seen performed in Russian, Italian, and English; and I had read Chekhov's letters about the play and David Magarshack's books. In fact, I knew the play well as a student and spectator but not as a participant. All very valuable as background material, but when rehearsals start it is the words on the pages of the script which are the important ones. Not just the memorizing of them, but becoming familiar with the character who thinks and speaks them.

Both Blanche and Madame Ranevskaya are beautifully and fully written characters. In fact, both plays are superbly written throughout. All the characters are observed and revealed with loving insight by Chekhov and Williams. Every facet of every person is there on the pages; the actor has to find and realize them all. It is hard to describe the joy of discovering the exquisite ambiguities of a character. There is not one scene in *Cherry Orchard* or *Streetcar* which is in one sustained mood, there are constant crosscurrents and one must find them all. This is what is fascinating, what makes it possible to play in a play like this for a long time. One never quite finishes. I think I've been extremely lucky in doing a great many very good plays. Sometimes, in a long run, you will elaborate if you're not careful, but what I think you must do is to simplify, to get the same or deeper effect with less.

N.   How do you feel about Repertory Theatre? You've played in it in England and for two seasons here at the Guthrie. What does it mean to you, as against the sustained single role?

❧   TANDY: Well, I don't think there's any such thing as "against." I feel there's a place for both.

I find it very stimulating to do different plays on consecutive nights. It's exhausting because of the preparation time. We've now been rehearsing for almost four months without stopping— on three plays. On the other hand, to go from diametrically opposed kinds of productions, parts, styles, keeps you on your toes. You learn a great deal. I don't think you should do it all the time, but there is also a place for a long run providing it's in a play that has some depth. If it's a matter of going to the theater to repeat, mechanically—if there's nothing in the part to dig for—it can be rather boring. But I really haven't had many experiences like that. I've almost always been lucky enough to have good parts and been deeply interested in what I was doing. Of course, a long run can be tiresome. But I think actors should be in long runs, in short runs, in repertory, on television, in motion pictures, on radio—all of it. There are millions of ways of doing things, and the more we spread ourselves in different kinds of work, the better it is for us.

N.   What do you look for, or want, in a characterization?

TANDY: All facets of it. Or as many as possible. Hume has a saying—and it may not be original with him— "When you're playing an angel, look for the devil; when you're playing a devil, look for the angel."

After all, we all have many facets in real life. We are complex. Our relationships are very complex; we aren't of one color. I don't think we should be of one dimension in theater. There are technical things to consider—you must almost be aware of a hidden musical score; the sounds must be interesting, dramatic, engaging, and the thoughts must be revealing and revealed. I can't answer this question very well. All I can say is that I want to get into the skin of the whole person. Sometimes the part isn't written that way. A broad cartoon may be necessary, not a complex character; then you've got to settle for that and find the dramatic values within the limitation.

N.   When you're playing a role do you feel a conscious obligation toward any particular person or entity?

TANDY: I believe my obligation is to the author. I think his meaning is of prime importance.

N.   I'd like to turn to the Guthrie Theatre now. You've worked here for two seasons. What reception have you felt? Do audiences differ, tangibly, from audiences in, say, New York or London?

✿   TANDY: The audiences the first year at the Guthrie Theatre had an enthusiasm which one is not likely to encounter in New York; there was an enormous will to absorb what was being offered here and a determination on the part of the audience as well as the actors that the venture should be successful. They probably met us more than half way. This third season, I think some of that rapturous enthusiasm has been changed into a more critical enjoyment. The audience still contributes much more than a New York audience, which is after all sated with entertainment of all kinds. The audience here comes not only for an evening's entertainment, but to see performances of the very best plays that have ever been written. No one can complain of the quality of the plays. The first year the audience was more willing to be dazzled by the spectacle than it is now. There is a deeper and more critical perception— all very good for the audience and even better for the company. We should grow together.

N.   What do you think of the health of theater on the whole? Here and (to be totally general) everywhere?

✿   TANDY: I assure you I am not an expert, but it seems to me that there is a growing awareness all over the country of the necessity of theater as part of the daily bread of life. The theater deals with human ideas and emotions. No one is trying to sell anything as on television and radio. James Bridie once wrote Hume this definition of a good play, "It tells a story, it's a poem, a philosophical demonstration."

Theater isn't just a spectator's sport. People go to the theater to share an experience, to hear the poetry and the philosophical demonstration may provide hours of stimulating discussion after the play is over.

Now all over the country there are people in many cities who understand the need for theaters of their own. There is a great theater-building spree going on all over. I am glad. It is a very healthy sign, but a lovely building isn't theater, and the people who build and administrate these buildings had better be very sure that they have inspired, dedicated and experienced leadership in every department. These theaters must succeed—for the good of everybody. I don't mean by putting on last year's Broadway comedy hit as insurance of success but by a program of the best that the theater has to offer presented, mounted, directed, and acted by people who have a respect for the intelligence of their audiences. Professionals who will not be here today and gone tomorrow but will stay and be responsible for the welfare of the theater. I firmly believe that good plays are within the intellectual and emotional range of an enormous number of people. These audiences all over the country have been ignored for a long time.

N.   What do you think of the level and effect of theatrical criticism?

TANDY: I think there are very few critics. There are reporters—lots of them. They write news, not criticism. Very few critics have an opportunity to function as critics. If they have to go to the theater, then rush to write a review in forty minutes, they are functioning as reporters. It seems to me that criticism takes more time.

There was a time when I never read criticism because I found that it was rarely possible to find anything constructive that would help me. Now, of course, one must read them to know whether the play has a chance of running. I read my notices now—with the thought, "Is this going to make people buy tickets?"

I wish it were possible for critics—and there are some extremely intelligent men who write well—to come to the theater, be part of the theater, watch what goes on in production and through rehearsals, to learn those separate areas of domain allotted the producer, the director, the writer, the actor. It would be difficult enough even if you were aware of all these things to know, when you see the finished play, that it was a foible of the director that pulled the play out of gear, or the insistence of the author who said, "This is the way it must be and I won't change the dialogue," or whether it's the actor who cannot encompass the dimensions of a part. Often it's heartbreaking to see the wrong person blamed for a fault in a production.

I think, too, that today (perhaps because the cost of tickets is so high, particularly on Broadway) people read the critics only to be assured that they will enjoy themselves. And the awful thing is that if they should read a notice that says, "Here is an original mind writing a marvelous first act about a fascinating subject," and then goes on to say, "the second act was not so good," you're dead and very few people are going to see that marvelous first act. So if the critic has become a reporter who runs a sort of shopping guide, it may be because that's what the public wants.

N.   The final question : If you were to give advice to the young actor—

❧   TANDY : I wouldn't. The irony is, Hume and I have to, right now, because our daughter Tandy wants to become an actress. Our advice was : "First of all, get the best education you can, because it will never be wasted—it can only enrich you. Second, make absolutely sure that you've got to be an actress or bust before you get into it, because it can be heartbreaking, and there are few rewards, or rewards for very few people. But if the work fascinates you, then do it. But if it's the success or the notoriety or the money or the glamor that fascinates you, it isn't worth it. It's only the work that is ultimately fascinating." I suppose the best advice is "Don't"—but that will not stop anyone who wants, really wants, to be an actor.